FOR THE PEOPLE

Inside the Los Angeles County
District Attorney's Office
1850-2000

For the People is a project of the District Attorney's Crime Prevention Foundation, which supports programs for at-risk children and crime victims.

FOR THE PEOPLE

Inside the Los Angeles County District Attorney's Office 1850-2000

Michael Parrish

foreword by Kevin Starr

ANGEL CITY PRESS
2118 Wilshire Blvd., #880
Santa Monica, California 90403
310.395.9982
www.angelcitypress.com

FOR THE PEOPLE
by Michael Parrish
Copyright © 2001 by District Attorney's Crime Prevention Foundation
Design by Maritta Tapanainen

First edition
10 9 8 7 6 5 4 3 2 1

ISBN 1-883318-15-7

Distributed in China and Hong Kong by Hong Kong Graphics and Distribution

LIBRARY OF CONGRESS CATALOGING-IN-PUBLICATION DATA

Parrish, Michael.
For the people : inside the Los Angeles District Attorney's office, 1850-2000 / by Michael
        Parrish.— 1st ed.
        p. cm.
Includes bibliographical references and index.
ISBN 1-883318-15-7 (alk. paper)
1. California. District Attorney (Los Angeles County)—History. 2. Public
        prosecutors—California—Los Angeles County—History. 3. Criminal justice,
        Administration of—California—Los Angeles County—History. 4. Crime—California
        —Los Angeles County—History. 5. Trials—California—Los Angeles County. I. Title.
    KF355.L6 P37 2001
    364.9794'93—dc21
                                00-010747
                                CIP

Printed in Hong Kong

The District Attorney of Los Angeles County, as a constitutional officer and the public prosecutor acting on behalf of the People, is vested with the independent power to conduct prosecutions for public offenses, to detect crime and to investigate criminal activity. The District Attorney advises the Grand Jury in its investigations. The District Attorney enforces the financial responsibility of parents to support their children. By law, the District Attorney sponsors and participates in programs to improve the administration of justice.

The District Attorney fulfills these responsibilities through the efforts of the employees of the Office of the District Attorney. Each employee of the District Attorney's Office shall adopt the highest standards of ethical behavior and professionalism. Each employee, moreover, is integral to achieving the mission of the Office and shares the District Attorney's obligation to enhance the fundamental right of the People of Los Angeles County to a safe and just society. At all times, the mission of the District Attorney's Office shall be carried out in a fair, evenhanded and compassionate manner.

Contents

District Attorney S. Ernest Roll watches as the county clerk administers the oath to the District Attorney's Bureau of Investigation, establishing them as Peace Officers, 1951.

The human desire for justice is instinctive—and a demand for a fair system of justice was at the core of the creation of the Los Angeles County District Attorney's Office in 1850. As Los Angeles grew from a dusty town surrounded by *ranchos* into a citified magnet for newcomers and international adventurers, the need for an organized process for achieving criminal justice grew more pressing. With the county's swelling population came a growing assortment of colorful criminals who required corralling and a citizenry that demanded more than vigilante justice. Answering the call for an established county prosecutor was William C. Ferrell, who was swept into the post of district attorney in an election in which 377 votes were cast.

One hundred fifty years later, the Los Angeles County District Attorney's Office has grown from a one-man operation into the largest local prosecutorial agency in the world, with more than thirty-five hundred employees, more than eleven hundred of whom are lawyers. Now serving a population of about ten million, the Office handles more than eighty-five thousand felonies countywide each year and two hundred fifty thousand misdemeanors. But the district attorney's mission remains the same: to seek justice, to protect members of the public, and to do the right thing.

For the People depicts the colorful history of the District Attorney's Office, whose broad jurisdictional reach across time enfolds much of the history of Los Angeles. Here are the justices and injustices of the American West, the sensational cases of the twentieth century, the scandalous travesties of Hollywood high-life, the corruption of political power, and the heartbreaking casualties of urban terrorism, of gang warfare, of untreated mental illness gone homicidal. Here are the greatest scourges of Los Angeles—conflagrations of racial tensions and civil unrest beginning in 1871 with the Chinese Massacre and including the Watts riots of 1965 and those that followed acquittals in the Rodney G. King beating trial in 1992. *For the People* shows how in the face of such unrest the criminal justice system—for better and worse—struggled to respond.

Chronicled here are L.A.'s most notorious criminal cases, from the 1922 trial of murderess Clara "Tiger Woman" Phillips, to the 1942 Sleepy Lagoon killing, to the conviction of Robert F. Kennedy's assassin Sirhan Sirhan, to the Manson murder trials, to O.J. Simpson. *For the People* shows how even in the most intense media glare, prosecutors, for the most part, did their jobs, seeking reparation for victims, seeking justice for those damaged or destroyed by evil or carelessness or greed, typically doing so with success.

As a veteran of more than thirty years in the District Attorney's Office, I believe knowing the history of this region instills a deeper appreciation for the community we, as prosecutors, serve. As a native Los Angeleno, my interest in local history is personal. My family's background is typical of many people who live in the region.

After my Italian grandfather was killed in the Mexican Revolution, my Aztec grandmother went north to the United States, eventually settling in East Los Angeles with her young son, my father. My mother's parents migrated from Sonora, Mexico, to Arizona to provide the promise of opportunity to their nineteen children born in America. I was born in the small home my parents shared with some of my aunts and uncles on 41st Street and Figueroa Boulevard in South Central Los Angeles. Before my mother turned my father around, he was a small-time gang member who later would boast of his arrest by an LAPD officer named Tom Bradley (who in 1973 became the city's first African-American mayor).

Immigrant families continue to stream into Los Angeles—a dynamic metropolis defined in large part by its diversity. In this melting pot that is Los Angeles, there is much to connect us with our past. My hope is that *For the People* does just that for those who work in the Los Angeles County District Attorney's Office, the employees to whom this book is dedicated. The reason for undertaking this history project commemorating the office's sesquicentennial is to enable the prosecutors, investigators and support staff to feel part of an organization with a great history and to give the public a greater understanding of the evolution of criminal justice in Los Angeles County. *For the People* shows how the Los Angeles County District Attorney's Office—with its legacy of cases that made national and even international headlines because of the fascinating circumstances involved or the legal ground broken—has consistently been at the center of storms in the criminal justice system. One daunting courtroom challenge after another is depicted in this hundred-fifty-year history. It provides a sense of continuity, illuminating the work of our predecessors, offering new insight into the professional challenges of the office and renewed inspiration in the present-day pursuit of justice. *For the People* shows that, time and time again, the District Attorney's Office carried out its mission to do the right thing, mindful of the enormous responsibility and the authority the people of the State of California have entrusted to it.

—Gil Garcetti
District Attorney
Los Angeles County
July 2000

Los Angeles Civic Center, circa 1967.

No office holds more power or authority than that of prosecutor. The power of protectoral office comes not only from its intrinsic authority, but from the large amount of discretion that is allowed a prosecutor in the matter of whether or not to press charges. Each prosecutor, then, is responsible to the law as the law relates to the facts of a case, and, more subtly, each prosecutor is also empowered to assess those ambiguous borderlands that can exist between the evidence and the law. The office of the prosecutor is at once based in the traditions and precedence of Anglo-American common law and in the sometimes impenetrable and intractable facts of a case. When a prosecutor is also an elected official, as in the case of the Los Angeles County District Attorney, yet another factor—society itself, which is to say, the general will as expressed through politics—can be of relevance; for in some cases, neither the law nor the evidence leads inevitability to a clear-cut conclusion, and the values of society must be called upon in the process.

For the People is about the Los Angeles County District Attorney's Office and some of the extraordinary cases that Office has prosecuted over the past hundred fifty years. From this perspective, it is a history of specific district attorneys and their deputies and specific cases. But it is also, by implication, a social and cultural history of Los Angeles. Criminal behavior while consistent in certain ways across the ages, also reflects a certain time and place. While the law is not sociology, it is shaped across the decades by shifting and developing social values and structures.

The response of the public to each crime can also vary as society alters and rearranges its attitudes and values. In the case of this history book, it is quite easy to observe, for example, a level of social violence in the frontier period, as expressed by a lynching and the massacre of innocent Chinese, that would be unthinkable in a later era.

So many of the early cases discussed in *For the People*—the Lugo case and the Vasquez case, for instance—deal with the interaction between Hispanic residents of the region and the newly established American hegemony. The temptation to the white majority in these years was the exploitation of the prior residents and vigilantism, as evidenced in the lynching of French ex-patriot Michel Lachenais in December 1870. Xenophobia reached its climax in the terrible massacre by a mob of nineteen Chinese in October 1871. This was the low point of Los Angeles public behavior in the nineteenth century and a chilling reminder of how society can degenerate when it detaches from the rule of law.

That rule of law, however, was established in the early years, 1850 to 1899, helped in great measure by a series of distinguished district attorneys. It was as if Los Angeles—a remote and sparsely settled frontier cattle town through the 1860s—explored its dark side in the 1871 massacres and realized that in this direction there was only chaos. Within a few short years, this same city, which had behaved so abominably, was building distinguished office blocks, paving streets, laying down streetcar tracks, opening schools, constructing its first cathedral and establishing the rule of law.

In the 1880s Los Angeles County entered the first of its many population booms. Between 1900 and 1919, the county absorbed more than a million new residents, while experiencing the profound social transformation of this era. Thus the District Attorney's Office had to deal simultaneously with the single greatest act of anti-newspaper terrorism in the history of the United States, the bombing of the *Los Angeles Times*; the effort to clean up local government—born of the Progressive Era—and a series of dramatic murder cases during the 1920s and the 1930s—born of the general social and personal instability of a population of residents from elsewhere, frequently eccentric, even grotesque, unbuttressed by community sanctions.

During those years Los Angeles County earned its well-deserved reputation as a place where crimes of violence could be especially grotesque and sociologically revealing. As this history shows, the record speaks for itself. Los Angeles, at least as far as crime was concerned, earned its reputation as a far-out place.

Seventy, even eighty years later, commentators had not tired of pointing to the Madalynne Obenchain case, the Tiger Woman case, the William Hickman case, the murder of William Desmond Taylor, the disappearance of Sister Aimee Semple McPherson and the Julian Petroleum scandal as studies in the distinctive, frequently bizarre, social texture of life in Los Angeles County. Indeed, in these tumultuous years, a district attorney himself, Asa Keyes, succumbed to the instability of the times, was tried and convicted and spent time in San Quentin.

All of America has courtroom trials, of course; but so many of the trials in this history are possessed of a vividness, a theatricality, a quality of *Grand Guignol*— the case of Rattlesnake James, for instance; the case of the lover in the attic, kept there for some ten years; the Winnie Ruth Judd trunk murder case—that suggest a certain crossover between fiction and reality, the believable and the improbable that has become part of the folklore of the region. Frequently, the cases in this history involve celebrities. A famous theater tycoon, Alexander Pantages and, later, movie star Errol Flynn are charged with rape. Singer Madonna is stalked and put on the stand to face the stalker. Hollywood's favorite gangster Benjamin Siegel is unsuccessfully prosecuted followed in time by equally unsuccessful efforts to convict Mickey Cohen. Robert Mitchum goes to the slammer, briefly, for smoking marijuana and emerges more popular than ever.

Sadly, ethnically based and ethnically biased prosecutions—the railroading of Pedro Gonzalez or the trumped-up Sleepy Lagoon charges, for example—testify to the continuing second-class status of whole sectors of the population. The 1950s was a decade of suppressed tensions and a certain existentialist edge. The trials, convictions and executions of Barbara Graham and Caryl Chessman captured the popular imagination (and then Susan Hayward played Graham in the movie *I Want to Live*, with one of the most horrific execution scenes ever) because these two cases revealed, most powerfully, the tensions and texture of the 1950s, at once the era of *Ozzie and Harriet* and a time bomb waiting to explode. That explosion occurred in the 1960s, beginning with the effort to prosecute comedian Lenny Bruce for obscenity. In such internationally significant cases as the Watts riots of 1965, the assassination of Senator Robert Kennedy in 1968 and the Manson murder trials of 1969, Los Angeles County was revealed as a seedbed of political and social tensions and dark obsessions that help define an era. The deaths of Ruben Salazar, the murder of Sal Mineo, the rape charges leveled against Roman Polanski, the bizarre rattlesnake trial involving Synanon (the second notable rattlesnake-as-murder-weapon case in Los Angeles County history) continued this cavalcade of cases revealing the underside of America—or at the least, the underside of Southern California into the 1970s.

This representative role continues, however begrudgingly, through the last two decades of the century. The cases from the 1980s through the 1990s have proven even more revelatory of the tensions being experienced by an entire society. America experiences the collapse of its savings and loan sector, and Los Angeles faces the Charles Keating trial. America becomes increasingly enamored with celebritydom, and as in the cases of the actresses Theresa Saldana, Rebecca Schaeffer and Madonna, celebrities are stalked, maimed, and even murdered by obsessed fans. As if to signal the rise of gratuitous murder in the final years of the century, the era opens with the Bob's Big Boy massacre of December 1980 and continues through the murders, arrest, trial, conviction and sentencing of Satanist Richard Ramirez. To this day, the McMartin Preschool case still lingers in ambiguity. Despite its inconclusive outcome, the McMartin case holds its place in the unfolding story of child abuse, real or imagined, a sad legacy of the century's last two decades. Then came the Rodney King beating, the acquittal of the indicted officers and the riots that followed in which Los Angeles once again, as in the Chinese massacres of 1871 or the Watts riots of 1965, looked the gorgon of social disintegration in the face—and almost blinked.

History is the record of what goes right and what goes wrong. In the cases discussed in this narrative, something went wrong, whether murder most foul, financial swindling, political corruption or other of the many forms of human misbehavior. In a variety of ways, each of the crimes discussed in *For the People* illuminates not just the criminal, the victim or the prosecutor—but society as well. Part of the fascination the rest of the world has with Southern California arises because of the frequently theatrical nature of its crimes and what these crimes tell us about the human condition in general, as well as with life in these United States—and how the two confront and affect each other in a place called Los Angeles County.

— Dr. Kevin Starr
State Librarian
Los Angeles, California
July 2000

Bella Union Hotel, 1871.

From Cow Town Beginnings

The pueblo of *La Reyna de los Angeles*, the Queen of Angels, and the great ranchos in the surrounding lowland, were prosperous and comparatively genteel in the final decades before California became part of the United States. But every society has its criminals. And the California-born offspring of Spanish and Mexican immigrants had begun using the term *Californio* in the 1830s to distinguish themselves from Mexican convicts and other scoundrels—in those days called *cholos*—who were being sent north by the Mexican government to help populate its distant colony. California was Mexico's Siberia.

Yet murder and robbery were still rare and for many, life was secure and comfortable. The *Dons* seldom kept count of their cattle, which thrived in gentle surroundings tended by low-cost albeit exploited Indian labor. In the final years of Mexican rule, a couple of thousand *Californios*, several thousand Native Americans, a few Yankees, French and other foreigners—and a hundred thousand cows—lived in the Los Angeles Basin. When *rancheros* felt the need to raise cash, they rounded up a few hundred head of cattle, carted the hides and tallow to the shoreline at San Pedro and sold them to trading vessels that plied the California coast, anchoring at its rudimentary ports. San Pedro's sandy, almost uninhabited shore "furnished more hides than any port on the coast," wrote

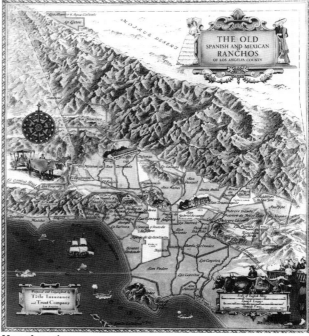

Map of *ranchos*.

Richard Henry Dana Jr. in *Two Years Before the Mast*. Dana worked as a common sailor aboard the Boston trader *Pilgrim* in 1834. He loaded hides at San Pedro, learning that "...about thirty miles in the interior was a fine plane country, filled with herds of cattle, in the center of which was the *Pueblo de los Angeles*—the largest town in California—and several of the wealthiest missions...."

Disputes and crimes were adjudicated at the local level under the Mexican judicial system by *alcaldes*, magistrates whose token of office was a silver-headed cane. *Alcaldes* were authorized to fine errant citizens up to twenty-five dollars and to sentence them to up to four days of work in the public interest. *Juezes del campo*, judges of the plains, straightened out the business dealings and small criminal matters of the *ranchos*. There were two jails—one for the accused, the other for the convicted. Typical sentences were a month in jail for slander; banishment, for vagrancy or adultery.

Much would change with the end of the Mexican-American War. Under the Treaty of Guadalupe Hidalgo in 1848, California was annexed to the United States. *Californios* were assured U.S. citizenship or resident status if they chose. In a two-year transition administered by the United States Army, the civic and legal systems of Mexico were replaced with American structures. It was a transition in form, but not always in people.

The last *alcalde* under Mexican rule, for instance, was Massachusetts-born Abel Stearns, who had become a Mexican citizen in 1828, moved to Los Angeles and converted to Catholicism to marry 14-year-old Arcadia Bandini. His home had doubled as the courthouse. So would the home of the first judge of Los Angeles under the new U.S. court system, the widely respected Agustin Olvera, a former *alcalde* under Mexican rule.

Los Angeles as a municipality changed in fundamental ways as well. In the traditional, family-oriented life of the *Californios*, Los Angeles had been a sleepy cow town where ranchers occasionally bought provisions to take back to the *rancho*, where social life was centered.

The home of Judge Agustin Olvera doubled as a courthouse.

Now, discharged soldiers from both sides of the Mexican-American War were loose on the streets—with guns, access to a collection of new saloons but few jobs.

Historian Paul M. De Falla credits the true starting point for Los Angeles's status as "a wide-open town in the fullest sense of the word" with the discharge from military service of Company E of Stevenson's Regiment, also known as the Bowery Company, in Los Angeles in 1848.

A year later, gold was discovered in California, and the southern, all-weather route for Forty-Niners from around the world ran through Yuma, Arizona, and the waystation of Los Angeles, as these fortune-seekers trekked to the northern California gold fields.

Minutes of first court session, 1850.

Los Angeles panorama, 1869.

Los Angeles became a rough, routinely deadly town. Gambling dens and prostitution provided a congenial atmosphere for crime. In 1850, murder was commonplace: almost one every day among a total population of only 8,329 residents. Matters were only to become worse. The historian H.H. Bancroft estimated by 1853, four hundred gamblers had been flushed out of San Francisco by

Document of the state legislature creating the District Attorney's Office, 1850.

vigilance groups and had ended up in Los Angeles. The first boatload of non-local prostitutes, again heading south from San Francisco, arrived the same year.

California's military government ended in December 1849. The previous September, a constitutional convention had created the new state structure, including a judiciary with a state supreme court; district courts which had jurisdiction over serious crimes and other powers similar to later superior courts; county courts which handled probate and heard appeals from justice courts, and the justices of the peace. Courts of sessions were panels composed of the judge of the county court and two justices of the peace. Courts of sessions had only limited criminal jurisdiction and many of their duties would be taken over later by the County Board of Supervisors.

The one holdover from Mexican rule was the *juez del campo*, the judge of the plains, an important position in the era of the *ranchos*. A *juez del campo* settled disputes over ownership of horses and cattle and presided at rodeos, important competitive business events as well as entertainment. The position of *juez del*

Agustin Olvera.

Agustin Olvera

The new County's first judge remains a prominent citizen and civic leader under Mexican rule, through the military transition and after California becomes a state.

Under the Mexican government, Agustin Olvera had been a member of the territorial assembly and commissioner of land distribution. During the transition to statehood, after the end of the Mexican-American War, the U.S. Army appointed Olvera to be Judge of the First Instance in 1849. Olvera was elected Los Angeles County's first judge in 1850, and while he learned English, the first sheriff of Los Angeles, bilingual George F. Burrill, was paid fifty dollars a month to translate the proceedings when court was in session. Olvera would be elected to the county Board of Supervisors in 1855. In 1877, the Los Angeles City Council changed the name of Wine Street to Olvera Street, in his honor. The neighborhood of his home, where he first held County trials, is now the historic Olvera Street marketplace and plaza.

William C. Ferrell.

William C. Ferrell, District Attorney 1850-1851

The first district attorney in Los Angeles County came from North Carolina and ended his days on an isolated mesa in Mexico.

District Attorney William C. Ferrell—elected April 1, 1850, in a contest in which three hundred seventy-seven votes were cast—was the people's prosecutor in the big First Judicial District, which included San Diego and Los Angeles counties. In fact, he lived in San Diego for the part of the one-year term that he actually served. He was age 39 when elected, and had just arrived from North Carolina, where he had been an attorney. His income as district attorney was largely derived from a ten percent cut of civil judgments as well as fees paid from guilty criminal defendants' fines. In October 1850, when it became clear that the state legislature would soon require a district attorney in each county—drastically cutting his income—Ferrell promptly quit. He would serve in other public positions in San Diego through the mid-1850s, on the first County Board of Supervisors, as county assessor and as district attorney for San Diego County. Then, apparently as a way to thwart his growing dependence on alcohol, in 1860 he moved to Mexico, building an adobe home with vegetable garden and a large vineyard on a remote mesa south of Tijuana. He died in Mexico in 1883.

campo was prestigious, and it continued for two decades after annexation, until the big *ranchos* were no more.

The state legislature created district attorney's offices on February 27, 1850. William C. Ferrell was elected the first district attorney in Los Angeles County on April 1. Two months later, on June 5, the new First District Court convened. The vast First Judicial District held sway over San Diego and Los Angeles counties. And at the time, Los Angeles County included what would later be San Bernardino and Orange counties, as well as parts of Inyo and Kern counties. At this first session, District Attorney Ferrell and several other attorneys were admitted to the new California bar—the first attorneys in Los Angeles to be made members

Abel Stearns remained in charge of the *alcalde* court until the new court system began to function. On July 8, 1850, in a rented room at the Bella Union Hotel, the first criminal calendar was called for the new Court of Sessions. The six cases heard that day ranged from larceny to assault. Three defendants pleaded guilty. The same six-man jury heard the three cases that went to trial, prosecuted by Ferrell. Two ended in conviction; one, acquittal. The guilty received fines of from one to five dollars.

Court sessions in those days were casual and occasionally raucous. One popular, sharp-witted judge of the county court, William G. Dryden, once lectured a guilty defendant on his crime, then sentenced him: "But the jury recommends clemency. Accordingly, I declare you a free man, and you may go about your business."

A comic in the audience shouted, "What *is* his business?"

"Horse-stealing, sir!" the judge shouted back. "*Horse-stealing!*"

Dryden did try to bring dignity to the courts, by issuing an edict: "It is ordered that hereafter attorneys while in attendance upon court will be required to wear a coat of some kind and will not be allowed to rest their feet on the tops of tables or whittle or spit tobacco juice on the floor or stove…." He didn't ban pistols or bowie knives, however, which were frequently carried into court by members of the audience, attorneys and other court principals, including the judge.

At a far more serious level, the transition to a new judicial system was complicated by rising tension between the *Californio* majority and the English-speaking minority. "If the Yankees and the *Californios* of the cow counties found certain areas of respect for each other, one matter in particular—the problem of crime and punishment—divided them with razorlike sharpness," observed historian Leonard Pitt in *The Decline of the Californios.*

Don Antonio Lugo.

The Lugo Case

The murder of two men in 1850 increases suspicion between the *Californio* majority and the new Yankee establishment.

In 1850, Patrick McSwiggen, an Irishman, and a Creek Indian named Sam were murdered in Cajon Pass, a long, wide canyon rising from San Bernardino to the Mojave Desert. The same day, Don Jose del Carmen Lugo, the wealthy and respected owner of the vast Rancho San Bernardino, three of his sons and a large party of ranch hands rode through the pass chasing a band of Ute Indians who had stolen some of their best horses. To Yankee members of the new Los Angeles law-enforcement community, the party of *Californios* became immediate suspects in the murders. Then a Mexican *vaquero* and thief from Sonora, who had been in the Lugo party, said that he, another Sonoran and three Lugo sons—Francisco, Benito and Chico—had killed the two men. The *vaquero* claimed that the Irishman had lied to the Lugo party, sending the riders up a canyon where the Utes were waiting to ambush them. One of the ranch hands had been killed. The *vaquero* said that the Lugo boys had come back and killed the two in revenge.

But the Lugos strongly denied the murders and were backed up by twenty witnesses. The Yankees still didn't believe them, however. Justice of the Peace Jonathan R. Scott eventually indicted the three Lugo sons and put them in jail. To the *Californios*, this was another highly suspicious Yankee move. First the Yankees had taken the word of an admitted Mexican thief over that of a respected *Californio* family. Now Scott, who hated the Lugos, had pressed the case in what seemed a personal vendetta. Scott and his wife, as it happened, had once stayed at the Lugo ranch. When Scott physically assaulted his wife during a domestic argument, Don Lugo and his son, Chico, pulled Scott away from his wife, a move Scott considered humiliating. Scott had the two Lugos convicted of assault and fined $2.50 apiece.

The murders were more serious, and the situation deteriorated. "Even more alarming than a prejudiced prosecutor and an inflamed public opinion," historian Leonard Pitt noted, "was the arrival in town of twenty-five meddlesome ruffians." A gang led by a former Texas Ranger, John "Red" Irving, came into Los Angeles, learned of the Lugo situation, and set out to extort money from the Lugo family. The Lugos had hired Yankee attorney Joseph Lancaster Brent as their defense counsel, assisted by future District Attorney Isaac Ogier. Brent firmly believed the boys to be innocent.

Now one of Irving's men told Brent that Irving wanted ten thousand dollars from the Lugos to keep the sons from being

Joseph Lancaster Brent.

Benjamin Hayes.

horses and cattle and apparently threatened women. This brought out a military unit stationed in the area. Now Irving cooked up another scheme to get at the Lugo's valuables. He sent a man to tell the Cahuilla Indians in the San Bernardino Mountains that a band of white men was coming to exterminate them. Irving expected that the Indians and the military unit would be too engaged in his engineered battle to notice that he and his men had returned to loot the Lugo estate.

The Lugos learned of the plan, however, and disappeared with their worldly goods. Irving arrived to ransack the place but found nothing valuable. As he and his band walked back out of the house, they found themselves surrounded by silent Cahuillas, led by chief Juan Antonio. The Cahuillas followed Irving and nearly a dozen of his men into a blind canyon, where they killed them all. Justice of the Peace Jose Maria Lugo, an old friend of Juan Antonio and the Cahuilla Indians, had secretly enlisted them as special police to dispense justice to Irving and his men.

A coroner's jury decided that Justice of the Peace Lugo and his Cahuilla policemen had gone beyond their authority. But with the agreement of County Attorney Benjamin Hayes, the jury pronounced the killings to be "justifiable." The charges against the Lugo sons were eventually dismissed by Judge Agustin Olvera, in the Court of Sessions, for lack of evidence.

It was a clear example, noted Pitt, "of the overlapping of old and new judicial philosophies." The Californios considered justice to have been done to the Irving gang. Yankees thought they should have been brought into court. District attorneys would be reconciling the old and new legal standards and philosophies at least into the 1880s.

lynched. Irving would escort them to safety in Sonora. It was a simple extortion attempt.

Brent came up with a better scheme. He arranged to have seventy-five armed *Californios* and Sonorans gather at a spot near the courthouse the night before the Lugo sons were to be let out on bail. And when a unit of the state militia happened by the next morning, Brent convinced the soldiers to deliver the Lugos intact from the courthouse to their armed friends. Acting District Attorney Thomas Sutherland came to court armed while bail was posted, to protect the judge and the proceedings. The courtroom, filled with Irving's men, remained calm because the soldiers stood by.

Frustrated, Irving and his men headed for Chino, where they stole

Vicente Lugo family at their Bell Gardens Home, about 1890.

The *Californio* tradition was informal but sought justice as a matter of honor and simple truth. Yankee justice was more structured, though prejudice during this period made a mockery of the idea of sticking to the letter of the law. One example was the explosive Lugo case (see page 24).

The new American judicial structure was imposed, no matter in the face of widespread skepticism. In the mid-1850s, for instance, one Spanish-American wit noted that the new Los Angeles criminal justice establishment had as many judges, prosecutors and constables as Cortes had soldiers when he subjugated the Aztec empire.

At the same time, the new legal system was far from judicial in the way rights were allotted to various new and old Californians, particularly among the ambitious gold-seekers. At the prodding of Yankee Forty-Niners, the state adopted the notorious Foreign Miners' Tax Law of 1850 to discourage competition from non-U.S. miners—many of whom came from Sonora, Mexico, and other parts of Latin America. In practice, the tax wasn't assessed on Irish or other European miners. And it was often unfairly imposed upon all Spanish-speaking miners, whether the native *Californios* or foreigners. Violent protests by angry, disenfranchised miners, and hard feelings among all parties, became common.

Los Angeles police officers in their first uniforms, 1890s.

The Land Act of 1851 was another early source of great hostility. The unfortunate law hastened the breakup of the old *ranchos* and fostered disputes over land and water that inflamed old and new residents. With expanding demand from Gold Rush miners, the old tallow-and-hide trade was overshadowed by a highly profitable market for beef.

Meanwhile, the guarantees of the Treaty of Guadalupe Hidalgo and the new state constitution were not always respected. The 1855 California Legislature simply refused to publish new laws in Spanish as well as English, despite the brand-new state constitution's requirement.

Aliso Street, downtown Los Angeles, 1899.

26

The Lynching of Michel Lachenais

A Frenchman who kills a popular local farmer in 1870 receives the County's last extreme example of frontier justice.

Though a mob would lynch and shoot to death nineteen Chinese men the next year, the 1870 lynching of Michel Lachenais was the last in which a vigilante group delivered summary justice to a criminal.

French ex-patriots had once constituted the largest non-Spanish-speaking minority in Los Angeles. But Lachenais had never been the best representative of the French community. He had twice been tried for murder—receiving a conviction for manslaughter and an acquittal. In one case, he had killed a fellow Frenchman at a funeral wake. In 1870, he shot and killed Jacob Bell, a well-liked elderly farmer, in a water dispute. They had been alone. The killer's identity remained a mystery until Lachenais made a drunken reference to it one night. He was arrested and jailed. The same night, outraged citizens formed a vigilance committee at Stearns' Hall. Attendees discussed

Lachenais's record of violence and voted for death. Three hundred armed men, led by a local barber and former city councilman, marched on the jail on the morning of December 17, broke down the doors with sledgehammers and dragged Lachenais to the Tomlinson and Griffith corral, across the street from the present-day Criminal Courts Building. Lachenais became the thirty-fifth man to be hanged from the timbers of the corral. The next month, County Judge Ygnacio Sepulveda charged the grand jury with determining the leaders of the mob, but the jury members declined, saying that had the law been faithfully executed, the lynching would have never taken place.

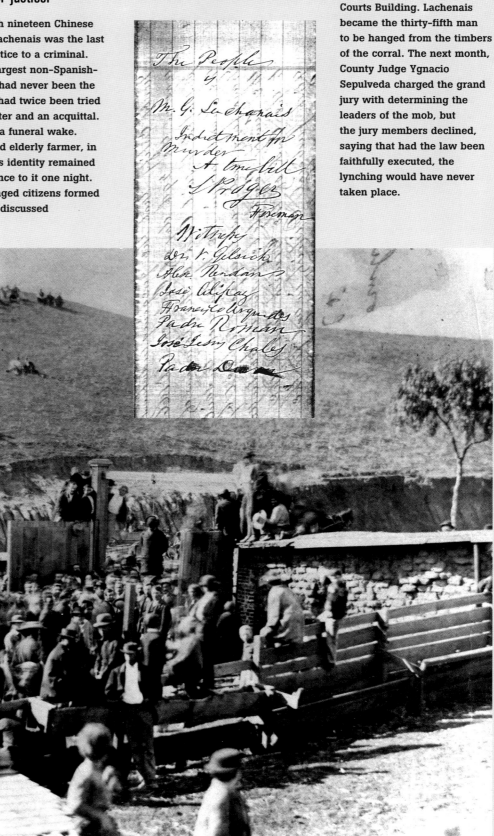

The lynching of Michel Lachenais, 1870; his indictment (inset).

Clara S. Foltz, 1911.

Clara Shortridge Foltz

Becoming the first female deputy district attorney in 1910 is only one of many milestones for a pioneering lawyer and for the District Attorney's Office.

Clara Shortridge Foltz, sister of U. S. Senator Samuel Shortridge, a long-time California Republican leader, had studied law at her father's law firm in San Jose. When she was denied admission to the all-male Hastings College of Law at the University of California, she applied for a writ of mandate to compel Hastings to admit her—arguing her own case through district court and the State Supreme Court, where she won. Foltz was the divorced mother of five children in 1878 when she drafted an amendment to the state Civil Code to admit women to the state bar. She vigorously supported the legislation and when it was signed into law she became the first woman attorney admitted in California. This made her only the third woman lawyer in the entire United States.

District Attorney John D. Fredericks had been persuaded to hire Foltz, then 61 years old, by Los Angeles women's groups. When she accepted the post, she described herself as "the only female

prosecutor in the world." She also became an advocate, in 1893, of a separate office of public defender. Her supporters had supposed that she would represent the interests only of women and children. But they had underestimated the woman who would become known in legal circles as the "Portia of the Pacific." Foltz announced, "I look at the field from a broader standpoint than my sisters do. When they advocated my appointment they were thinking only of the women and little ones. But the law appeals to me broadly and I will do whatever is given me by Captain Fredericks."

On national political issues, she was a staunch advocate of woman suffrage and was pivotal in the successful campaign to get women the vote in California in 1911. She was against Prohibition and was anti-Communist. Foltz ran for governor in 1930. When she announced her candidacy for U.S. Senator in 1933 she said, "That a woman should seek this office is not extraordinary, since women have been counted among the law-givers of the world from Deborah who, tradition says, ruled Israel."

Lita Belle Hibben.

The second female deputy district attorney was Lita Belle Hibben, who joined the office in 1915, at age 29. Women joined the office in the early years to work in juvenile delinquency and family units. (In fact, it wasn't until 1932 that District Attorney Buron Fitts hired Deputy District Attorney Terrys Olender, the first female prosecutor to try general felony cases rather than focusing on delinquency and family cases.) In 1915, the new child-support operation dealt with forty-five hundred cases of "lazy" dads, as the newspapers then called fathers who refused to pay court-ordered child support. Almost two hundred of these dads ended up on a County chain gang after conviction for failure to provide.

The District Attorney's Office has maintained the largest local child-support enforcement program in the United States. Over the

May Allison, first "Failure to Provide" trustee, 1915.

years, automation of the unit has drastically increased the amount of money recovered. In 1976, the program was reorganized to form the Bureau of Child Support Operations, which grew to involve fully a third of all District Attorney's Office employees. From 1976 to 1992, child-support collections in Los Angeles grew from $30 million to more than $124 million. In 2000, the California State Legislature relieved all of the state's district attorneys' offices from the civil aspect of family support collection, to allow concentration on prosecution of cases that have become criminal matters.

Biases hardened. Several celebrated *Californio* and Mexican-American bandits set out on the outlaw trail during this period. At the same time, Yankee newcomers to Los Angeles, even civic leaders, took up unorthodox law-enforcement methods. In the 1850s, vigilante groups were formed, including the Rangers, the most prominent group. Roy Bean, who would later be known in Texas as "Judge" Roy Bean, was an early Ranger. So was Isaac Stockton Ogier, the county's second district attorney.

Cover of early promotional booklet on Los Angeles.

Yet by the late 1860s, longtime residents of good will—*Californios*, Mexican immigrants and Yankees alike—had begun to improve the legal system. A gradual influx of church-going Americans also helped to settle the town into more respectable ways. In 1870 prostitution was outlawed in the central business district.

Over the decades, new technologies and new attitudes brought different criminal scenarios.

The Southern Pacific railroad connected Los Angeles to the rest of the nation, as well as to San Pedro Harbor in the mid-1870s. It soon became both a boon to business and a continually corrupting influence on public officials in a position to further the railroad's ambitions. When the Santa Fe rail line reached Los Angeles in 1885, a fare war between the two made tickets to Los Angeles irresistibly cheap. Thousands of newcomers, many from the midwest, moved to the county—sparking wild speculation in new townships and, often, bogus land deals.

The pastoral ranching and fruit-farming region was gradually transforming into a patchwork of urban and industrial neighborhoods. The two decades from 1880 to 1900 saw spectacular growth, with the county population booming from

```
             SEMI-ANNUAL REPORT
OF J. D. FREDERICKS, DISTRICT ATTORNEY OF
                LOS ANGELES COUNTY
FOR THE SIX MONTHS ENDING DECEMBER 31, 1914.

                - - - - -

1.   Convicted, - - - - - - - - - - - - - - - - - - -  55
2.   Plead guilty, - - - - - - - - - - - - - - - - - - 174
3.   Acquitted, - - - - - - - - - - - - - - - - - - - -  9
4.   Insane, escaped, died, dismissed, - - - - - - - - - 80
5.   Pending trial, - - - - - - - - - - - - - - - - - -  21
6.   Sentenced to death, - - - - - - - - - - - - - - - -
7.   Sentenced to State's Prison, - - - - - - - - - - - 72
8.   Sentenced to other institutions, - - - - - - - - - -32
9.   Fines, sentence suspended, probation, - - - - - - - -122
```
Status report on cases, 1914.

33,381 to more than 170,000 residents. Streets were paved and Los Angeles was electrified—with street lighting for homes and businesses, electric trolleys, electric power for manufacturing plants. The telephone—"the new invention to facilitate speaking at a distance," as Harris Newmark called it in his memoir, *Sixty Years in Southern California, 1853–1913*—became a popular instrument by the late 1880s.

The Los Angeles Aqueduct, completed in 1913, provided water and inexpensive electric power for even more growth. By now, district attorneys were no longer working to domesticate an unruly cow town but to build a professional agency able to apply

Earliest known group photo of the District Attorney's staff, 1924.

First Public Defender

Walton J. Woods becomes the nation's first public defender.

In 1914 the Board of Supervisors created the new post of public defender. Though District Attorney John D. Fredericks, and many others in the legal community, were skeptics at first, the duty of the Public Defender's Office to ensure the rights of defendants became essential in trials. In the early days, Walton Woods split his time between criminal and civil cases. In 1920, Woods became a judge in the Superior Court.

Woods, 1914.

the law to an exploding population. In 1911, the district attorney's and deputy district attorneys' jobs became full-time positions—with private practice on the side no longer allowed. In the same period, employees of the office came under civil-service regulation and the first branch office was opened, in Long Beach. The first female deputy district attorney, Clara Shortridge Foltz, was hired in 1910. Five years later, Lita Belle Hibben became the second. In 1913, the District Attorney's Office turned over civil prosecutions to the newly created office of County Counsel. In 1914, the County created the first public defender's office in the nation, again focusing the role of the District Attorney's Office.

The county continued to grow. After 1915, Los Angeles received what historian Robert M. Fogelson called "two welcome windfalls": an oil industry and the motion-picture business. After World War I ended in 1919, big oil reserves were discovered in Huntington Beach, Seal Beach, Montebello, Santa Fe Springs and Long Beach. At that time, the wells in these fields constituted Los Angeles's leading industry, supplying nine percent of U.S. oil demand—and five percent of the world's. But along with this new industry came more new arrivals, many of them rough, oilfield roustabouts. Thousands more came when auto-related companies including Goodyear, Goodrich and Firestone picked Los Angeles over San Francisco and Portland, Oregon, for new manufacturing plants.

Broadway, looking south, 1928.

Movie producers liked the freedom from an East Coast monopoly that had tried to control the new industry—as well as Southern California's good, clear weather, wide variety of accessible scenery, and relatively easy distribution to the rest of the country. By 1930, fifty-two motion picture studios were in operation, employing fifteen thousand workers.

Meanwhile, city leaders increased regulation of saloons, prostitution, gambling and related pastimes. In the 1890s, Compton, Ontario, Long Beach and other Southern California cities, backed by the powerful Anti-Saloon League of California, voted to ban alcoholic beverages. In 1899, Los Angeles limited itself to two hundred saloons. By 1910, there was hardly a saloon left in Los Angeles County, and the City of

Bureau of Investigation

The unsung heroes of many major prosecutions got their start in 1913, with authorization to hire three detectives.

The County Board of Supervisors approved the hiring of the first District Attorney's Office investigators, along with a small support staff, in 1913. The first chief of detectives was Sam Browne, who, during the term of District Attorney J. D. Fredericks, had made the key arrest during the *Los Angeles Times* bombing trial—an apprehension that led to bribery charges against defense attorney Clarence Darrow.

The need for more investigators soon became clear. By 1920, a dozen detectives were at work. District Attorney Buron Fitts officially organized the group into the Bureau of Investigation after he took

office in 1928, using federal Justice Department investigations units as models. He split the Bureau into two forces. One, known familiarly as the Booze Squad, concentrated on liquor law and vice enforcement. The other handled all other criminal investigations. By 1950, the Bureau had sixty-five investigators; by 2000, there were more than two hundred.

In the early years, investigators' duties included probing murders and protecting witnesses. Now the investigators, who have full peace-officer authority equal to a sheriff's deputy, process witnesses and develop evidence for crimes ranging from murder to insurance fraud to child abuse. Specially designated investigators work directly in teams with prosecutors in the Hardcore Gang Division, Special Investigations Division—which is assigned to public corruption and police-misconduct cases— the Family Violence Division and other units.

Since its inception, the Bureau has been crucial in a long line of cases prosecuted by the District Attorney's Office. Bureau investigators found the body of Grace Young, hidden in a cistern by her husband, Dr. Thomas Young, in 1925. A female investigator from the Bureau for weeks protected Eunice Pringle, the key witness in the 1929 Alexander Pantages rape case. Investigators pieced together the bizarre tale of Robert "Rattlesnake" James, who killed his wife and tried to make it look like an accidental drowning. In later trials—the Ennis Cosby and Charles Keating cases, for example—Bureau investigators developed evidence and witnesses that were crucial to the trial prosecutors.

District Attorney's Bureau of Investigation of 1933.

Scenes of the Action

County Courthouses move, improve and expand over the decades.

In the early 1850s, the first County court sessions were held in rented rooms in the Bella Union Hotel and private homes. Then in 1859, John Temple, an early Los Angeles businessman, built the yellow brick Market House on the current site of the Los Angeles City Hall. Just as he completed construction, Temple made a generous addition. "Thanks to the public spirit of Mr. Temple, a clock has been erected in the tower of the Market House," the *Los Angeles Star* wrote in appreciation, "The bell is fine-toned and sonorous, its notes being heard all over the city. This is a very great accommodation for the public." The first floor was filled with market stalls, and the County rented the second floor for courtrooms.

Temple died in 1864. The County bought the building for twenty thousand dollars in 1867. All County offices were now brought under one roof. Lawyers' offices, restaurants frequented by the legal community and associated businesses concentrated in the neighborhood. And for three decades, whenever court was in session, the custom was for lawyers and witnesses to wait below. When their turn in court came, the bailiff would stick his head out a courtroom window and call out the name, three times. When the bailiff called an attorney, he always added the term "Esquire."

As the county's population boomed in the 1880s, the judicial system was forced to again rent rooms scattered around downtown Los Angeles. In 1886, voters passed a two-hundred-thousand-dollar bond issue to build a new courthouse on Poundcake Hill, the later site of the Criminal Courts Building at Spring and Temple Streets. The five-hundred-thousand-dollar, three-story courthouse opened for judicial business in 1891, with the district attorney's offices on the third floor and the sheriff's department in the basement. The face and hands of the old clock from the Clocktower Courthouse

The first court sessions were held in the Bella Union Hotel.

Clocktower Courthouse, 1880.

Southern view of the Clocktower Courthouse.

The half-million-dollar Red Sandstone Courthouse opened in 1891.

were installed atop the new courthouse. The building boasted an inside elevator. Later, an outside elevator with windows was added— known as the Honeymoon Tower because it bore couples up to the marriage-license office.

The Red Sandstone Courthouse, as the structure was called, became overcrowded in the first years of the new century. In 1911, the District Attorney's Office, the County jails, municipal courts and superior court criminal divisions moved into the new Hall of Records, just south of the courthouse. In 1926, the District Attorney's Office moved again, to the fourteen-story, $6.5 million Hall of Justice. In 1971, the District Attorney's Office, the Public Defender's Office and municipal and superior criminal courts relocated to the Criminal Courts Building, back to the site of the old Red Sandstone Courthouse, which had been razed after it was severely damaged in the 1933 earthquake.

Early photograph of Hall of Justice.

Angels had elected a "dry" mayor, George Alexander. The rest of the country banned alcohol with the advent of Prohibition, which lasted from 1919 to 1933. Unhappily for the Progressives and Temperance groups which sought to dissuade citizens from indulging in the evils of drink, Prohibition served better to foster a new criminal class, as well as the sassy, unconventional spirit of the Roaring Twenties.

Horses and stages gave way to automobiles through these years, and the auto changed Los Angeles more than most U.S. cities. Inevitably, this handy machine was put to use in robberies. Another widespread crime wrought by the automobile, Prohibition notwithstanding, was drunk driving. In 1930, for example, the District Attorney's Office obtained convictions in nine murders, seven cases of manslaughter and three hundred seventy cases of driving while intoxicated.

This period also marked the first chapter in the career of one of the best-known Los Angeles deputy district attorneys ever, J. Miller Leavy, who joined the office in 1932 and served for four decades. A dozen men and one woman—the notorious Barbara Graham— were executed after Leavy obtained their convictions for murder. "He was the epitome of the hard-drinking, savvy, ethical, driven trial lawyer and he really trained a whole generation [of prosecutors]," Deputy District Attorney Michael Genelin recalled after Leavy's death in 1995.

In the 1940s, racial tension returned, with friction primarily between Latinos and Anglos. In the post-war economic slump in Los Angeles, led by a decline in military aircraft production, many blamed a boom in crime on out-of-work aircraft workers. True or not, crime had increased and the District Attorney's Office expanded to take on the new case load. In 1940, the District Attorney's Office had a staff of one hundred seventy-five and an annual budget of six hundred eighty thousand dollars. Two decades later, the staff had grown to four hundred employees, with a budget of more than $3 million.

In the next decade, the felony caseload doubled—to forty thousand cases a year. By 1979, the office had twenty-three hundred employees, five hundred fifty of whom were prosecutors. A big challenge for the District Attorney's Office through this period came from the changing legal landscape for the death penalty. It was first overturned by the California Supreme Court in 1972, which declared execution to be cruel and unusual punishment, in violation of the state constitution. This changed the sentences of one hundred seven Death Row inmates to life in prison—in most cases, with the possibility of parole. A similar court decision in 1976 reinforced the ban. But in 1977, the California Legislature restored the death penalty and the next year, state voters approved an even broader statute that replaced the 1977 law. The first use after the sentencing option was restored was the execution in 1992 of San Diego murderer Robert Alton Harris.

Gangs, drug violence, family violence, hate crimes, serial killers and stalkers were the focus of extensive prosecutorial efforts in the final two decades of the century. Tougher sentencing laws for rape, domestic violence and aggravated assault helped to contain these crimes but also increased the costs and complexities of many trials.

The District Attorney's Office developed along with the County of Los Angeles as it grew to almost ten million by the year 2000. The District Attorney, one of three elective positions in the County system, prosecutes all felonies committed in the county; prosecutes misdemeanors in unincorporated areas; appears before and advises the Los Angeles County Grand Jury and remains charged, as in the earliest days, with the broad mandate to improve the administration of justice.

California overturns the death penalty, 1972.

Hall of Justice; various stages of construction.

Defendant Barbara Graham.

Thieves and Killers

Theft is an ancient temptation and, no matter the natural bounty of the Los Angeles region, those with a larcenous eye have never had quite enough personal wealth. Sometimes the criminal doesn't stop at stealing. All too often, what begins as a robbery deteriorates into more serious, sometimes deadly crime.

The Forty-Niners passing through town, for instance, were joined by "vagabonds from every quarter of the globe," wrote San Gabriel resident Hugo Reid to a friend in 1849. "Scoundrels from nowhere, rascals from Oregon, pickpockets from New York, accomplished gentlemen from Europe, interlopers from Lima and Chile, Mexican thieves, gamblers of no particular spot, and assassins manufactured in Hell for the expressed purpose of converting highways and byways into theaters of blood... "

In 1855, the *Los Angeles Star* tallied the arrests and convictions passing through the County jail over a six-month period: "Forty were convicted. Sent to state prison 6; to wit, 1 American, 2 Indians, 3 Mexicans. Sent to County Jail six months or less 4; three months or less 9; less than one month or fined 21; whipped 2; on bail, or in jail waiting the Grand Jury 5."

Robbery and larceny statistics increased along with Southern California's population. In 1998, Los Angeles County counted 226,987 crimes, not including federal cases. By far the largest number—174,049—were larceny-thefts. Robberies, that is, thefts performed in person with violence or the fear of violence, accounted for another 31,041 incidents.

Yet, as the century progressed, the picture was improving in the county. Between 1992 and 1996, reports of murder, rape and robbery—the most violent crimes—dropped thirty-two percent, far more than the twenty-percent drop in California as a whole. District Attorney Gil Garcetti attributed this progress to better policing; fewer young men as a percentage of the total population (young males are the most likely to commit violent crime); tougher laws, including California's 1994 "Three Strikes" law, and, far from least, the track record of the District Attorney's Office, which at the year 2000 convicted ninety-four percent of the offenders that it prosecuted.

Tiburcio Vasquez

The charm of an early celebrity bandit is not enough to save him from the noose.

As Tiburcio Vasquez awaited trial in a Los Angeles jail in 1874, a newspaper editorial writer lectured fellow citizens on right and wrong. The journalist found it "difficult to rationally account for that fickle quality in human nature which makes the majority of people look with a sentiment akin to admiration upon individuals who have become notorious, no matter at what cost of infamy. When Vasquez and his gang were prowling around the State, red-handed with the blood of their victims, robbing defenseless passengers and making raids upon peaceful rancheros, none of the puerile sympathy and reprehensible adulation, which now seems to surround the captive chief, could be discovered among our people. But since he has been secured, and has had the chance to egotistically recapitulate his misdeeds with a plausible tongue, we find a very general sentiment of commiseration for the fallen bandit."

Indeed, the writer had a point. For more than two decades, Vasquez, charismatic leader of an audacious band of thieves, had stolen live-stock, company payrolls, robbed passengers in stage coaches, stolen old men's gold watches at gunpoint and looted entire towns up and down the new state of California. Shortly before his final capture in the Santa Monica Mountains ten miles from downtown Los Angeles, he was said to be planning to raise a bandit army of two hundred men to capture and ransack Los Angeles and San Diego.

Yet Vasquez always claimed that he had never killed anyone during his robberies, though some in his band clearly had. And he blamed unfair treatment by the new Yankees in Northern California for his turn to a life outside the law. Handsome and outgoing, proud of what he considered his chivalry, he had a notoriously winning sense of humor and was what was once known as a ladies' man. Certainly, he was a born master of public relations. Within moments of being jailed in Los Angeles, a sympathizer had brought a bottle of whisky to his cell. He

complimented his captors, including Los Angeles Sheriff William R. Rowland, who had cleverly engineered the arrest, and Vasquez generously toasted the president of the United States. He returned a gold watch to one victim who came by. He also made arrangements to raise money to hire a lawyer by endorsing a local retailer. That evening's newspaper carried the advertisement: "Vasquez says that Mendell Meyer has the Finest and Most Complete Stock of Dry Goods and Clothing." He also made a deal with a local photographer, who sold portraits of Vasquez for twenty-five cents. Enamored local women brought him flowers. The Merced Theater quickly staged a short play, which was performed after excerpts from *Hamlet* and *Othello*— "The new local farce entitled *The Capture of Vasquez*." He wanted to take the lead role himself, but Sheriff Rowland wouldn't release him to perform. So Vasquez coached the actor who played his part, even loaning him a suit of his own clothes for authenticity.

The most serious criminal charges against Vasquez, however, involved a raid at Tres Pinos, near Monterey, in which several victims were killed. He was taken north on the coastal vessel *The Senator*, convicted of the murders—though he denied to the end that he was responsible—and was hanged on March 19, 1875. His last word, given with characteristic bravado to his executioner, was "Pronto!"

Vasquez Rock as the bandits' hideout was known; Tiburcio Vasquez.

Vasquez (bottom, center) and his captors.

Bob's Big Boy Restaurant crime scene.

The Bob's Big Boy Robbery and Murder

In 1980 a robbery turns into a massacre.

The robbery was set for 2:00 a.m., closing time at the Bob's Big Boy restaurant on La Cienega Boulevard. Ricardo Rene Sanders, 25, planned the attack using information from his girlfriend, Carletha Ann Stewart, a former waitress at the restaurant. Sanders and Franklin Freeman Jr., Stewart's cousin, invaded the restaurant with shotguns. Stewart waited outside in a car. The cashier, Ahmad Mushuk, asked "Hey, what's going on?" One of the robbers hit Mushuk over the head with a gun butt. He slumped to the floor, and there was no more resistance. The two collected about thirteen hundred dollars from restaurant manager Michael Malloy then ordered two customers and the eight conscious employees to the rear of the restaurant. "We're going to the back," Sanders told them. "You're going to get hurt." The victims were ordered into the restaurant's walk-in frozen-food locker, where they were robbed of wallets, watches and jewelry. Then the two robbers ordered the victims to face the wall, and to kneel. They fired at their backs with a sawed-off shotgun and a .32-caliber pistol, until they ran out of shells.

The carnage was terrible. A customer, a waitress and Mushuk, the cashier, were dead. A busboy was critically wounded and died several months later. Malloy lost an eye from a gunshot wound. A customer was left partially paralyzed from wounds to her back and spine. A waitress who had pleaded "Don't hurt me, don't hurt me," was left brain-damaged. Two other waitresses had been hurt, one with a gunshot wound to the arm and the other with the need for extensive psychological therapy.

Within days, people who had heard the robbery being planned had tipped off the police. Investigators found a shotgun and shotgun shells in Sanders's bedroom closet, and at Stewart's house they found money, some of it still in Bank of America wrappers like those used at the restaurant. Four survivors of the freezer identified Sanders as one of the killers.

Deputy District Attorney Harvey Giss, who prosecuted the case, called the murder scene a "holocaust." The courtroom battles with renowned Los Angeles defense attorney Leslie Abramson became so strident that Los Angeles Superior Court Judge James M. Ideman threatened both attorneys with contempt. Each defendant was tried separately and the trials went on for four years. Sanders was convicted in 1982 and was sentenced to death. "The belief of the court is this defendant is not fit to live even within a state prison," said Judge Ideman. "The death penalty in this case is not only the appropriate penalty—it is the only penalty." A hung jury in the separately tried Franklin Freeman case voted eleven to one for death. In the end, he was sentenced to life without possibility of parole. Stewart, the former Bob's waitress who drove the getaway car, got four concurrent life sentences.

Clockwise from top: Deputy District Attorney Harvey Giss; *Herald Examiner* headline on Ricardo Sander's death penalty sentence; Sanders with defense attorney Leslie Abramson; defendants Stewart and Freeman.

41

Lionel Ray Williams

What started as a robbery ends with the death of actor Sal Mineo in 1976.

Sal Mineo became a household name after his brilliant and distinctive performances in movies that included *Rebel Without a Cause* in 1955, and *Exodus* in 1960. But his career fell off gradually and by February 1976, he hadn't made a movie in five years. On February 12, in his most recent attempt at a comeback, he was in rehearsal for the Los Angeles run of the play

Sal Mineo, 1969.

P. S., Your Cat Is Dead, at the Westwood Theatre. For the past three years, he had been living quietly in West Hollywood in a modest apartment on Holloway Drive, just off the Sunset Strip.

Mineo came home from rehearsal about 10:00 p.m. that night, a week before the play was to open, and parked in the garage. Then his neighbors in the two-story apartment building heard screams—"Oh God! No!"—and sounds of a struggle. The first neighbors to reach Mineo said, variously, that they had seen a man running away: a white man, or a man in dark clothing, or a man with blond hair, or with long, dark hair. Mineo was gasping and in pain from a deep wound in his chest. By the time paramedics arrived, he was dead.

For a year and a half police investigated the killing with little success until the wife of Lionel Ray Williams, a former pizza delivery man and career criminal, told police that her husband had come home covered with blood the night of Mineo's murder and had told her that he had killed "this dude in Hollywood." They had turned on the television to watch the news and saw pictures of Mineo's body being loaded into the coroner's van. That was the "dude," Williams had told his wife.

Police were skeptical at first because Williams was black—contrary to most of the eyewitness accounts. But investigators began to find other connections to the case, including more instances of Williams claiming to friends, cellmates (a guard overhead him), and a female relative—in one case even to police, who were investigating another crime—that he either committed or knew about the Mineo murder.

In January 1978, Williams was charged with first-degree murder for killing Mineo, as well as ten counts of armed robbery for other brutal attacks that occurred around the same time. A year later trial began, with Deputy District Attorney Michael Genelin prosecuting the case. Genelin argued that Mineo's murder fit the pattern of the other strong-arm robberies, in which Williams used guns, knives and a hammer. Williams was a "predator," Genelin told jurors, "... a night marauder who would kill you if he had to—or kill you even if he didn't have to. He is a person who likes to inflict pain."

The knife used to kill Mineo was peculiar, which made it possible to match it to Mineo's wound. When Williams was in prison in Michigan for another crime, he had a rendition of this unusual knife tattooed on his arm. Genelin told jurors that Williams had "put the mark of Cain" on himself.

Genelin presented seven victims who each identified Williams as their attacker. He also called to the witness stand a personal friend of Williams who had committed at least one robbery with Williams. By then in the U.S. Marine Corps, the friend showed up in court in uniform and told in detail how Williams had described killing Mineo and running away before he could rob him. Genelin also made the point that Williams was a light-skinned black man, who could easily have appeared white in the darkness of the murder scene.

Williams was convicted of second-degree murder and the ten robbery counts, receiving a sentence of fifty-one years to life. With California's "set-term" sentencing law that was recomputed to fourteen years. He was released on parole in 1990. Williams was later sent back to prison, convicted of yet another robbery.

Haing Ngor

After a complex trial, three killers of a Cambodian humanitarian get long sentences.

Haing Ngor learned about brutality from the Khmer Rouge, the fanatical Communist movement that took over his country in 1975. At the time, Ngor was a young, well-off physician in Phnom Penh, Cambodia's capital. He was forced to flee so abruptly when the Khmer Rouge entered the city that he left a dying patient on an operating table. In the countryside, where he was designated a "war slave," and with the Khmer Rouge routinely slaughtering all educated people, he posed as a cab driver. He survived despite torture, starvation and grinding labor as a field hand. Among more than a million other Cambodians, his father, his wife and other family members died in the horror. Indeed, he watched helplessly as his wife died of complications from malnutrition during pregnancy, at the hands of untrained medics. Had he revealed that he was a doctor, and had he attempted to save her, he and his wife and all members of his family would have been killed on the spot by the Khmer Rouge.

Ngor moved to Los Angeles in 1980. Three years later, he was working as a four-hundred-dollars-a-month jobs counselor for refugees at the non-profit Chinatown Service Center when he was offered a major role in the movie *The Killing Fields*, about the Cambodian massacres. He won an Oscar for his supporting role in the film. And though he showed up at the service center at 8:30 a.m. the next morning, to help more refugees find work, he also went on to other acting jobs in movies as well as television programs including *Miami Vice*, *China Beach* and *Highway to Heaven*. He donated much of the income and royalties from his Hollywood work, as well as his fees as a lecturer, to help start two refugee organizations; to provide medical services to Cambodian refugees and other displaced persons; to support Cambodian orphans; to make investments to support new businesses in Cambodia; to champion human rights, and in the United States, ironically, to counter gang violence. Even after he became wealthy again, he continued to live in an unpretentious Chinatown apartment. And there, in his carport, on February 25, 1996, he was shot and killed, apparently when he turned over a six-thousand-dollar Rolex watch but refused to give robbers a small locket that held a photo of his dead wife.

Haing Ngor, 1986.

Three members of a Chinatown street gang who called themselves the Oriental Lazy Boys were charged with the crime—Tak Sun Tan, 21, who had a previous conviction for robbery; Jason Chan, 20, whose first criminal conviction came at age 13, and Indra Lim, also 20. Because Superior Court Judge J.D. Smith ruled that some pieces of evidence could only be admitted against a specific defendant, each defendant was tried before a separate jury, simultaneously. Under the complex arrangement, Deputy District Attorney Craig Hum, a specialist in gang

prosecutions, presented some of the evidence to all three assembled juries and other evidence to only one panel. Hum gave three separate closing arguments in the case.

The available evidence and testimony made the case difficult as well. The Rolex watch and 9-millimeter Glock handgun used in the murder were never found. Witnesses who first tied the men to the killing scene in statements to the police later claimed to be unable to remember what they saw at the time, or had told investigators— even when tape recordings of their police interviews were replayed at the trial. Two witnesses who first said they had given Chan, Lim and Tan a ride when they saw them running from Ngor's apartment complex, later changed their stories. Hum told jurors that this was common for gang members fearing retaliation. Indeed, Thol "T-Bone" May, often connected with the Oriental Lazy Boys, admitted that he had seen Chan with a Glock pistol. During a preliminary hearing, he announced: "My life is over. If they want to kill me, go ahead. But I just want to say to all my homies, I'm sorry."

"What these defendants did was take the life of an unbelievable human being, doctor, Academy Award-winner and great humanitarian," Hum said in one of his closing arguments. All three juries voted to convict the defendants, although the Chan jury declined to name him as the shooter.

Judge Smith sentenced Jason Chan to life without chance of parole, Tak Sun Tan to fifty-six years to life, and Indra Lim to twenty-six years to life. Prosecutor Hum put the case in its larger perspective: "This man survived genocide in the killing fields of Cambodia only to be murdered on the killing streets of Los Angeles. He was killed by gangsters looking for money to buy drugs. Truly sad."

Louis Bundy

A hot-tempered juvenile thief in Highland Park adds murder to his crimes in 1913.

A high-school dropout and neighborhood bully, 17-year-old Louis Bundy had been arrested for stealing from a local department store and was suspected of other thefts, including the robbery of a vegetable gardener. To raise cash for a Christmas present for his girlfriend, Bundy set out to rob a local drugstore that made deliveries around Highland Park. On a dark, damp night, he phoned in an order for a fifty-cent bottle of magnesia water, telling the druggist that he would also need change for a twenty-dollar bill. The delivery boy, Harold Ziesche, 15, lashed his new flashlight to his bicycle before setting off. The flashlight was a gift from his father, who was worried that Ziesche might not be easily seen at night by the new and growing throng of automobile drivers around town.

Bundy was waiting in bushes by the side of the road. When he saw Ziesche, he leaped out and beat him unconscious with an ax handle and a rock. The worried druggist traced Ziesche's path after he failed to return and took the boy to a receiving hospital at First and Hill streets, where he died. Ziesche had been a likable, enterprising young man and the case outraged the town. Police investigators hunted house-to-house through Highland Park while William B. White, Highland Park's local patrolman, took a plaster of Paris cast of the killer's shoe prints at the crime scene. A shoe repairman identified one heel cast as matching the brand of heel he had put on Bundy's shoes the week before.

Bundy did have a terrible temper. Enraged when he heard that White planned to arrest him, Bundy and two friends pulled a strand of heavy wire across the Avenue 60 bridge. Then Bundy telephoned police anonymously, claiming that a U. S. Post Office on the other side of the bridge—also in White's patrol territory—had just been robbed. Bundy expected White to jump on his motorcycle and to race across the bridge in response, to be ripped from his bike by the nearly invisible wire.

But White had already heard of Bundy's plan from a neighborhood source and he stayed away from the bridge. He went right ahead and arrested Bundy and Bundy gave a jailhouse confession. Bundy told White that he felt he had to kill Ziesche because Ziesche had seen his face in the flashlight's glare, and could identify him.

Earl Rogers, the well-known Los Angeles defense attorney, defended Bundy at trial, using the unusual argument that chain-smoking cigarettes—Bundy smoked three packs a day—had damaged Bundy's youthful, still-growing brain, causing him to commit the robbery and murder while insane. But when three physicians testified that Bundy had been sane, District Attorney Thomas Lee Woolwine pressed for conviction, and for Bundy's execution as soon as he became 18 years old. The jury convicted.

Rogers was shocked at the verdict and he regretted his decision to keep Bundy off the witness stand during the trial. The boy was so obnoxious that he alienated everyone with whom he came in contact. But now that his client faced the gallows, Rogers said that he should have put the boy in front of the jury. His crazed, "mad dog" anger might have brought a verdict of not guilty by reason of insanity.

Bundy was hanged at San Quentin in 1914. In the aftermath, the Los Angeles Police Department set up the first crime-prevention program for juveniles in the world, the City Mother's Bureau.

Victim dabs away tears after hearing sentence.

Caryl Chessman

The "Red Light Bandit," an adroit career criminal, becomes a cause célèbre before his execution in 1960.

In 1947, a man impersonating a police officer was on a spree, robbing couples parked in lovers' lanes in the Malibu Colony, on Mulholland Drive overlooking Los Angeles, around the Rose Bowl in Pasadena, and in the hills above the small, wealthy suburb of Flintridge. He flashed a red light from his car when he pulled up behind his victims, demanded the couples' wallets and purses ostensibly for identification, and pulled a .45-caliber automatic when he announced, "This is a stickup." In several robberies, he also kidnapped women, took them off alone, and threatened them unless they performed oral sex.

"Sometimes, in an atonal monotone, he would repeat over and over, insanely, 'If you don't do what I say they'll carry you away in a casket.' Sometimes he would carry off and criminally assault the woman. If she begged him to show mercy, he would listen without interrupting, his face expressionless. Then he would ask in a lifeless monotone, 'You through?' If she said she was, he repeated his demands. If she burst into tears he sat unmoving and waited until she finished crying. 'You through now?' that terrible voice then would ask."

That description comes from *Cell 2455 Death Row,* a best-selling book written by the man who was charged and convicted of—but denied to the end—committing the series of crimes. Caryl Whittier Chessman, was a 26-year-old son of a Los Feliz florist, and self-described professional criminal—burglaries, robbing liquor stores and the like. Chessman was on parole from San Quentin when he was captured in a chase through Hollywood in a stolen Ford club coupe that matched the victims' description. At first, Chessman confessed to the police that he was the man they were looking for. Later he recanted, saying that he had confessed only because he had been subjected to "third-degree methods" by his interrogators. Chessman claimed that the Ford had actually been stolen by another man, who had jumped out and got away before police surrounded the car. Chessman refused to identify the other passenger, however, declaring that he needed only to prove that he wasn't guilty himself—not who the guilty party was.

At trial, a cocky but intelligent and articulate Chessman, who had picked up a jailhouse legal education in prison, represented himself. "I was in the mood to give the state a good battle for my life," he wrote. The case was handled by the widely known Deputy District Attorney J. Miller Leavy, an implacable prosecutor and strong supporter of the death penalty. Though no one had died in the robberies, three of the eighteen felonies charged were potential capital cases under a state law that allowed the death penalty for kidnapping to commit robbery.

The trial itself, in May 1948, was little-noticed at the time by Los Angeles journalists. Only one reporter from a small Hollywood newspaper sat through it every day. And though that reporter, a steadfast opponent of capital punishment, might have been expected to be sympathetic to Chessman, he wasn't. "Chessman was the most unbearably insolent defendant I've seen in court, before or since," the reporter later told the *Los Angeles Times*. "He sneered at the judge, he sneered at the prosecutor, he even sneered at his defense advisor."

Chessman acts as his own attorney.

For his part, Leavy presented convincing material evidence as well as eight victims who identified Chessman. Meanwhile, Chessman's dual role as defendant and defense attorney did not always serve him well. One of the victims of what was then referred to as a "sex perversion" refused to treat Chessman as anything but the man on trial. At one point, Chessman asked her, on the witness stand, "How long were you in the Ford?"

She tartly replied, "In the car with you? Is that what you mean?"

Chessman turned to the judge. "I object to that," he complained. "It is not responsive to my question."

"Objection overruled," said Superior Court Judge Charles W. Fricke, "the witness has asked you to qualify your question."

"Well, the defense maintains its innocence… " said Chessman.

"I don't care what the defense maintains," said Fricke. "The objection is overruled."

"Well, I wasn't there, so I don't know what she means," Chessman sparred.

"I don't know whether you were there or not," said an exasperated Fricke. "That is the question we are here to decide. I do not want any more argument after I have ruled. Ask your next question. You would get along much better if you would respect the court's rulings."

Chessman's principal alibi also withered in court. He brought in his crippled mother to swear that while one "Red Light Bandit" crime was being committed, Chessman had been at home all day, installing a kitchen floor. But Leavy produced evidence that on the same day, Chessman had hocked jewelry at a distant pawnshop.

"This young man is completely worthless," Leavy told the jury. "Since he was 16 he has abused every privilege of society." The jury returned guilty verdicts on seventeen of eighteen counts—on their first ballot. The same jury later voted for the death penalty on two of those counts.

But that was just the beginning of the Chessman case. In his various appeals, over the next dozen years, Chessman cited the fact that he had been denied daily trial transcripts during the trial and that indeed, there never was a complete record because the court reporter died before transcribing all his notes. Chessman also argued that the court reporter appointed to finish the transcription turned out to be a relative of Leavy, the prosecutor; a man with a spotty work record, and a heavy drinker who may even have been intoxicated while he worked on the transcript. Chessman's appeals went all the way to the U.S. Supreme Court, several times, and in all he received eight stays of execution.

Meanwhile, as Chessman continued to study law in prison, he wrote his four books—one a novel—using vivid anecdotes to ultimately contend that even the worst criminals could be rehabilitated. His campaign made him an international symbol for death-penalty foes. His supporters included Eleanor Roosevelt, Norman Mailer, California Governor Pat Brown and his son (and later governor) Jerry Brown, as well as intellectuals, Hollywood personalities and others who opposed capital punishment—particularly for anyone who had not been convicted of murder.

On May 2, 1960, another execution date set in the protracted struggle, a federal judge agreed to issue yet another stay, to hear more legal arguments. But this time the judge's assistant dialed the wrong phone number to deliver word to Death Row. Chessman died in the San Quentin gas chamber just after 10:00 a.m.

Prosecutor J. Miller Leavy with strangler's towel; Graham's victim, Mabel Monohan (inset).

Barbara Graham

A robbery turns into brutal murder in a case better known for a movie than the facts.

In 1953, Mabel Monahan, a former vaudeville dancer and professional skater, was living alone in a small Burbank bungalow. Monahan, an elderly, crippled widow, was also the former mother-in-law of Tutor Scherer, a Nevada gambling kingpin. Rumor had it in the Los Angeles criminal underground that Scherer had hidden one hundred thousand dollars in cash in Monahan's house.

On the night of March 9, Monahan heard a woman scream outside her front door. When she opened the door, Barbara Graham, a 29-year-old convicted prostitute and perjuror, rushed inside, followed by a strong-armed gang that included ex-convict Emmett Perkins, Jack Santo, John L. True and Baxter Shorter, a former member of the Mickey Cohen mob. They threw a pillowcase over Monahan's head, tied her hands behind her back and Graham beat her in the face and skull with a pistol butt while Perkins and Santo strangled her, trying to get her to tell them where the money was. They tore the house apart but still couldn't find any cash. They left Monahan to die.

Less than a month after the killing, Graham, consistently described as a voluptuous blonde, was arrested. Shorter had gone to the police and become a key informant in the Monahan murder. Nine days after Graham was brought in, Perkins kidnapped Shorter at gunpoint from Shorter's downtown Los Angeles apartment building. Burbank Police

Chief Rex Andrews told reporters, "I'm afraid they will kill him, if he isn't already dead. We told him at noon today to get out of town or they'd kill him." Shorter was never seen again.

Deputy District Attorneys J. Miller Leavy and Adolph Alexander tried the case against Graham, Santo, Perkins and, originally, True. True would be given immunity and appear as a star witness for the prosecution.

Leavy described the beating of Mabel Monahan to the jury: "Mrs. Monahan looked as if she had been hit by a heavy truck traveling at high speed. The savage brutality of that attack is like nothing I have seen in twenty years of experience. I can scarcely believe that human beings could do that to an elderly woman, against whom they had nothing, merely because they wanted money."

True's testimony as a member of the gang was damning, but so was a revealing set of conversations secretly recorded between Graham and an undercover police officer. Leavy and Alexander introduced them into testimony from handwritten notes and a wire recording (a precursor of magnetic tapes that stored sound on a thin wire, and the origin of the term "wired" for a person carrying a surreptitious listening device). The conversations involved Graham trying to arrange an alibi for the murder night by promising payment to a hotel clerk and to the undercover officer. Graham and the officer discussed the arrangement in three conversations held in the county jail visitors' room.

Graham handwriting sample; Graham with defendants Santo and Perkins.

San Quentin's gas chamber.

At one point, the officer and Graham set out the essential alibi—that they had spent the night of the murder together at a motel, in a love tryst.

The officer asked: "How would it be if I picked a city out of town for a motel where we could say we spent that particular night together?"

Graham replied: "That would be swell, and at the next meeting we have you can describe it to me so we can get together on our stories."

"Do you know how much this job is going to cost you?" the officer asked.

"Yes, Donna told me you wanted five hundred dollars."

In their conversations, the officer acted concerned that the missing Baxter Shorter might suddenly show up in court, to contradict their story. But Graham strongly suggested that she knew Baxter was dead, though the newspapers had speculated that the prosecutors had Shorter in protective custody.

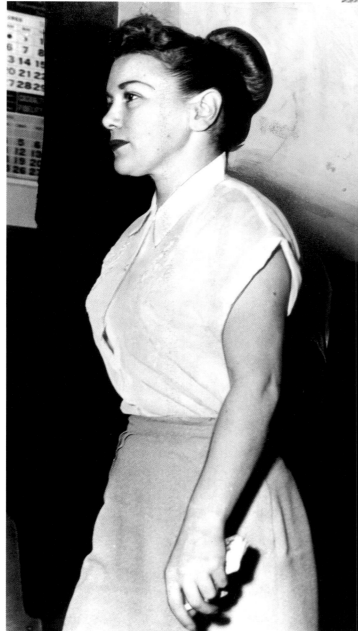

Graham's "last walk"; letter to husband.

"Every time I read that, I laugh," Graham told the officer.

"You do? You know what happened to him?" he asked.

"Uh huh," Graham said.

"You do?"

"Uh huh. Just don't worry. He won't show up."

In another conversation, Graham said: "Yes, he's been done away with, and I can assure you he won't be at the trial."

Graham, Perkins and Santo were convicted. And on June 4, 1955, all three were executed at San Quentin. Barbara Graham refused to tell police what happened to Baxter Shorter even after her last appeal was denied. When she walked into the gas chamber, one of the death-watch guards advised her to take a deep breath as soon as she sensed the gas, because it would make her death easier.

"How the hell would you know?" she wisecracked.

A very different tale—of an unlucky prostitute and petty criminal who is framed for the Monahan murder—was presented three years later in the movie *I Want to Live*. The movie was acclaimed for making a strong case against the death penalty. Susan Hayward, in a moving lead performance, won an Academy Award. That screenplay's version of Barbara Graham's story was the only version that many people ever heard.

But Leavy's comment after Graham's execution comes closer to the view of those who followed the real trial. "Barbara Graham tied Mabel Monahan's hands behind her back, pistol-whipped her and left her to die. Sending her to the gas chamber didn't bother me at all."

Cosby's Mercedes-Benz on Skirball Drive.

Ennis Cosby

An impatient, drug-hyped robber kills entertainer Bill Cosby's son while he changes a flat tire.

About 1:15 a.m. on January 16, 1997, a raw, rainy night just off the San Diego Freeway in Bel-Air, Ennis Cosby stopped to change a flat tire on his father's Mercedes convertible. After hours of delays, he had finally gotten on his way for a late supper with Stephanie Crane, 48, a screenwriter from an old Hollywood entertainment-industry family and a new friend Cosby had met by chance the week before at a party. Now, ten minutes from Crane's Sherman Oaks home, he had blown a tire. Cosby, a 27-year-old Ph.D candidate at Columbia University Teachers College, in New York, called Crane from his cell phone and she volunteered to come to help. Then three people in a car stopped near and asked if he was all right. "Yeah, everything's cool," said Cosby. When Crane got there, she waited in her black Jaguar with the heater running and trained her lights on Cosby while he broke out the jack and went to work. "It was freezing cold and a little bit rainy," Crane recalled later in court. "Ennis leaned down and hugged me and said, 'Hello, friend.'... He said he liked working on cars. I said, 'I can't believe you're doing this.'"

The three in the other car were Mikhail Markhasev, a 19-year-old Ukrainian immigrant and gang member, Eli Zakaria, 24, and Zakaria's girlfriend Sara Ann Peters, 22. They had stopped at a pay phone in the nearby park-and-ride lot to call a Bel-Air drug dealer, to see if he was home—apparently so they could rob him. When the three, high on heroin and cocaine, couldn't get in touch with the dealer, Markhasev drifted off, leaving the impression with Peters that he might rob someone else.

The next thing Crane knew, a man in a light-colored knit cap loomed next to her window, saying, "Get out of the car or I'll shoot!"

In a panic, Crane quickly locked the door and drove off a few yards. But then she turned around and went back to shine her lights on the robber, hoping to scare him away from Cosby.

In grand jury testimony later, Markhasev's friend Michael Chang explained to jurors what Markhasev told him happened: Markhasev had walked over to Cosby, sticking a gun in his face and demanding money. Cosby told Markhasev that no one had ever pointed a gun at him before, and he said to "kick back, to hold on." Markhasev told Chang that Cosby didn't get his wallet out fast enough. "It was kind of like, 'Can you believe what he said to me?'" Chang told the grand jury. "He just blasted him" At the trial, Crane testified that by the time she turned around, Cosby had been shot in the head. He was laying in a pool of blood when her car lights fell on the Mercedes again. Crane saw a man run to the other car, jump in, and then it was gone.

Peters told the grand jury that she had heard what sounded like a car backfire, then Markhasev had run back to their car and said, nervously, "Let's go. We've got to get out of here. Let's go." Zakaria, she remembered, had yelled, "What's going on?," but Markhasev didn't answer. They drove to a wooded area in North Hollywood where police later found the murder weapon, a .38-caliber pistol, wrapped in a knit cap. Then, said Peters, they went to a friend's house and turned on a television. Markhasev was scared and transfixed by the news coverage of Cosby's killing. Peters recalled that Zakaria was angry because he realized what Markhasev had done. She remembered Markhasev asking himself out loud, "Why did it have to happen? Why did I have to do it?"

Testimony also revealed that two days later, Markhasev asked Chang, whom he had first met in a juvenile detention facility, to go back with him to the woods and to help hunt for the gun. A friend of Chang's, Christopher So, drove them out to the San Fernando Valley spot, but they couldn't find the gun. Markhasev told Chang and So that he'd killed a black man: "It's big. It's all over the news." Chang was startled—"You killed Cosby!"—So remembered. So also knew that

Cap with gun (above). Markhasev letter from jail (below).

the *National Enquirer* had offered a one-hundred-thousand-dollar reward for information about the gun used to kill Cosby. He says he called the tabloid and left his pager number. The *Enquirer* passed on that number to the police. So took them to the wooded area in North Hollywood. Police found the gun and arrested Markhasev charging him with one count of murder and one count of attempted robbery.

In his opening statement, Deputy Alternate Public Defender Henry Hall promised jurors he would prove that Zakaria, not Markhasev, had killed Cosby. Stephanie Crane had failed to pick Markhasev out of a lineup, and Hall contended that her final description of the killer more closely resembled Zakaria. Yet Crane's early depiction, given to detectives putting together a composite drawing, did fit Markhasev, argued Deputy District Attorney Anne Ingalls, who prosecuted the case. Ingalls also faced the challenge of getting jurors to consider credible her four other major witnesses—Zakaria, Peters, Chang and So—despite their criminal backgrounds. But Ingalls had other evidence to make her case.

Her first witness, Los Angeles Police Department Detective John Garcia, introduced letters that he said Markhasev wrote to people he knew in a Mexican prison gang. Some of the correspondence made reference to the Cosby killing. "The crime happened in Bel-Air," one letter stated. "A robbery gone bad... I went to

rob a connection and obviously found something else." It was signed "Peewee." Some of the letters had been retrieved from the trash at the home of a jailhouse informant's girlfriend; others Markhasev had given to a jailer, who gave them to investigators instead of mailing them. An LAPD handwriting expert testified that while the writing showed normal variations, on the whole, individual characters were similar to those in other known Markhasev correspondence. Other LAPD criminologists testified that the gun found in the wooded area had fired the bullet that killed Cosby, and that a hair found in the cap wrapped around it matched hair taken from Markhasev when he was arrested.

Christopher So, who was forced to testify under court order, said that Markhasev had been panicked when he and Chang couldn't find the gun. "'I got to go back. I got to find that gun,'" he quoted Markhasev. So also said that he was afraid for his life, fearing retaliation from Markhasev's gang friends, for calling the *National Enquirer*—the act that had set investigators on Markhasev's trail. Apparently sharing the same fear, Michael Chang sat silent in the witness box, refusing to testify, even when held in contempt of court. Zakaria also refused to testify, claiming his Fifth Amendment right against self-incrimination. But in what was widely deemed a smart move by Ingalls, she brought Zakaria into court anyway, as silent proof that Markhasev, not Zakaria, looked like Crane's first impressions of the killer.

Ingalls deliberately kept the trial low-key and there was no grandstanding on the part of the defense—though Markhasev himself smirked at jurors and the Cosby family sitting in the audience. (Bill Cosby attended only one day of the proceedings, saying that he didn't want to take the focus off Markhasev.) The trial took only two weeks. And in the end, Hall was forced to admit that he hadn't proved that Zakaria was the true killer. The jury returned a guilty verdict after fewer than six hours of deliberation.

Markhasev was sentenced to life without parole, with an additional ten years tacked on because he had used a gun in the failed robbery. Bill Cosby, in a statement added to Markhasev's probation and sentencing report, showed the depth of his anger at his only son's killer: "The malice, hatred and ill will leading to his murder must be kept off America's streets forever."

Deputy District Attorney Anne Ingalls.

Reenactment of double murder in which Deputy District Attorney Jack Kirschke was convicted.

Crimes of the Heart

n 1881 in downtown Los Angeles, a beautiful young singer, Lastania Abarta, shot to death well-known womanizer Francisco "Chico" Forster when he declined to marry her, as promised, the morning after taking her virginity. Abarta was judged not guilty by reason of insanity. A reputable local doctor testified that, "Any virtuous woman when deprived of her virtue would go mad, undoubtedly." Just five years later, Hattie Woolsteen, known to detractors as "Wicked Woolsteen," was accused of killing her dentist lover, who had originally seduced her by drugging her in the dentist's chair. She was charged with shooting him, then burning a barn down around his corpse, after learning that the dentist was married. She was acquitted of what one reporter called "a tale of a young girl's sorrow and a man's lustful brutality."

Still today, love in all its permutations can be deadly. The bedroom is all too often transformed from a safe haven for optimism, passion and intimate togetherness into a killing ground for those deranged by, or newly bereft of love. And Los Angeles has always displayed a singular flamboyance when it comes to crimes of the heart. Perhaps this makes sense in a town where tales of romance and death are standard themes, formed and groomed by an entertainment industry that has for decades shown the rest of the world how life in its most dramatic version should be lived.

Los Angeles has also produced plenty of glamorous real-life characters who have caught the public's attention. Sometimes men are the central figures in these true-crime dramas, but more often women have taken center stage. In Los Angeles in the Roaring Twenties, for instance, being a beautiful young "murderess" only enhanced a woman's mystique as yet another "homicidal lady," as they were often described in the press.

To prosecutors, these defendants have always posed an unusual challenge. While the guilty partner in a straightforward domestic violence case is often easy to identify and to convict, many crimes of passion are complicated and heavily based on circumstantial evidence. Of even more concern is the potential for "homicidal ladies" and the like to be viewed by the public and the jury with compassion, even admiration. Experienced prosecutors take care not to create inappropriate sympathy by seeming to be too tough and insensitive with these defendants, murderous as they may be.

Walburga "Dolly" Oesterreich

A bizarre saga of obsession, sex, and a secret lover in the attic began to unravel on a late-summer night in 1922.

Dolly Oesterreich always had a man in her life—usually more than one. Fred Oesterreich, her husband, was a hard-living, hard-drinking and wealthy manufacturer of women's clothing, primarily kitchen aprons. The couple first lived in Milwaukee, then moved to Los Angeles. Following them out was Dolly Oesterreich's secret live-in lover, Otto Sanhuber. In 1913, when Dolly was a housewife in her early thirties, she had seduced Sanhuber, age 17, who was then working as a sewing-machine repairman in her husband's factory. Oesterreich began the affair by calling her husband at work to tell him that her sewing machine was broken. When Sanhuber arrived at her home to fix the machine, she was wearing only stockings and a silk robe.

The owlish, slight Sanhuber, who later described himself as Oesterreich's "sex slave," not only became fixated on the domineering housewife but he moved into the house, quietly retreating to the attic each evening when Fred Oesterreich came home from work. And wherever the Oesterreichs moved, for the next decade, so did Sanhuber. During the day, Sanhuber made the beds, did other housework and kitchen chores, made bootleg gin and fulfilled his duties as a lover. He

lived on scraps he was fed in the kitchen. At night, in the attic, he lived another, solitary life, reading murder mysteries by candlelight and writing fiction—adventurous tales of lust and romance that he eventually sold to magazines. When the strange tale became publicly known, the newspapers called Sanhuber the "ghost in the garret" and "Bat Man."

The Oesterreichs frequently quarreled, but a particularly loud argument, and the sounds of a physical struggle, finally brought Sanhuber out of his attic late on the night of August 22, 1922. Fearing for his lover's safety, Sanhuber grabbed two small pistols and came down to confront Fred Oesterreich. The undoubtedly surprised husband recognized Sanhuber from years before, when he'd ordered him to stay away from his wife. Oesterreich grappled with Sanhuber and in the struggle was shot three times, once in the back of the head.

The lovers decided to feign an attack by burglars, whom Dolly Oesterreich would claim had killed Oesterreich when he resisted their demands. Sanhuber locked Dolly Oesterreich in a bedroom closet, threw the key into the hallway, hid Fred Oesterreich's expensive diamond watch, then retreated to his attic hideout. Dolly Oesterreich screamed for her husband—"Fred! Oh Fred!"—but was slumped on the closet floor when police arrived, alerted by neighbors who had heard the gunfire.

For almost a year the story held, though detectives were suspicious. For one thing, Oesterreich had been killed by a .25-caliber handgun, a petite weapon that few armed robbers would choose.

Oesterreich with Chief District Attorney Investigator Blayney Matthews.

The owlish Otto Sanhuber (center).

Dolly Oesterreich, meanwhile, moved to another house in the neighborhood, installing Sanhuber again secretly in the attic. She also struck up an affair with the attorney settling her husband's estate, Herman S. Shapiro. As a gift to her new lover, she gave Shapiro her late husband's diamond watch, which he recognized. Oesterreich explained that she'd found it under a seat cushion in the house, but didn't think she needed to tell the authorities about it.

Then Oesterreich added a third lover, a businessman named Roy H. Klumb. From Klumb, she wanted a favor. Would he dispose of an old gun similar enough to the one used to kill her husband that it might be embarrassing if the police found it? Klumb threw it into what turned out to be a shallow spot in the La Brea Tar Pits. She asked a neighbor to do her a similar favor, and he buried the other gun under a rose bush in his backyard.

By July of the next year, however, a detective had learned that Shapiro had the watch. And Klumb, after breaking up with Oesterreich, had told police of disposing of one of her guns. They retrieved the first gun from the tar pits. With the case back in the newspapers, the neighbor brought in the gun from under the rose bush. Dolly Oesterreich was arrested for murder.

In jail, Oesterreich begged Shapiro to take food to the still-hidden Sanhuber. When he did, and the two men began talking, Shapiro learned of Sanhuber's ten-year obsession. Shapiro threw him out of the house.

Meanwhile, in hearings that dragged over months, Chief Deputy District Attorney Buron Fitts and Deputy District Attorney Harold L. Davis searched for a motive and more evidence, as well as an explanation of how Dolly Oesterreich could have locked herself in her bedroom closet and still deposited the key outside the door. Both guns were also rusted and damaged; it was impossible to prove that either one was the murder weapon. Then Oesterreich became so ill that she was reported to be dying. Eventually she was released on bail. Soon, all charges were dropped for lack of evidence.

Shapiro, her remaining lover, moved into Oesterreich's house, and they lived together in a tumultuous relationship for the next seven years. Finally, in 1930, Shapiro moved out and told the authorities about Sanhuber, the "ghost in the garret." Oesterreich and Sanhuber were both arrested this time—Oesterreich being charged with conspiracy while Sanhuber was charged with murder. The jury found Sanhuber guilty of manslaughter, but since it was now a year beyond the statute of limitations for him on a manslaughter conviction, Sanhuber was freed. In a separate trial prosecuted by Deputy District Attorney James Costello, Oesterreich was saved by a hung jury. Lacking more convincing evidence, new District Attorney Buron Fitts ended the long melodrama by declining to try her again.

Sanhuber disappeared. Oesterreich apparently bridled her passions, living quietly with the same man for the next three decades, until her death in 1961.

Jack Kirschke

A deputy district attorney kills his estranged wife and her lover, catching them in compromising circumstances in 1967.

Jack Kirschke, a widely known prosecutor, and his wife, fashion designer Elaine Terry Kirschke, ran with a fast, hard-drinking crowd—yacht owners, people who flew their own airplanes, people who knew how to have a good time at the trendy parties they gave in their Spanish-style home in the coastal community of Naples. When relations became strained between the Kirschkes, Elaine Kirschke began an affair with Orville Drankhan, a reckless electronics manufacturer and pilot. Drankhan, who had been recently arrested for flying his plane drunk, had also had a steady mistress for the past four years. Elaine Kirschke, however, could hold her own in the relationship, as a heavy drinker and member of the self-anointed Jolly Girls, a group of women in the yacht-club set who supported each other with alibis to hide their extramarital affairs.

Early in the morning of April 8, 1967, Elaine Kirschke and her lover were embracing on the round bed in the Kirschke home when they were shot to death. Jack Kirschke was the logical suspect, and he was

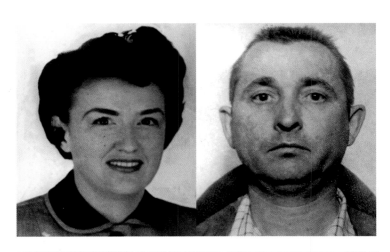

Clockwise from top left: Elaine Kirschke, Drankhan, and Kirschke.

charged with two counts of murder, though he claimed that at the time he had been in Las Vegas at a Rotary Club convention.

Because Kirschke was a deputy district attorney, the case was prosecuted by the California Attorney General's Office. At trial, Deputy Attorney General Albert W. Harris contended that Kirschke had obtained a pistol that had been evidence in a 1960 case prosecuted by Kirschke for the District Attorney's Office. Then, he said, Kirschke had hidden in wait in his home. When his wife and her lover appeared after a night of drinking and dancing at the Long Beach Yacht Club, and had begun to make love in the bedroom, Kirschke opened fire.

Kirschke's attorney, Albert C. S. Ramsey, countered with a series of witnesses who said they had seen Kirschke the night of the killing. Kirschke said that he had gone to the airport that evening, to try to catch a plane to Las Vegas, but had missed the plane. He decided to drive to the convention instead. And five witnesses were called to testify to back him up: a bartender and a woman who said that Kirschke talked to her little boy at the airport that night, a San Bernardino waitress who remembered him from later the same night, and two gas-station attendants who said they saw him in Yermo on the highway to Las Vegas, sometime before 4:00 a.m. on the morning of the shooting. Ramsey told jurors that if they believed even one of the witnesses, they would have to have reasonable doubt that Kirschke could have committed the murders.

But criminologists had difficulty setting the exact time of death. And Harris, the prosecutor, showed how Kirschke could have killed the pair and still have been seen by the witnesses—there were loopholes in the timing. Harris also called witnesses who testified that Kirschke was furious about the affair. And while both sides called experts who gave conflicting testimony about the gun, which was never found, Harris made a powerful point with the jury in a simple statement. "It was Jack Kirschke's gun, it was his house, it was his bed, it was his wife, and it was his wife's lover," he said. "If Jack Kirschke didn't do it, then who did?"

Jurors voted twelve-to-nothing on the first ballot for a murder conviction. They also had little trouble agreeing on murder in the first degree for both counts. Kirschke had expected acquittal and even those who had anticipated conviction had predicted reduced charges.

Kirschke dismissed his attorney and handled the penalty phase himself. Ever aggressive, he attacked several jurors by name, referring to one woman juror as "Madame Defarge," a reference to a cold-hearted character in the Charles Dickens novel *A Tale of Two Cities*, who contentedly did her knitting next to people being decapitated on the Paris guillotine. Finally, he dared the jury to give him the death penalty. After four hours of deliberation, they did.

Albert Ramsey, his attorney through the main trial, said he was astonished. "There isn't a sane person in the world who could say a man should die for a crime of passion such as this," Ramsey said outside the courtroom.

Superior Court Judge Kathleen Parker, concerned that jurors may have been prejudiced by Kirschke's angry final argument—though the jurors denied this to reporters—reduced his sentence to life imprisonment.

In prison, he romanced Sarah James, a church-going single mother of two children whom he had met when she was a bookkeeper for the Long Beach Yacht Club. In 1976, they were married, and his new wife worked hard to get Kirschke out of prison. His sentence was commuted and he left prison on parole the next year, after ten years of incarceration. But the marriage didn't last. When they began living together, James said, "He turned into this tyrannical, coldhearted stranger... And when I stood up to him, he left me for one of my best friends."

Lana Turner, Johnny Stompanato and Cheryl Crane

A stormy, exploitive romance ends when Turner's gangster lover is killed by her 14-year-old daughter.

Johnny Stompanato, a handsome ex-Marine and former bodyguard for mobster Mickey Cohen, was far from an ideal boyfriend. Actress Lana Turner, describing her turbulent one-year romance with Stompanato, admitted that he had stolen thousands of dollars from her, "not counting the tabs I picked up for him." And he had a legendary, violent temper. Not long before his death, he showed up on a movie set with a gun, threatening Turner in a jealous rage. Actor Sean Connery threw a fast punch and decked him. Stompanato had hit Turner on occasion. And he had threatened several times to cut up her face with a razor, or cripple her, if she ever left him.

The lovers' final round of fighting began just before the 1958 Academy Awards ceremony. Stompanato, who loved to see his picture in the paper, wanted to accompany Turner to the Oscar ceremonies. Turner, then 38, had been nominated for an award—for her role as a neurotic mother in *Peyton Place*—which was her first nomination in two decades of movie-making. Though Turner had done memorable work in such movies as *The Postman Always Rings Twice*, she was more often known as a sex symbol, promoted from her early years as the "Sweater Girl." In any case, she declined to attend the Oscar ceremony with a hoodlum lover in tow, which deeply angered and hurt Stompanato, according to friends. For days after the event (she didn't win the Oscar), they had violent arguments.

Finally, on April 4, 1958, a Friday night, in a battle more bitter than usual, Stompanato again threatened Turner with violence. Turner's 14-year-old daughter, Cheryl Crane, ran into the kitchen and came back to Turner's bedroom with an eight-inch bread knife. Afraid that this time Stompanato would seriously harm her mother, Crane stabbed him in the stomach. The knife entered at a peculiar slant, severing his lower aorta. He died in a matter of minutes. Beverly Hills Police Chief Clinton H. Anderson said that when he got to the star's home, Turner was standing at the top of a stairway, pleading: "Can't I take the blame? I want to take the blame for my daughter for whatever happened." Crane told another investigator, "I didn't mean to kill him, I just meant to frighten him."

Crane was taken to juvenile hall, where an attendant quoted her saying: "I know this is a terrible thing, of course, but I did not know what was happening at the time. I feel so sorry for Mommy, but I did it to protect her. I love her more than anything."

A week later, a coroner's inquest was held in the Hall of Records, with Deputy District Attorney William McGinley conferring with the coroner's office. Even before the inquest, most law-enforcement officials familiar with the case didn't expect Cheryl Crane to be prosecuted, which angered Stompanato's old boss, Mickey Cohen. Cohen had liked Stompanato and he retaliated by leaking love letters from Turner to Stompanato to the *Los Angeles Herald Examiner*. "Know how dearly I love you angel... ," read one excerpt. "...hold me dear lover *mi macho*."

And during the inquest itself, an unidentified man jumped up and claimed that Crane had killed Stompanato because she was in love with him herself, stabbing him in a jealous fit. Despite all Cohen's meddling, the Coroner's jury pronounced the killing "justifiable homicide." After a custody hearing, Crane was returned to her mother.

Turner, Stompanato and Crane; Stompanato's body at stabbing scene (below).

Madalynne Obenchain

A troubled beauty of the Jazz Age is accused of murdering the man she had planned to marry.

By all accounts, dark-eyed, 28-year-old Madalynne Obenchain had only to wink at a man to get her way. And these were not just momentary effects. Even the men she abandoned remained loyal to her. A former college sweetheart and a former husband both came to her aid when she needed them. *Los Angeles Times* writer Harry "Doc" Carr observed that she "puts men gently aside when she tires of them and they yield with a smile of pain. When she wants them again, they throw aside careers, freedom—everything, in answer to her nod."

Obenchain needed help after her boyfriend, J. Belton Kennedy, was found shot to death on August 5, 1921, outside his fashionably rustic cabin on Beverly Glen Boulevard, near the Los Angeles Country Club. Madalynne Donna Connor had been single when she met Kennedy in 1917, after she moved to Los Angeles from Chicago. Kennedy was an insurance broker at his affluent father's firm. Kennedy proposed marriage, but his mother opposed the union.

After two years of promises but no wedding date from Kennedy, Connor accepted the standing marriage proposal of Chicago attorney Ralph Obenchain, whom Connor had met at Northwestern University. But in less than a week, she was back in Los Angeles and back in Kennedy's bed. Kennedy again promised marriage, and Connor asked Obenchain for a divorce. Ralph Obenchain—whom prosecutors would later mock as a "human doormat"—not only agreed to an uncontested divorce but was willing to provide his transient wife with alimony and extra money when she needed it.

Once again Kennedy and Madalynne Obenchain couldn't set a date for the wedding, though exactly why becomes a matter of dispute. And from there the story splits into two versions.

Madalynne and Ralph Obenchain.

In Madalynne Obenchain's rendition, at just before 10:00 p.m. on the night of Kennedy's murder, she came to the Beverly Hills police station to sob out the news that Kennedy had been killed from ambush in front of his cabin. She said that she and Kennedy had returned there after a drive, and that as they walked up the front steps, she had asked him to go back to the car to get matches. He was halfway back down the steps when she heard two shots. Kennedy called out "Good night, Madalynne" before he died. Obenchain said that she saw two "roughly dressed" men running off behind the house.

Investigators pieced together a different account after the proprietor of the Russel Hotel, on South Broadway in downtown Los Angeles, told police that a guest registered as Arthur C. Burch had been anxious to rent a room from which he could watch Kennedy's office, across the street. Burch had also left the hotel on the day of the murder with a long package under his arm, and had returned after midnight. And he had been visited beforehand by a woman who had also peered out across the street with him from the hotel room.

Arthur Burch, it turned out, had been in love with Madalynne Obenchain since he had met her when he was a track star at

Northwestern. He, too, had proposed marriage. Investigators believed that Obenchain became enraged when Kennedy refused to marry her even after she had divorced her husband. She had gotten in touch with Burch, they surmised, who brought a shotgun out from Chicago to avenge this offense against a woman that he considered a "goddess." Burch, investigators said, had waited in ambush and used both barrels of the shotgun on Kennedy when he stooped to retrieve a lucky penny that Obenchain told him she had left under a rock.

Burch was arrested in Las Vegas and returned to Los Angeles to stand trial with Obenchain for Kennedy's murder. Ex-husband Ralph Obenchain quit his job and came west to defend the object of his abiding love. He also tried to marry her again in her jail cell, but the trial judge wouldn't allow it. Smitten admirers of Madalynne Obenchain sent hundreds of flower arrangements and other gifts to brighten her jail cell at Christmas.

Before her first trial, the prosecution's theory was undermined when Ralph Obenchain released a handwritten exchange of notes between Madalynne Obenchain and Kennedy. As she had consistently maintained, far from being a "woman scorned," she had been the one to call off their proposed marriage. "Madalynne, dear, won't you please reconsider your decision not to become my wife?" Kennedy had written. "…I appreciate and admire your feeling in not wanting to marry me over the objections of my parents… But after all, Madalynne, dear, I want you to marry not my parents but me."

Obenchain replied: "…I cannot and will not marry you under any circumstances… Please do not annoy me any more, as I intend to return to Ralph."

In all, five juries over sixteen months heard separate trials of Obenchain and Burch, prosecuted by Deputy District Attorneys Asa Keyes and Charles W. Fricke. In the lengthy Burch trials, prosecutors painstakingly listed the cars used, garages rented, and other details of Burch's trip from Chicago to Los Angeles. Witnesses testified that they had seen him in the glen near Kennedy's cabin. His defense attorneys, faced with a compelling rendition of the evidence, shocked the first jury by announcing that they had come to believe Burch was insane, and therefore not guilty.

Obenchain's second trial reached a new level of sensationalism when it was revealed that she had now begun a passionate correspondence with a convicted robber, also incarcerated, named Paul Roman. Ostensibly, Roman was no more than another admirer in love with the intoxicating Madalynne—though he knew a lot more about her than met the eye. "Your nearness as I try to sleep seems like a caress," she wrote in a letter later made public. Roman's responses were less subtle. In one he noted, "What you need is a lot of attention, and I'm the guy to give it to you."

Obenchain allegedly bribed Roman to testify that he had overheard two men talking of killing Kennedy. But Roman's motives were murkier—and apparently were never cleared up at the trial. To the surprise of all concerned, a costume-shop owner testified that Kennedy and Roman regularly rented female clothing from her. She also recalled that just before his murder, Kennedy had said that Roman would beat him if he ever got married.

A *Los Angeles Times* account of the rambunctious deliberations by one of the Obenchain juries gives an idea of how heated the arguments became: "Battle after battle was waged in the jury room to win votes to the young woman's side… Threats were made. At one time the opposing camps nearly came to blows and were only prevented by the women on the jury."

All five trials ended with hung juries. The Burch panels hung because each contained reluctant jurors who believed that even if Burch had killed Kennedy, he was not guilty by reason of love-crazed insanity. Critics of the Obenchain hung juries claimed that by the time they went into deliberation, all the men had fallen in love with the defendant. In the end, all charges were dropped against both Obenchain and her steadfast suitor, Arthur Burch.

District Attorney Thomas Woolwine publicly attacked the jury, particularly one holdout female juror, after the first Burch trial. Madalynne Obenchain, cool as always, only remarked that, "Mr. Woolwine does not take his defeat very gracefully."

Attorney William Bierne displaying headline on Obenchain case years after he defended her.

Clara "Tiger Woman" Phillips

A beautiful but jealous Roaring Twenties wife caught the city's attention when she hammered her suspected rival to death in 1922.

Clara Phillips, an attractive former showgirl and dancer, had a passionate possessive streak, especially when it came to her new husband, Armour Phillips, a wealthy Los Angeles oil-stock broker. But her jealousy rose to a lethal level when she learned—from angry comments made by her husband, and listening in on a spare telephone— that there was more than casual flirtation in the attention he was paying to a pretty young widowed bank clerk, Alberta Meadows. In fact, Armour Phillips had apparently told his wife that he loved

hence the "Tiger Woman" label. At Phillips's trial, during closing arguments, Deputy District Attorney Charles W. Fricke acted out his scenario of the young bank clerk's final, violent moments. He held his hands together as if choking someone, telling the jury, "Clara Phillips grabbed the dying girl by the throat as she lay on the ground, and burying her thumbs into her flesh, choked her and said 'Die, you —.'"

After the murder, Clara Phillips told her husband that she had killed Meadows. He helped her to hide Meadows' car and then got her on a train headed for Mexico. But the next morning, Armour Phillips had second thoughts about becoming an accessory to a murder, and he went to his attorney's office. The attorney called well-known Undersheriff Eugene Warren Biscailuz, who later would serve as sheriff of Los Angeles County for more than two decades. Police officers in Arizona took Clara Phillips off the train at Tucson and returned her to Los Angeles to be tried for murder.

Left to right: two unidentified men, District Attorney Woolwine. Sheriff's Deputy Netti Yaw, Phillips and Judge Frederick Hauser.

Meadows and had thought of running away with her.

In 1922, after an early-summer afternoon spent drinking in a Long Beach speakeasy with her friend, Peggy Caffee, an infuriated Phillips, with Caffee coming along, went to the bank where Meadows worked. When Meadows emerged, they asked for a ride from her. Meadows, who didn't know Phillips, headed as directed for Montecito Heights, a quiet, isolated area north of downtown Los Angeles. There Phillips got Meadows out of the car and attacked her with a claw hammer. She hit her in the face and head, used the claw hammer head to disembowel the young woman, then hit her in the head again with such force that the hammer head snapped off in her skull. Finally Phillips strangled Meadows, prosecutors later claimed. The corpse, nauseated newspaper reporters decided, appeared as though it had been attacked by a tiger,

In court, Clara Phillips's attorney at first tried to prove that her friend, Peggy Caffee, had given Meadows the death blows. Then he tried for an insanity defense. Both sides called psychiatrists, then known as alienists, to make their respective cases. Prosecutor Fricke focused jurors' attention on Clara Phillips's "off-again, on-again memory" and dismissed the testimony of her alienists as "medical bunk." Phillips's attorney, according to the *Los Angeles Times*, "compared the prosecution alienists to the defense alienists as an ordinary mechanic might be compared to Edison." The defense attorney added that the mutilation of Meadows' body could only be the work of an insane person—and that Phillips shouldn't be held criminally responsible.

Fricke countered that, "This defendant, Clara Phillips, personally beat that poor girl out there on Montecito Drive. Her thought was to come back and brag to her husband of what she had done 'to the girl you love.' But undoubtedly she realizes that her violent temper has got her in a position where there is only one thing she can expect, and that is the punishment she deserves. She knows she is going to get it. And all she is hoping for is that it won't be the death penalty."

The jury convicted Phillips of second-degree murder, with a sentence of ten years to life in state prison.

But Phillips had always displayed great tenacity, resourcefulness and charm, traits that she reportedly shared with her sister, Etta May Jackson. Clara Phillips had plenty of admirers, before and after her conviction. They stuffed her jail cell with flowers and candy. And some offered more practical support. One of these was a man named Jesse Carson.

Though just how the matter was accomplished was subject to much speculation, Carson admitted helping Phillips to escape from the old

were going to set the two free. The police chief even had gunboats patrolling the Honduran harbor of Puerto Cortes to keep them in the country. But Lavine argued with Phillips that if she were truly innocent, she should come back to Los Angeles and prove it. He didn't mention the fact that her lawyer was now dead and had filed her appeal too late to be considered. In any event, Phillips agreed to return voluntarily, and Biscailuz, who spoke Spanish fluently, smuggled the two sisters out of the country aboard a fruit cargo vessel that landed in New Orleans.

More than two thousand celebrity-struck Los Angelenos met the train from Louisiana that brought Phillips back in June 1923. Standing on the observation platform of a railroad car, she and her husband kissed and embraced for the benefit of press photographers. But with no appeal possible, the train moved north, taking her to San Quentin.

Phillips retained her high spirits and active life during twelve years

A *Los Angeles Examiner* photo showed a potential Phillips jail-escape route.

Los Angeles County jail eight days after her conviction. She hid out for a while, then she, her sister and Carson made their way to Mexico and then Honduras.

Morris Lavine, a reporter for the *Los Angeles Examiner*, tracked Phillips to Honduras. Contacted through the Honduran consulate in Los Angeles, officials in the capital, Tegucigalpa, took Phillips and her sister into custody to await extradition. Lavine, Biscailuz and Biscailuz's wife went down to bring them back. But by then, Phillips and her sister had become as popular among some powerful Hondurans, including the Tegucigalpa chief of police, as they had been in Los Angeles. Many influential Hondurans, in fact, were reluctant to see the sisters leave. And with the country near revolution, and no U.S. extradition request yet formally in hand, it looked as though the Hondurans

in prison. In San Quentin, she played the saxophone and organized and conducted a seven-piece orchestra of women inmates, wrote and performed in a theatrical production and learned to be a dental assistant. When she was moved to the new women's prison in Tehachapi, she was equally at the center of prison social life.

But she didn't return to the front pages when she was paroled in 1935. She went to La Mesa, near San Diego, and moved into her mother's house, where she lived with her mother and three of her sisters. In 1938, she divorced her husband Armour Phillips, whose whereabouts by then were not known. Phillips announced that she would marry another man, though he was never publicly identified. Phillips worked as a dental assistant around San Diego until 1961, when she moved to Texas and dropped from sight.

McPherson.

Aimee Semple McPherson

The lively evangelist and faith healer is charged with criminal conspiracy and publicly disgraced by a sex scandal and faked kidnapping in 1926.

Aimee Kennedy's spiritual awakening came as a teenager in Canada. She heard a handsome Pentecostal evangelist named Robert James Semple give a stirring sermon and speak in tongues. As she heard more, she fell in love, as he reinspired her apparently lagging faith. At age 17, in 1908, Aimee Kennedy married Semple. As they conducted revivals around the United States and Canada, it became clear that Aimee was a powerful preacher in her own right. But the marriage was short-lived. Robert Semple died suddenly in Hong Kong— of typhoid fever, malaria or dysentery, according to various sources—as the two were about to enter China as missionaries. Aimee and their new daughter returned to the United States, where she began her own career as an evangelist with the Salvation Army. She married again in 1912, to Harold "Mack" McPherson, a Rhode Island accountant. They had a son. But life as a housewife proved dull compared with the flashy world on

stage that she began to envision for herself. Mack McPherson didn't like the tent-revival life, however. They would eventually divorce.

Meanwhile, in 1918, calling herself Aimee Semple McPherson, she preached her way across the country to what she would always describe as the City of Angels. She stopped along the way to deliver sermons to groups of subscribers to one of her earliest enterprises, the *Foursquare Monthly* magazine, drawn from her own teachings, the Foursquare Gospel.

She could really pack a house. A mesmerizing, erotically charged strawberry blonde, McPherson relied on music and theatrics—what she called her "illustrated sermons"—to make her points during services. She once wore a police uniform, riding into the auditorium on a motorcycle to deliver her sermon—on "arresting sin." She dressed as George Washington at Valley Forge, as a University of Southern California football player, as a nurse praying for the sick. McPherson could also raise money. She was fond of telling her followers, when the collection plate was passed, that "Sister," as she called herself, "has a headache tonight. Just quiet money, please"—in other words, bills not mere coins.

By 1923, she had expanded from rented halls, constructing her own Bible school, administrative center and theater-style church— the massive Angelus Temple, overlooking Echo Park Lake, with seating for fifty-three hundred worshippers. It had a Miracle Room full of wheelchairs, canes and crutches discarded by believers McPherson had cured. In the main auditorium, McPherson preached from center stage on a red velvet throne, when she wasn't traveling the city in luxurious open touring cars performing one promotional stunt or another.

In 1926, her church, a rare female-led ministry, was expanding dramatically in part through affiliations with other churches around the Southwest. At one point, she had founded 411 congregations, half of them led by women preachers. In 1926, McPherson was also a striking and powerful woman, in her glory at age 36. But KFSG, for Kall FourSquare Gospel, the church radio station, became the enterprise of her undoing. Almost no one contests the evidence linking McPherson romantically to Kenneth G. Ormiston, a married man whom she met when he was an engineer at the radio station.

Arrangements for a secret tryst, which ultimately made their adultery public, had all the dramatic elements of other McPherson productions. On May 18, she disappeared as she was swimming near Venice Beach. Her followers maintained a vigil on the beach, fearing that she had gone under. A professional diver as well as a church volunteer both drowned during an intensive, but fruitless search. More than a month passed. Then on June 23, three days after her stricken followers held a memorial at the Angelus Temple, McPherson showed up in the tiny town of Agua Prieta, across the Mexican border from Douglas, Arizona. She claimed she had been kidnapped and kept hostage at a shack in the Sonoran Desert. More than a hundred thousand people took to the streets of Los Angeles to greet McPherson when she returned in an automobile covered with roses.

District Attorney Asa Keyes was less enthusiastic. The grand jury questioned McPherson and her mother, Minnie Kennedy. McPherson said she had been kidnapped by "Jake," "Rose" and "Steve." But suspicious investigators and the press traced Ormiston's movements and found that he had spent a month with a woman in a cottage in Carmel. District Attorney's Office investigators produced a "little blue trunk" containing black satin, high-heeled slippers and a blue serge dress that closely resembled a dress McPherson had been photographed wearing on a tour to the Holy Land that January. Keyes also showed grand jurors a grocery list found in the cottage that clearly was in McPherson's handwriting, though McPherson refused to give fresh handwriting samples. The McPherson camp countered with the signed affidavit of a woman who claimed to have been Ormiston's companion in Carmel.

McPherson, her mother and four others were charged with conspiracy to obstruct justice by manufacturing false evidence—"falsely, wickedly and maliciously." In mid-September 1926, when her mother surrendered to arrest and arraignment, McPherson and her doctor said that she herself was unfortunately too sick in bed to surrender. "Although too ill to remain on her feet for more than a few seconds," the *Los Angeles Times* reported, "Mrs. McPherson came to a little balcony at the front of the house and thanked her faithful for their expressions of love and confidence."

The press kept the story alive, as details came to light here and there. But in January 1927, Keyes dropped all charges—unable to gather enough evidence, he said, to win against such a well-known public figure. Critics questioned whether Keyes had been bought off by McPherson's followers. Though that was never proved, the accusation prompted an investigation of the entire tenure of Keyes as district attorney, which ended in his conviction for taking bribes in another case—and spending nineteen months in San Quentin. Another casualty was Superior Court Judge Carlos Hardy, who was impeached for accepting a twenty-five-hundred-dollar "love offering" from Angelus Temple for his extraordinary and extra-legal support of McPherson, which included intimidating a witness, practicing law while serving on the bench, obstruction of justice and unethical conduct.

For McPherson, the embarrassing publicity began a downward spiral in her popularity, and many former believers turned away from her church. She was widely ridiculed when she traveled the country on what she called her Vindication Tour.

In 1931, McPherson married again. David Hutton was a vaudeville and cabaret singer who had performed in an Angelus Temple production. But he was also known as a womanizer who drank alcohol—not a popular image in the Foursquare Gospel world. The two would later divorce. A string of scandals dogged her through the following years. In 1944, Aimee Semple McPherson, touring Oakland, California, to preach to a group of her dwindling admirers, died from an accidental overdose of sleeping pills.

McPherson trial, District Attorney Asa Keyes (right), 1926. Sister Aimee in action (background).

Christian Brando

The son of a famous actor kills his half-sister's Tahitian lover in a complex case that ends with a plea of voluntary manslaughter.

As actor Marlon Brando described it, at about 10:40 p.m., May 16, 1990, at his expansive hilltop estate above Hollywood, his oldest son, Christian, came into Brando's room "looking weird" and told his father, "I killed Dag. He's dead, Pop. I didn't mean to do it. He went for the gun and it went off." Marlon Brando said he went immediately to the den where Dag Drollet, his daughter Cheyenne Brando's long time lover, had been shot. Drollet was on a sofa with a gunshot wound in the cheek. In one hand he had a television remote control and in the other, tobacco, rolling papers and a cigarette lighter. Marlon Brando tried mouth-to-mouth resuscitation. He dialed 911.

Marlon Brando lived much of the last several decades of the twentieth century in Tahiti as well as in Los Angeles. And Tahiti was home to 20-year-old Cheyenne Brando, long a troubled young woman, who had already achieved some modest fame as a model. Before the killing, Cheyenne Brando had been living for more than a year with Dag Drollet, the 26-year-old son of a well-known Tahitian politician. She was seven months pregnant with their child at the time of the shooting. They had separated two months before. Drollet was said to be trying to distance himself from the Brando family. Yet Drollet had come to Los Angeles with Cheyenne Brando in early May, and they had moved into the hilltop home with her father, while she underwent

Marlon Brando kisses son, Christian, in court.

psychological counseling. Known for her exotic beauty, Cheyenne Brando had been particularly depressed after her disfigurement that spring in an auto accident in Tahiti.

Christian Brando, a 32-year-old self-employed welder, claimed that the shooting was an accident—that he had become enraged because he had been told that Drollet had been "slapping around" his pregnant half-sister Cheyenne. Brando's attorney said that he had flourished a gun to show Drollet that he meant business. Drollet was imposing, at six feet, seven inches and more than two hundred pounds. As the two men had argued, and then struggled, Brando's gun had gone off.

Prosecutors, however, considered the death to be a premeditated killing. They found no evidence of a struggle before the shooting. And they maintained that Christian and Cheyenne Brando had discussed the alleged beatings at length earlier that evening, over dinner at the Hollywood restaurant, The Musso & Frank Grill. Christian Brando had also been drunk when he later confronted Drollet, with at least a .27 percent blood alcohol level (more than three times the legal limit for someone driving an automobile in California.) Drollet's parents, who attended all the hearings, also adamantly maintained that their son had never beaten Cheyenne Brando.

Prosecuting for the District Attorney's Office were Deputy District Attorneys Steven Barshop and William Clark. Robert Shapiro, who would later defend O. J. Simpson, represented Christian Brando.

Barshop considered Cheyenne Brando to be the prosecution's star material witness, since she knew her brother's state of mind before the shooting. And she reportedly had told police investigators that the gunshot "was not an accident. It was a murder, in case you don't know it." Marlon Brando had assured the police that Cheyenne would stay in Los Angeles during the proceedings. But Cheyenne Brando simply got on a plane to Tahiti, where she bore her child. In Tahiti, she added to the controversy by saying that her father and her brother's girl-friend had played roles in the death. Shortly thereafter, she was admitted to a psychiatric hospital.

To prosecutors, the major problem was that none of this testimony could be heard in court unless Cheyenne Brando were physically there,

Victim Dag Drollet.

to be cross-examined by the defense. And not only could she not be subpoenaed in French-controlled Tahiti, but she had been charged in a Tahiti court herself as an accomplice in Drollet's death. The French refused to let her leave until their own case was resolved.

Meanwhile, police investigators had failed to read Christian Brando all his Miranda rights before he admitted that he had stopped at his girlfriend's house to pick up his gun just minutes before the shooting—which would have bolstered prosecutors' arguments that the killing was premeditated. Then, as prosecutors battled to have Cheyenne Brando returned to Los Angeles to testify, she overdosed on drugs and went into a coma in a Tahiti hospital. When she revived, briefly, she tried to commit suicide by hanging herself. Prosecutors petitioned the Superior Court, Second District Court of Appeal, the California Supreme Court and U.S. District Court to compel Cheyenne Brando's return—but all refused. In late December 1990, Santa Monica Superior Court Judge Joel Rudof declared her to be "mentally disabled," which, as a practical matter, ended attempts to force her to testify in a Los Angeles court.

What had once seemed a strong case for premeditated murder now looked tough to prosecute. The prosecutors agreed to a plea bargain—Christian Brando would plead guilty to voluntary manslaughter, including a special allegation that he had committed the crime with a handgun. Barshop, the prosecutor, was "personally disappointed," he said. But without Cheyenne Brando, "we cannot legally prove malice, and without being able to prove malice, this case is a provable manslaughter. With her, this case is a murder—at least a triable murder."

At the hearing before Christian Brando was sentenced, his father gave an emotional, if discursive account of how he and his first wife had failed their son, Christian, describing him as a "basket case" and drug- and alcohol-abuser. A probation officer recommended only a three-year sentence, saying that Christian Brando evidenced chemically induced brain damage. The maximum penalty was sixteen years in prison.

In their brief, prosecutors listed previous violent acts, a "pattern of ever-escalating violence," including allegations that young Brando shot and wounded a man in a car in Brando's driveway; that Brando smashed a car's headlights with a hammer when he thought the man had tried to hit him; and that he had allegedly threatened his former wife and her mother. "Christian Brando is a serious danger to society," prosecutors pleaded to the judge, "not only because he is vicious, but also because he thinks the law does not apply to him."

Testifying for the defense, Christian Brando's ex-wife and former mother-in-law disputed that he had seriously threatened them. His ex-wife said that he had acted like a "brat" during the divorce. What prosecutors had termed a loaded rifle, pointed at the mother-in-law, the woman who had known Christian Brando since he was a young boy described as a toy plastic rifle that had been left in the house by a babysitter. "My daughter and he," she told the court, "they fought like brother and sister all the time." In the end, the courtroom was stunned to hear a sentence of ten years, more than most observers had expected.

Marlon Brando visited his son on Mondays, not the official visiting day at the California Men's Colony at San Luis Obispo, a state prison, arriving in a limousine or Rolls Royce. Otherwise, Christian Brando spent his time getting a high-school diploma equivalent and reading the Bible and *War and Peace*. Cheyenne Brando committed suicide by hanging in Tahiti in 1995. Dag Drollet's parents took over the care of the baby, Tookie. Shortly after midnight on January 11, 1996, after just short of five years in prison, Christian Brando was released on parole.

Lance Helms, child abuse victim.

Family Violence

n 1861, Jose Alvitre and his wife were in their sixties. They had raised twelve children together. Yet through all those years, as the *Los Angeles Star* reported, "The old man was in the habit of taking sprees, and when intoxicated he seemed to have an insane desire to abuse his wife." Early in 1861, Alvitre had been jailed for four months for assaulting his wife in an attempt to kill her. In May, out of jail and drunk again, he succeeded, stabbing her seven times. He tried to escape but his neighbors caught him. They knew the family's sad history and decided that no further criminal investigation was needed. They promptly lynched Alvitre. In an editorial, the *Star* noted that recently in Los Angeles three women had been "assaulted and treated in an inhuman manner"—two by their husbands and one by a stranger. "We think the promptness of justice in these parts will soon cure their propensity to abuse or kill women," the *Star* announced optimistically.

Unfortunately, family and intimate-relationship violence continue to devastate people from all walks of life in Los Angeles County. Both men and women in families harm each other as well as their children. Still, women and children are more often victims not offenders. The FBI estimates that a third of all women homicide victims in the United States are killed by their husbands or ex-husbands.

Since the early 1990s, prosecutors and police departments have become much more aggressive in investigating and prosecuting these crimes, however, and in aiding victims before the abuse becomes deadly. Some patterns and danger signals have emerged. Many abusers make open comments to fellow workers about what they've done, or intend to do. In recent years, many victims have understood their danger well enough to approach the authorities—obtaining temporary restraining orders or even court orders barring their abusers from owning a gun or other weapon. For abusers such as Donald Bohana and John David Sweeney, there have been clear tipoffs to their histories of abuse. Dolores Jackson's family had noticed black-and-blue marks on her after she started dating Bohana. Actress Dominique Dunne had also suffered bouts of abuse at Sweeney's hands before his fatal attack.

In 1994, the Los Angeles District Attorney's Office set up a toll-free hotline for all county residents, called Safe Way Out. Available in six languages, the hotline connects victims with shelters. The District Attorney's Office also operates Special Assistance to Victims in Emergency, or S.A.V.E., which offers food, shelter, clothing and financial assistance to crime victims and their families.

These supports—as well as a much wider awareness of the problem since the death of Nicole Brown and the trials of O. J. Simpson—have contributed to a decline in the level of family violence in Los Angeles County. In 1993, county prosecutors were filing one domestic-violence homicide case every five days; in 2000, that had dropped to one case filed every fourteen to fifteen days, a third of the former rate.

Griffith J. Griffith

A mining and real-estate tycoon tries to kill his wife in a drunken argument and is sentenced to prison in 1903.

Trained as a journalist in his native Wales, Griffith Jenkins Griffith came to San Francisco in 1873, where he became a mining reporter. He learned the mining business and gave up newspapers to become a mining consultant and investor, making an impressive fortune in just a few years. When he moved to Los Angeles in 1881, he bought the Rancho Los Feliz. As a Christmas present to Los Angeles in 1896, and to avoid paying property taxes, Griffith donated more than three thousand of the *rancho*'s four thousand acres to the city, for what would become Griffith Park. Through these years, he was becoming increasingly eccentric, hot-tempered and alcoholic,

Griffith J. Griffith

however. By the 1890s he was drinking as much as two quarts of whiskey daily. He was also having ferocious arguments with his wife, Tina, a descendant of the pioneer Verdugo family and an inheritor of giant Rancho San Rafael. One point of contention was religion. Tina Griffith was staunchly Catholic; Griffith was a zealous Protestant. And in 1903, vacationing in the presidential suite at the four-story Arcadia Hotel, a seaside resort in Santa Monica, a drunken Griffith brutally accosted his wife.

Griffith entered his wife's room and told her to kneel, while he held her prayer book. With his other hand, he pointed a pistol at her and accused her of slowly trying to poison him. He demanded that she swear that she had been faithful to him. Though Tina said she had, and pleaded for her life, he shot her anyway. At the last second she turned her head and the bullet hit her in the forehead at an angle, blinding her in her right eye. To save herself, she jumped out the window. One floor below, she landed on the wooden piazza of the hotel owner. She had broken her arm in the fall. The owner and his wife hauled her through their window. Griffith was now at their door, claiming that Tina Griffith had accidentally shot herself. The owner put in a call to the sheriff.

District Attorney J. D. Fredericks charged Griffith with attempted murder. At the time, it was common practice for supporters of the victim to pay for their own lawyers to help in the prosecution. Tina Griffith's angry family hired a former judge, J.W. McKinley, former California Governor Henry T. Gage

and Isadore B. Dockweiler, a prominent attorney, to act as special prosecutors to help Fredericks in the case. Renowned defense attorney Earl Rogers defended Griffith. The courtroom battle was essentially between Rogers and Gage.

The trial opened in February 1904. Gage contended that Griffith was sane, though drunk, and trying to murder his wife. He was responsible for his actions. Rogers portrayed Griffith as the victim of "alcoholic insanity," that he became a "crazy drunk" when he drank, a condition which had caused him for years to live a "Dr. Jekyll and Mr. Hyde" life. The concept that alcoholism could be a disease, not a personal failing, was a new idea, at least in the Los Angeles courts. Rogers brought in doctors—alienists, as psychiatrists were then known— and authorities on drinking, including such practical experts as bartenders, bellboys and even Griffith's barber.

But Gage asked the jury, "Are we to say that because this man has been a drunken hog in secret most of his life, he may in this beautiful state of ours slaughter the innocent with impunity?" He also, with considerable drama, unveiled the disfigured face of Tina Griffith to the court. And then he challenged the jurors. "No *rich man* has ever been punished for such a crime in these United States," he said. "A *rich man* thinks he cannot be punished."

Though many in the trial audience were sympathetic with Rogers's idea that alcoholism was a disease, and many agreed that as the *Los Angeles Times* said, Griffith was "as crazy as a woodtick," the jury convicted him of the lesser charge of assault with a deadly weapon. Judge George H. Smith, who called the crime "revolting," gave Griffith the maximum term in San Quentin, two years. Though most observers considered the result a victory for the defense, Earl Rogers was distraught at the verdict and the sentence.

Griffith served his time and returned sobered and subdued. Many of his former acquaintances rebuffed him. But as a Catholic, Tina Griffith wouldn't divorce him. They lived under the same roof in a seventeen-room mansion until 1919, when Griffith died. Before his death he tried to make another philanthropic donation, one hundred thousand dollars for an astronomical observatory. The City refused the money. Only after his death would his money be used to build Griffith Park Observatory and the Greek Theater.

John David Sweeney

Actress Dominique Dunne breaks off an abusive romance with a restaurant chef. He strangles her to death in 1982.

Dominique Dunne, 22 years old, met John Sweeney, 27, at a party. She was an actress with a growing reputation. She had been featured in a major movie, *Poltergeist*, and was about to begin work on a television mini-series, *V*. Dunne was also the daughter of writer Dominick Dunne and the sister of movie writer-director Griffin Dunne. Sweeney was head chef at the fashionable west side restaurant Ma Maison. They began seeing each other romantically. But Sweeney, it turned out, had an uncontrollable temper.

Ellen Griffin Dunne, the actress's mother, would later describe to the court the scene when her daughter came to her house after the first time that Sweeney beat her. Dominique Dunne lay on the floor of her mother's hallway in the fetal position and told how Sweeney had hit her head on the floor and pulled out bunches of her hair. She was clearly terrified, said her mother. The beatings continued. One night after an evening out together, he choked her so hard that he left bruises on her neck. At the time, she was playing a battered child on an episode of the television show *Hill Street Blues*. She joked to a friend that she wouldn't need makeup to look abused, and she didn't.

After that, Dunne broke off the relationship and changed the locks on the house she had been sharing with Sweeney. Sweeney was enraged. Five weeks later, on October 30, 1982, when Dunne again refused to renew their romance, Sweeney came to her home. She was practicing a scene from the TV mini-series with fellow actor David Packer. Sweeney pulled her off her front porch and dragged her around to the side of the house, where they argued violently before he strangled her. Packer couldn't see what was happening, but he was alarmed enough at the struggle, and frightened enough of the big, angry chef, that he called police. He also called a friend and left a message on the answering machine: "If I die tonight, it was by John Sweeney." Dunne never regained consciousness. Five days after the attack, she was taken off life support.

District Attorney Robert H. Philibosian assigned Deputy District Attorney Steven Barshop to try the case. Sweeney was charged with murder, as well as felony assault for his choking attack five weeks before the murder. Deputy Public Defender Michael Adelson would defend Sweeney, assisted by Joseph Shapiro, an attorney hired by the Ma Maison restaurant. Superior Court Judge Burton S. Katz, who as a deputy district attorney had been one of the prosecutors of the Manson family, would preside.

Adelson argued that Sweeney, an otherwise "ordinarily reasonable person," had killed Dunne in a moment of passion when she refused to take up their relationship again. That would mean that Sweeney was guilty only of manslaughter. Sweeney now claimed that he couldn't remember the killing at all. And every day he brought a Bible to court with him, often weeping ostentatiously, in apparent remorse.

Barshop contended that Sweeney deserved a murder conviction because he showed malice and premeditation. Sweeney had confessed the killing to a sheriff's deputy soon after the crime. "'Man, I blew it. I killed her,'" Deputy Frank De Milio testified Sweeney told him. "'I didn't think I choked her that hard, but I don't know, I just kept on choking her. I just lost my temper and I blew it again.'" And in his opening remarks to the jury, Barshop gave a dramatic example of how Sweeney acted more methodically than in a mindless passion. The coroner had estimated that it took Sweeney four to six minutes

to strangle Dunne. Barshop held a watch before the jury and said, "Ladies and gentlemen, I am going to show you how long it took for Dominique Dunne to die." For four excruciating minutes, everyone in the court was aware of how much time Sweeney had to decide to take his large hands from her throat.

Barshop also learned of another woman who had been abused in a relationship with Sweeney. This, too, showed a man with an uncontrolled, violent temper—an abuser, not a man driven to killing in a moment of passion and rejection. In a hearing without the jury, Lillian Pierce, a woman in her thirties, told Judge Katz of ten separate beatings over her two-year relationship with Sweeney. She had suffered a broken nose, punctured eardrum, a collapsed lung and had twice had to be hospitalized. He'd thrown rocks at her, broken up furniture and even foamed at the mouth in his uncontrolled anger. And when Barshop hit a raw nerve in Sweeney with one of his questions, the court, though not the jury, got a first-hand view of his temper. Barshop believed that Sweeney was drawn to women from prominent, wealthy families. When he asked Pierce whether she was from a well-to-do family, because "I am trying to establish a pattern," Sweeney jumped up, infuriated, and headed for a rear door. The bailiff and four armed guards struggled with him until he relaxed and was handcuffed to his chair.

Actress Dominique Dunne.

Judge Katz, however, ruled that Lillian Pierce's injuries couldn't be told to the jury under any circumstances. And so in a development that was strongly criticized by women's rights and victims' rights groups, as well as the Dunne family, the jurors would reach verdicts without knowing that Sweeney had battered other women.

And in a last setback for the prosecution, after Barshop's final arguments, Adelson petitioned Judge Katz to eliminate first-degree murder from the jury's options, arguing that, "There is no premeditation or deliberation in this case." Judge Katz agreed. Second-degree murder would be the most serious verdict that jurors could choose.

The jury, in fact, decided that Sweeney had killed in the heat of passion and it settled on a lower-order verdict, voluntary manslaughter. The assault charge was lowered to misdemeanor assault. The verdicts were widely criticized. Protesters from five victims' rights groups, including Theresa Saldana, who had barely survived a knife attack by an obsessed fan, gathered outside the courthouse to hear Sweeney's sentencing. Judge Katz now called the Dunne killing "a case, pure and simple, of murder, murder with malice." He gave Sweeney the maximum penalty under the reduced charges, six and a half years in prison.

Sweeney was released after serving three and a half years. He became engaged to marry a woman in Florida until her father recognized Sweeney's name and intervened. Sweeney has since changed his name.

Slow-speed Bronco chase; (below) Judge Ito with prosecutors and defense attorneys.

O.J. Simpson

In a trial under the hot lights of the international media, a former football star is acquitted of the 1994 murders of Nicole Brown and Ronald Goldman.

On a Sunday afternoon, June 12, 1994, Orenthal James "O.J." Simpson and his houseguest, Brian "Kato" Kaelin, were talking. In the course of their conversation, Simpson told Kaelin that, after protracted attempts at reconciliation, he and his ex-wife, Nicole Brown, weren't "together anymore." A few hours later, both Simpson and Brown separately attended a dance recital featuring their daughter, Sydney, at nearby Paul Revere Junior High School in Brentwood where Brown and Simpson lived in separate residences. Their relationship had been punctuated by a number of well-documented incidents of domestic violence, including Simpson's 1989 misdemeanor conviction for spousal battery. After the dance recital, Simpson was told that he

was unwelcome at a Brown family gathering. He returned home and ran into Kaelin, again mentioning that he had seen his ex-wife.

Nicole Brown had dinner with her family at the restaurant Mezzaluna, then went home about 8:30 p.m. An hour later, Brown called the restaurant because her mother had forgotten her prescription glasses. Brown's friend Ronald Goldman, a Mezzaluna waiter, said he would bring them to her house later. At about the same time, Kaelin and Simpson pulled into the drive-through lane of a McDonald's. By 9:45 p.m., Kaelin and Simpson were back at Simpson's home, where they parted company and ate separately. Five minutes later, Goldman left the restaurant to return the glasses.

Just under an hour later, chauffeur Allan Park, who had been waiting outside Simpson's dark, quiet house to take Simpson to the airport, decided to buzz the intercom at one of the estate's entrances. He got no response. At about the same time, Kaelin heard a thumping sound on his rear wall. Shortly afterward, Park saw a person he later described as black, six feet tall and about two hundred pounds cross the driveway and go into Simpson's house. Park said the figure

Simpson Not Guilty
Drama Ends 474 Days After Arrest

Case Had Many Holes, Juror Says

■ **Panel:** Group agreed with forensic expert Lee that there was 'something wrong' with prosecution's evidence, he reports. Opportunities for contamination are cited.

■ **Verdicts:** The ex-football star expresses gratitude and returns to his Brentwood estate where friends and family celebrate. Relatives of the victims react with pain and grim silence to the jurors' decision.

By JIM NEWTON, TIMES STAFF WRITER

Bringing one of history's most riveting courtroom dramas to a stunning climax, O.J. Simpson was acquitted of two counts of murder Tuesday, verdicts that set the football Hall of Famer free 474 days after he was arrested and charged with a brutal double homicide.

At 11:16 a.m., Simpson returned home to his Brentwood estate, embracing his longtime friend Al Cowlings in the same driveway where the two were arrested on June 17, 1994. As night fell, crowds of well-wishers and detractors gathered beyond police barricades while the Simpson entourage partied inside the famous home.

Within hours of the verdicts— broadcast live and bringing busi-

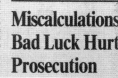

Miscalculations, Bad Luck Hurt Prosecution

Los Angeles Times acquittal headline on the morning after Simpson's October, 3, 1995 acquittal.

was in dark clothing, and he couldn't tell whether it was a man or a woman. Meanwhile, Park buzzed the house again, and this time a voice told him that he would be coming out soon. Four or five minutes later, the lights in Simpson's house went on, Simpson walked out and Simpson and Kaelin loaded Simpson's bags into the limousine. Park delivered Simpson to Los Angeles International Airport, where his flight to Chicago departed at 11:45. Shortly after midnight on June 13, Nicole Brown's dog led neighbors to the extraordinarily bloody scene where the bodies of Goldman and Brown were sprawled.

Thus began one of the most celebrated murder cases ever tried in Los Angeles County. Covered by the international media, the events through the investigation and trial were irresistible to millions of television viewers. Based on physical evidence—including a bloody glove found at Simpson's estate, blood drops leading from the bodies and blood inside Simpson's Ford Bronco and inside his home— it became clear that Simpson would be arrested as the prime murder suspect. Then, five days after the killings, and contrary to an agreement to surrender himself to the police, Simpson slipped out of friend Robert Kardashian's home, carrying, among other things, money, a passport and a disguise. He later was spotted in his white Ford Bronco with friend and former college teammate, Al Cowlings, near John Wayne Airport, in Orange County. They went on a long, slow drive, during which Simpson threatened suicide. Police followed and cleared a path in front, as the Bronco eventually returned to Simpson's home, where he was arrested without further melodrama.

There would be plenty of theater in the courtroom, however, as Deputy District Attorneys Marcia Clark, William Hodgman and Christopher Darden led the prosecution team. In defense was what would be known as the "Dream Team" of lawyers—including Robert Shapiro, Johnnie L. Cochran Jr., F. Lee Bailey, Alan M. Dershowitz and Barry Scheck. Superior Court Judge Lance Ito, a former deputy district attorney, would preside over the trial.

The tortuous story was laid out over months of testimony. Prosecutors argued that a mountain of evidence showed that no one else but Simpson could have, or would have the motive to kill Goldman and Brown. Particularly damning was DNA testing that showed both

victims' blood mixed with Simpson's inside the Bronco, as well as on the bloody glove.

The defense team presented evidence to suggest that the DNA samples had been contaminated. And in a dramatic moment, Simpson, standing at the defense table, pulled on the bloody glove and quickly declared it "too tight" to have been his. He did not testify in his own defense. The defense team argued to the predominantly black jury that much of the physical evidence had been planted by police, notably LAPD detective Mark Fuhrman, who was captured on audiotape making racially pejorative comments.

On October 3, 1995, following ten months of trial recorded in forty-eight thousand pages of transcripts, the jury took just three hours to acquit Simpson of the two murder charges.

In a civil suit brought later against Simpson by the families of Goldman and Brown, Simpson testified, denying that he was the killer. On February 4, 1997, the civil jury found Simpson liable for the deaths of Brown and Goldman and awarded more than $32 million in damages to their families.

Nicole Brown.　　　　Ronald Goldman.

Donald James Bohana

Dolores Jackson, former wife of singer Tito Jackson, is found dead in businessman Donald Bohana's swimming pool in 1994.

Just before dawn on August 27, 1994, the nude body of Dolores "Dee Dee" Jackson, age 39, was found propped up against a tree near the swimming pool of her new boyfriend of seven weeks, Ladera Heights businessman Donald Bohana, age 58. Jackson was the former wife of seventeen years of singer Tito Jackson, who with brother Michael and other family members constituted the Jackson 5 pop-music group. Sheriff's homicide detectives investigated the scene, but based on Bohana's statements the death seemed a simple accidental drowning.

But, the coroner's office released an opinion that indicated that Jackson died in an "assisted drowning," though the exact mode of death was still "undetermined." At the time of her death, Jackson had had a high blood-alcohol level of .22 percent. The coroner also found that she had suffered more than fifty traumatic injuries around her head, face and neck—including a ripped ear lobe, tongue that was bitten through, two black eyes, multiple contusions and extensive internal damage to her neck. The case languished, however, for several months until it was presented to the newly formed Family Violence Division Special Unit. Deputy District Attorney Lori-Ann C. Jones directed the reinvestigation of the case, which brought out significant new evidence that Bohana had committed murder.

Donald Bohana had always been considered a potential suspect in the death, but had never been arrested. Bohana was a prominent businessman in the Watts-Willowbrook area of Los Angeles, and active in civic organizations. But most of his recent business ventures had failed.

On March 7, 1997, sheriff's department homicide investigators arrested Bohana for Jackson's murder. At his indictment, the District Attorney's Office revealed that he owed debts of more than $4 million and had declared bankruptcy twice.

The Jackson family was relieved at the news of Bohana's arrest. Dee Dee Jackson had a well-known, long-standing fear of being in the water and never learned how to swim. So when Bohana had explained to the family that she had drowned while swimming laps and making "Olympic-style turns" in his pool, her family and friends didn't believe him.

Jackson family members and friends also testified at the trial that they began to notice suspicious black-and-blue bruises on Dee Dee Jackson's upper arms shortly after she began dating Bohana. The week she was murdered, Jackson had confided to a close friend that Bohana was being physically abusive to her and that she planned to break up with him.

But defense attorney Harland Braun contended that Jackson died as a result of a botched rescue attempt. Bohana saw Jackson in trouble, dove three times to try to pull her out, and resorted finally to the ten-foot pole of a leaf net to try to save her. The pole, argued Braun, caused Jackson's injuries. Bohana also claimed that when he did get Jackson out of the pool, he administered CPR until he heard her gasp and she started breathing. Then he went into his house to call for help.

Superior Court Judge Patricia J. Titus was then a deputy district attorney in the Family Violence Division. She prosecuted Bohana. Titus established that when Bohana called in the emergency, he gave the wrong address. When the paramedics arrived, they had to jump over the back fence to get into the backyard. Bohana had by then dried Jackson's naked body and propped it up against the tree.

Titus also showed jurors the pole net that was supposed to have caused such damage to Jackson's face and neck—clearly it couldn't have caused her injuries. The prosecutor argued that Bohana simply beat Jackson and threw her into the pool. Titus reminded jurors of Jackson's fear of the water. "The defense wants you to believe that unbeknownst to her entire family, except the defendant, that she could swim and swim well," Titus said. The jury returned a guilty verdict for second-degree murder.

At Bohana's sentencing, Superior Court Judge Morris B. Jones called Bohana "less than generous with the truth," and noted that there was medical evidence that Dee Dee Jackson had been strangled. He sentenced Bohana to fifteen years to life.

Deputy District Attorney Patti Titus.

David Helms

In a case that changed state child-abuse laws, a mother campaigns to have her batterer son convicted of the murder of her young grandson, Lance Helms—and to have his girlfriend released from prison.

Gail Helms was not only a mother but a devoted grandmother. When she couldn't save the lives of her daughter and grandson, she became determined to seek justice—even at the expense of her son. Gail Helms and her daughter, Ayn, had raised Lance Helms from the time he was five days old to the moment almost two years later when the Los Angeles County Dependency Court gave him back to his father.

The County Department of Children's Services had placed the baby in the care of Ayn Helms because he had been born heroin-addicted. Ayn's brother David and his girlfriend, the boy's mother, were addicts, and, in any case, in no position to raise him. The mother was headed to prison for robbery. David Helms, 37 years old, had a long criminal record of his own.

By all accounts, the young boy flourished in his aunt's care. Then in August 1994, Lance's father, now living off-and-on with a new girl-friend, Eve Wingfield, 21, went to the Department of Social Services and the Los Angeles County Dependency Court and regained custody. State child-abuse laws at the time placed more emphasis on family reunification than on child safety.

Gail and Ayn Helms began to find scrapes and bruises on the young boy's body when they visited him. Gail Helms took photographs of the injuries and kept notes in a diary, which she used in an attempt to get help from the Department of Social Services. But Lance Helms was still in the custody of his father on April 6, 1995.

That day, Wingfield was home in the couple's North Hollywood apartment, caring for Lance Helms and Wingfield's son, 4-year-old Calvin, both of whom were ill with stomach flu. Late that afternoon, David Helms came home and told Wingfield to go to a pawnbroker down the street, to redeem a few items for him. When Wingfield left, Lance Helms was talking to his father and sitting up on the couch. When she came back fifteen to twenty minutes later, the boy's lips were blue and he was slumped down. He was dead when the paramedics arrived. A coroner's report said that he looked like he'd been in an automobile accident, he was so badly beaten. Deputy Los Angeles County Medical Examiner James K. Ribe also concluded that the child had died a half hour to an hour after he was beaten.

To prosecutors, that meant that he had been beaten while in Eve Wingfield's care, before David Helms came home. She was charged with murder, and on the advice of her public defender, plea-bargained no contest to a count of child endangerment causing death. Otherwise, the attorney had warned her, she risked a life sentence for murder in a jury trial. Wingfield was sentenced to ten years in prison.

Gail Helms knew that an injustice had been done. Her daughter, Ayn, who suffered from lupus, died from the disease five months after Lance Helms died. Gail Helms was convinced, however, that her daughter had died from a broken heart over Lance's death. She proceeded alone in a campaign to have her son convicted of the boy's murder. She knew his history of violence, including the telling characteristic that even as a boy, he had focused on punching his brothers in the stomach when they fought. Lance Helms's injuries—including a broken rib, a liver that was split in pieces, a six-inch tear in the structure that anchors the intestines to the spine, and a

bruised diaphragm—came from hard punches to the stomach.

Helms pressed her campaign until LAPD Detectives Terry Lopez and Steve Bernard agreed to reopen the investigation. At the same time, Ribe, the medical examiner, remained troubled. On his own, and using his own funds, Ribe had continued to try to more narrowly set the time between Lance Helms's beating and his death. When Lopez and Bernard contacted Ribe about his first autopsy report, he had already concluded that Lance Helms had died almost immediately after he was beaten, making David Helms the more likely killer. In September 1997, Eve Wingfield, who had served twenty-one months of her prison sentence, was ordered freed, based on the new evidence. Seven months later, David Helms was charged with one count each of murder, assault on a child causing death and child abuse likely to produce great bodily harm and death.

In the trial, Ribe delivered a convincing account of why he changed his opinion about the boy's time of death. But defense attorney Jack Stone termed his testimony "tailoring his scientific opinion to coincide with the facts." Stone argued that if Ribe had now been able to estimate two times of death, this alone cast a reasonable doubt as to who beat the boy.

Deputy District Attorney Eleanor Hunter called medical experts to support Ribe's new report, as well as Eve Wingfield and other witnesses who had seen David Helms hitting his son—once, so hard that he was knocked out of his baby carriage. Yet Hunter later said that the most telling evidence was what David Helms did after the boy died. "He didn't say anything," Hunter pointed out. He didn't act like a father whose girlfriend has just murdered his son. Helms was convicted on all counts and sentenced to twenty-one years to life in state prison.

At the sentencing hearing, Gail Helms told the court that her son "is a serial batterer who has beaten every woman he has known. That includes his sister, his grandmother, his girlfriend...and me." In 1999, nominated by Hunter, Gail Helms was given the California District Attorneys Association's Patricia Lewis Witness of the Year Award, named for a woman who testified in a murder case despite numerous threats on her life. Meanwhile, the California Legislature passed a law requiring that a child's safety be the highest priority in custody cases.

Lance Helms with aunt, Ayn.

Savings and loan magnate Charles Keating.

For Financial Gain

Criminals have always found creative ways to make money outside the law. In too many cases, the idea has been as simple and dreadful as killing one's spouse for the insurance. Or as Edwin Seth Brown did, taking advantage of someone who is obviously vulnerable. Beginning in 1991, Brown, 45 years old, inveigled more than two-hundred-fifty thousand dollars—virtually her life savings—from Olive Ruby, a Santa Clarita Valley widow in her eighties, who was partially incapacitated from a stroke. Brown, who was prosecuted in 1998 by Deputy District Attorney Ardith Javan, was convicted of elder financial abuse and sentenced to four years in prison.

The sprawling expanse of Los Angeles County has historically offered unearned rewards on a grand and varied scale. Los Angeles was particularly profitable for bootleggers during Prohibition, for instance, because of the size of the market and the proximity of Mexico, where alcohol was legal. The oil boom in the 1920s was as exciting for ordinary investors of the day as corporate junks bonds would be in the 1980s.

The District Attorney's Office fraud divisions specialize in welfare, auto insurance, real estate and workers' compensation, which was for a time the bane of California business leaders. Deputy District Attorney Allen Field, who in 1997 became a bureau director in charge of the District Attorney's Office fraud units, recalled the workers' comp crisis. "The cost to employers was skyrocketing, out of control," said Field. "In some cases, the cost of workers' compensation insurance exceeded the payroll costs of companies—because there was so much fraud going on, with false claims, phony doctors, crooked lawyers. A state assemblyman once said to me, 'I'll bet you never thought that your job as a deputy district attorney was to save the California economy.' And he was very serious."

Field and colleague Edward Feldman helped to draft legislation to beef up worker's-comp fraud enforcement. The effect was dramatic. In 1992, the first year of the new program, with only the Los Angeles County District Attorney's Office yet implementing its provisions, fraudulent claims for worker's compensation insurance in California dropped by $2 billion.

Money, sadly, is often not the only valuable lost to greed. In too many of Los Angeles's most notorious crimes for financial gain, the greatest toll was in human life.

William Edward Hickman

Self-styled "The Fox," a college student kidnaps for ransom the 12-year-old daughter of a banker in 1927.

William Hickman chose a gruesome way to raise money for his college education—kidnapping the young daughter of a bank manager with whom he had once worked. Hickman, 19, took Marion Parker from Mount Vernon Junior High School after telling teachers that he was there to pick her up because her father, Perry M. Parker, had been injured. Then he sent a ransom demand to Parker demanding fifteen hundred dollars in twenty-dollar gold certificates.

Parker came to the rendezvous with the money, but he had told the authorities. He was followed to the site by police cars. Hickman didn't appear. The next day, Hickman sent another letter, upbraiding Parker for going to the police. That night, Parker appeared alone with the money. He gave it to a man in a car, after seeing his apparently live daughter sitting inside. The car pulled forward and moved down the street, then stopped. The man inside placed a parcel at the curb. It contained the limbless half-torso—the eyes sewn open, face powdered and hair combed—of Marion Parker.

The town was aghast at the news. A wide-spread manhunt found the car, but little else. Four days later, an LAPD sergeant identified Hickman from fingerprints on the ransom letters. Flyers were sent around the West Coast, offering rewards totaling fifty thousand dollars. The next day, one of the gold certificates

was cashed by a men's clothing store, which reported it. Hickman was captured the day after that, near Pendleton, Oregon.

District Attorney Asa Keyes brought Hickman and a collection of reporters back from Oregon on the train. On the way, Keyes elicited a full confession. Hickman had strangled her with a towel after the first failed rendezvous. But realizing afterwards that he would need her body as proof to get a ransom from her father, he put her in the bathtub, cut off her limbs and the lower half of her body. He dumped the body parts in Elysian Park.

Hickman pleaded not guilty by reason of insanity. It took a jury thirty-six minutes to find him to be sane. On October 19, 1928, ten months after the crime, Hickman was hanged at San Quentin.

Left to right: William Hickman in court (center); kidnapping note demands; victim Marion Parker.

Lyle and Eric Menendez.

The Menendez Brothers

After two difficult trials and six years of legal maneuvers, Lyle and Erik Menendez are sentenced to life for the shotgun killings of their parents.

The day after killing their unsuspecting parents with shotguns as they sat on a couch watching television, Lyle and Erik Menendez took the safe from their parents' house over to an attorney's, where they tried to open it in search of a will. When that failed, they hired a safecracker, who got it open. But the brothers were disappointed to find no will inside. The two did gain access to their parents' money, however, and promptly went on a spending spree—Rolex watches, a Porsche, a three-hundred-thousand-dollar down-payment on a New Jersey restaurant.

The saga began on the night of August 20, 1989, when Erik Menendez, 18 years old, called 911, shrieking that he and his brother, Lyle, 21, had just come home to find their parents dead. Their parents, Kitty and Jose Menendez, were multimillionaires. The brothers were suspected from the beginning. But until they confessed—in a taped conversation—to their psychiatrist, L. Jerome Oziel, police investigators had been stalled hunting for evidence for the first few months after the killings. Oziel's former lover, Judalon Smyth, told Beverly Hills police of the taped confession. More evidence accumulated and in 1993, the brothers were tried with separate juries for murder. Deputy District Attorney Pamela Bozanich, as lead prosecutor, assisted by Deputy District Attorney Lester Kuriyama, prosecuted the case. They argued that the murders ultimately resulted from long-standing, sometimes violent tension with their father, combined with the boys' greed. Both boys basically wanted their father out of their lives. They killed their mother, prosecutors said, because they didn't believe she could live without her husband.

Attorney Leslie Abramson defended Erik Menendez and Jill Lansing represented his brother, Lyle. In the first trial, the defense portrayed the brothers as convinced that their parents planned to kill them on the night of the murders, after years of psychological and sexual abuse. Both Lyle and Erik testified that their father had abused them, beginning at age 6 in each case. They killed their parents in terror and in self-defense, both said.

Prosecutors played the taped confession. On it, the brothers complained of their father's frequent infidelity and said they killed their mother to "put her out of her misery," but neither mentioned that they had been sexually abused, or were afraid of their parents that night. Both trials ended, after six months, with hung juries, split almost equally in half, unable to choose between murder and manslaughter for the two killers. The defense called for a plea-bargain. But District Attorney Gil Garcetti adamantly refused. He said he felt an "ethical, professional and moral responsibility to go forward... We're going to seek justice in this case."

The second trial, with a single jury this time, began in 1995. Deputy District Attorneys David Conn, as lead prosecutor, and Carol Najera tried the case. Erik Menendez was again defended by Leslie Abramson; Lyle, by Public Defenders Terry Towrey and Charles Gessler. The first trial was televised and was melodramatic, particularly when the brothers tearfully described their home life and the killings. The second trial, without television coverage, more often resembled a typical murder case. The prosecutors went into the killings in detail, arguing that even if the brothers had been provoked by their domineering father, and had shot him while in fear for their lives, how could they have been afraid of their mother? And the brothers had not only shot her several times in the first moments of the attack, but when she was on the floor and helpless, they reloaded their guns and shot her in the face.

Both were convicted. In the penalty phase of the trial, Conn called for a death sentence, emphasizing the brothers' "cold, calculating decision." He told jurors, "They chose death on Friday when they went shopping for shotguns. They chose death on Saturday when they reloaded their shotguns with more lethal ammunition. They chose death Sunday when they shot their parents to death. And now they want you to choose life for them?" The brothers were each sentenced to two consecutive sentences of life without parole, meaning that they will spend the rest of their lives behind bars. And for the first time, because of a state prison policy to keep crime partners apart, they will spend those lives in separate institutions.

Court clerk reads guilty verdicts.

Julian Pete

A company created by a charismatic promoter swindles thousands of investors and takes a district attorney down with it in the roaring Los Angeles oil boom.

Los Angeles offered a great advantage to brokers, honest and crooked, who peddled petroleum-company stocks during the 1920s oil boom—the wells were near at hand. Only a short bus ride from downtown Los Angeles were such giant fields as Signal Hill and Huntington Beach. Promoters wooed small investors with oil-field tours. With working oil wells as a dramatic backdrop, they gave free lectures, free lunches, parachute shows, appearances by stars including Norma

Left to right: District Attorney Fitts, D.A. Investigator Jack Chriss, Julian case witness.

Talmadge, and always the pitch to invest, delivered in crowded canvas shelters known as "sucker tents." Typical newspaper ads coaxed the vulnerable with, "See the Gushers at Santa Fe Springs," "Delicious Beef Barbecue," "Band Concert Entertainment," "Realize what fortunes are pouring out of the ground." The bus drivers were instructed to take routes that passed the mansions of wealthy people, particularly oil barons, to give potential investors a sense of what they could gain. It was the right environment at the right time for a flamboyant Canadian and former Texas oil-well field hand, Chauncey "C.C." Julian, who had just arrived in town.

Julian first speculated in oil leases, with uncanny success. Then his goal became to build an integrated oil company—a company that finds and pumps the oil, refines and sells the gasoline—just like Standard Oil. Julian was a spectacular promoter. In four months in 1922, "C.C." induced forty thousand mostly small Los Angeles investors to trust him with $11 million of their money to create Julian Petroleum Corporation, better known as Julian Pete. Julian promoted his new enterprise as an oil company for the common man. "You'll never make a thin dime just lookin' on!" he wrote in one of his daily newspaper ads, his personal memo to Los Angeles. When the first Julian rig was ready to drill for oil, Julian announced, "Come down to the field Sunday and look it all over from cellar to Crown block and see me spud this baby in. Seeing is believing." Investors and potential investors who took him up on that Sunday invitation had as much champagne as they could drink. And later when the drilling equipment broke, Julian strengthened his image as an honest man of the people with another ad that had the candor of a personal letter. "FOLKS," he announced after the drilling rig was back in operation, "At three o'clock this morning... my 'Bearcats' are again rambling to that 'Gusher' oil sand...I'm a little groggy but had to scribble you the word before hitting the hay." He was a highly popular if eccentric figure, driving around town in expensive cars, wearing flashy suits and spreading his money around. He had a fist fight in a bar with Charlie Chaplin; he gave a woman he met in a nightclub a new Cadillac.

But aside from this, his company Julian Pete's big draw was the promise of thirty dollars for every dollar of investment, when the wells began to produce. And the first Santa Fe Springs well did produce petroleum, at a small profit. The first investors enjoyed impressive cash and stock dividends. Julian used this proof of progress to raise more money selling stock to more small investors—at inflated prices, a trick known as watering the stock. By now, the big oil companies had begun to pressure newspapers to stop running Julian Pete ads, and the state corporation commissioner had started to clamp down on the company's ability to issue stock. Julian "began to water his stock and juggle his books," historian Kevin Starr noted in *Material Dreams: Southern California Through the 1920s.* "It took Harry Chandler of the *Times* and the FBI some three-plus years to make it convenient for Julian to remove himself to Oklahoma." Julian ended up in Shanghai, in 1934, where, after enjoying a farewell dinner that he didn't pay for, he went to his hotel room and committed suicide.

Before Julian left Los Angeles, however, a larger drama was about to play out. At a shareholder's meeting in the Hollywood Bowl, he had turned over the company to S.C. Lewis, a stock manipulator then under federal indictment in Texas. Lewis had arrived in Los Angeles in 1924—with one suitcase. Jacob Berman, who used the name Jack Bennett in Los Angeles, became Lewis's partner in the company. Berman was expert at what is known as a bucket-shop operation— an illegal, unlicensed brokerage.

Julian Pete was nearing the cliff's edge. Lewis and Berman used ostensibly exclusive stock pools to lure new investors. If one were from old Los Angeles money, one might be invited to invest in the top tier,

to their city. But no one had been able to nab him. Finally, in negotiations with Chief Deputy District Attorney Harold "Buddy" Davis, Berman surrendered in San Francisco and returned to Los Angeles.

C.C. Julian, who was still in town, was not judged a defendant, in large part because the company had been in the black when he left it.

Keyes assigned Davis, an inexperienced personal friend, to try the complex case, with assistance from Deputy District Attorneys Julian Richardson and E.P. Van Cott. The defendants hired an imposing team of talented attorneys. In an embarrassing, but telltale move, Keyes had dismissed criminal usury charges against some well-known investors in the Bankers Pool after they "put back" their profits. The grand jury had promptly indicted them again. Then Keyes, to the surprise of Richardson and Van Cott, walked into court and asked the judge to dismiss charges against several of the defendants,

Jury in Julian trial.

in one of the "banker's" pools. There was a "Jewish pool," for Jewish stockbrokers and merchants, a "Tia Juana pool," for gamblers, and so on. When Berman and Lewis ran out of real stock to support the pools, they forged stock certificates.

On May 6, 1927, the bubble burst. Julian preferred stock that had once sold at $36 a share, tanked at $2.88. An auditor had discovered the "overissue" of stock. The Los Angeles Stock Exchange halted trading. And the next day, the state corporation commissioner pulled the company's permit to issue more shares. Investors had poured $40 million into $150 million of now virtually worthless stock. Bewildered investors milled around the downtown business district in a daze.

In January 1928, District Attorney Asa "Ace" Keyes took on his last big case in office—prosecution of the ten defendants whom the grand jury considered primarily responsible for the Julian Pete swindle. All were charged with conspiracy to violate the state Corporate Securities Act as well as obtaining money under false pretenses. They included S. C. Lewis and Jacob Berman, the principals in the second incarnation of Julian Pete.

Berman had disappeared from Los Angeles four days before the crash. For a time, he had kept popping into view briefly in New York, Paris and London. Keyes had hired private detectives to follow Berman on his travels, and had arranged for New York City police officers to wait at the docks whenever Berman was supposed to be returning

including Ed Rosenberg, who was at the heart of the swindle. The judge declined.

The defense lawyers were so confident that they presented little testimony. S.C. Lewis testified on his own behalf, however, turning upon the others by putting the blame on Berman. Most of the defense lawyers quickly rested their cases. Keyes had been so disinterested in the trial that at one point the judge had lectured him for not helping Chief Deputy Davis to wade through a complicated point of securities law.

By the end of the trial, Keyes had also announced that he wouldn't seek re-election. Many observers expected a lackluster performance in the prosecution's closing argument, which Keyes intended to deliver. Yet, according to Jules Tygiel, in his account of the Julian case, *The Great Los Angeles Swindle*, "Keyes amply displayed his talents in his excoriation of S.C. Lewis." In a peculiar, two-hour speech, Keyes loaded all the blame on Lewis, whom he said had "issued stock like sausage coming out of a mill." The other defendants he portrayed as innocent in varying degrees—directly contradicting many of the arguments of his own attorneys who had tried the case. The confused jury found all the defendants not guilty. Later, jury members blamed the botched prosecution for their verdict. As it turned out, the prosecution was not so much botched as bought. Keyes and Davis would be convicted of taking bribes from Rosenberg and other defendants to guarantee their acquittals.

Robert "Rattlesnake" James

A barber is convicted and sentenced to death for killing his wife in a particularly gruesome fashion. A moment of panic takes place in the courtroom when Lethal wriggles free.

He was born Major Raymond Lisenba, in Alabama, but became Robert James after his first wife divorced him and several pregnant women with whom he had affairs pressed him for money. He changed his name and headed west. He was always attracted to women and liked to lavish money on them, more money than he was willing to make as a barber. He also dressed impeccably and had other expensive tastes, as well as a magnetic southern charm. On his first western tour he married twice more, and in the process discovered the money to be made in causing accidents to happen to people. When he killed his third wife, in a cabin in the Canadian woods, he collected fourteen thousand dollars from various insurance policies, two of which he had taken out himself. The police treated the woman's death as an accidental drowning.

By 1934, James was in Los Angeles, where he opened a downtown barber shop. James had driven west this time in an expensive Pierce-Arrow convertible with his attractive 17-year-old niece, Lois Wright, whom he had seduced and now introduced as his wife. While Lois became a manicurist in his shop, James went on the prowl for other women. Though he was making a good income from his five-chair barber shop, his spending on serial affairs demanded more cash. He married another woman in 1934. But he had the marriage annulled when he learned that she didn't believe in life insurance. Then he became involved with Mary Busch, 25, whom he also hired as a manicurist. They married and moved to a secluded house in La Cañada. Mary James became pregnant. Then in August, James brought two friends home for dinner. They had to search for James's wife, whom they found by flashlight, face down and dead in a backyard fish pond. Her left leg was swollen and purple.

The coroner termed the death accidental drowning and dismissed the purple leg as an insect bite. The insurance company paid, but a suspicious insurance investigator told Jack Southard, the District Attorney's Office chief investigator, that the claim seemed shady. Southard traced back to the death of James's third wife, in Canada, which sounded like murder. Chief Deputy District Attorney Eugene Williams had investigators begin full-time surveillance, including the use of listening devices in his house and renting the home next door. They learned not only that he was a sexual sadomasochist, with

Investigators peruse backyard pond at murder scene.

many women partners, but that he was also still having intercourse with his niece, Lois, which is incest.

"Williams was certain that Mary had been murdered," noted Marvin Wolf and former Deputy District Attorney Katherine Mader, in their book, *Fallen Angels*. "He decided to shake the tree and see what might fall out." Williams had James arrested one night while having sex with his niece. Then he gave the story—including the sadomasochism and the suspicious parallels between the two wives' deaths—to the newspapers. The tactic worked. After arduously tracking down a tip, investigators found Charles Hope, an ex-sailor turned short-order cook in Hermosa Beach. He had a grisly tale.

Hope had met James when Hope came into his shop for a haircut, on credit. As James cut his hair, he brought up the subject of rattlesnakes and told Hope he would pay him one hundred dollars if he obtained two. It wasn't easy, but Hope eventually bought two snakes, named Lethal and Lightning.

Meanwhile, James had convinced his wife to have an abortion—on their kitchen table, since abortions were illegal. Hope would play the doctor. On a Sunday, James gave his wife whiskey to drink as an anesthetic. He taped her eyes and mouth shut, ostensibly to ensure the anonymity of the doctor doing the abortion. He also tied her down to the table so she couldn't move. Hope brought the snakes in,

in a box with a sliding side. James put his wife's left leg into the box, where a snake bit her.

Hope took the snakes back and resold them to their first owner. Then he returned in the evening to the James house. Though in agony from the rattlesnake venom, Mary James was still alive. James and Hope went into the garage and drank, waiting for her to die. Finally, James said, "The snakes were no damned good," and he convinced Hope to help him drown the nearly comatose woman in the bathtub. Then they placed her body in the fish pond.

They were both tried for first-degree murder. Deputy District Attorneys Williams and John Barnes prosecuted. Former Deputy District Attorney Russell Parsons defended James. Walter Winchell and other notables were drawn by the spectacle and sat in the audience. Peter Lorre, the actor, studied James in preparation for a movie role as a psychotic killer. The snakes were brought in as evidence. There was a tense moment when Lethal briefly broke free in the courtroom. But no one was bitten and Lethal was recaptured. Hope was given life in prison. When James's attorney told him to brace himself before his verdict was announced, James coolly replied, "I can take it." James was given the death sentence. On May 1, 1942, "Rattlesnake" James, as reporters had dubbed him, became the last convict executed in California by hanging.

James (center) as verdict is read; (inset) rattlesnakes Lethal and Lightning.

Deputies escort Scott; Scott traveling with wife, Evelyn.

L. Ewing Scott

A paint salesman is accused of killing his wealthy wife, whose body can't be found. The conviction, in 1957, sets a legal precedent.

It might have been a routine murder case, had there been a body.

L. Ewing Scott was a good-looking but not particularly successful paint salesman who had married wealthy Evelyn Throsby Scott in 1950. Scott was 59; his wife, 63. With her money, they lived a comfortable life in Bel-Air. On May 16, 1955, the Scotts went to a local car dealer,

tried out a Mercedes-Benz, then returned home. Scott went out again to buy a can of tooth powder for his wife, Scott said, and when he returned, she had disappeared.

Evelyn Scott's friends and family were suspicious. The District Attorney's Office began what it termed a "discreet investigation" that July. Investigators from the office interrogated Scott—he would later claim "brutally." In one incident, Scott said through his attorney, investigators picked him up at the Jonathan Club, took him back to his house, interrogated him for eighteen hours without letting him eat,

money, taking preliminary steps to liquidate her assets. This prompted the grand jury to indict Scott on thirteen counts of forgery and grand theft in April 1956. District Attorney Roll warned Scott, in an announcement to the press, that, "Definite and positive action" would be taken against him as soon as Chief Deputy District Attorney Adolph Alexander returned from the East Coast, where he was still investigating certain aspects of Scott's handling of his wife's trust funds. Chief Parker warned Scott that if he left California without permission, it would be considered "flight to avoid prosecution." Scott promptly fled.

The stakes in the case were raised when Scott was charged with murder. He was caught trying to enter Canada from Detroit about a year later and extradited to California for trial.

Deputy District Attorney J. Miller Leavy prosecuted the case. P. Basil Lambros defended Scott. Lambros argued that, lacking a body, Evelyn Scott could still be alive. In a surprise move at the end of his arguments, Lambros called Leavy to the stand, where he admitted that the authorities were still looking for the woman. Rumors abounded that she had been buried in a freeway off-ramp or support pillar.

An urban legend about the trial has Lambros telling jurors that Evelyn Scott, "might walk through this courtroom door at any minute," which caused almost everyone in the chamber to glance at the door— evidencing doubt. Then, as the story has it, veteran prosecutor Leavy trumped the defense attorney by noting, "Every head in this courtroom turned toward that door just now—except one, that of the defendant. And he didn't bother to look because he knows she's not going to walk through that door. He killed her."

Years later, Leavy told the *Los Angeles Times*, "It didn't happen that way at all. What we did was prove 'the suddenly interrupted life pattern' of Evelyn Scott." While Evelyn Scott had no reason to suddenly leave, her husband had a strong motive to kill her—financial gain. The circumstantial evidence was also convincing. Evelyn Scott's charred eyeglasses, dentures and garters were found in the Scott home incinerator, for example.

Scott was convicted and sentenced to life in prison, though Leavy had argued for the gas chamber. After twenty-one years incarcerated, eighteen of them in San Quentin, Scott was released at age 81 because he was too ill to continue life in prison. In 1984, just before he died, Scott confessed in detail to writer Diane Wagner, who was writing a book about the

Clockwise from top: Co-prosecutors Art Alarcon and Leavy with District Attorney McKesson; Chief Deputy D.A. Adolph Alexander with crime lab chief, Ray Pinker.

and at one point hit him over the head with a phone book. They also grilled Scott's brother-in-law, E. Raymond Throsby, though Throsby didn't complain of his treatment.

The Los Angeles Police Department didn't learn that Evelyn Scott was missing until March 1956, eight months after the fact, when Throsby, her brother, filed a Superior Court petition for trusteeship of Evelyn Scott's six-hundred-thousand-dollar estate. LAPD Chief William Parker, enraged that District Attorney S. Ernest Roll hadn't told him of his investigation, began a large-scale manhunt for the missing woman, but with no luck.

Meanwhile, Scott was maneuvering to gain control of his wife's

case. "I hit her in the head with a mallet, a hard rubber mallet. Just once. On the head, right on top," Scott told her. Then he put her body in the trunk of his car and drove to Las Vegas and then further into the desert, burying her six miles east of the town. Leavy was surprised at the confession and wondered if Scott knew what he was saying. He had always stoutly denied that his wife was dead.

The case is often erroneously cited as the first murder conviction obtained without the victim's body being found. But Leavy pointed out that the true legal landmark was that this was the first "no-body" murder case won in California in which the killer did not admit that the victim was dead.

Billionaire Boys Club

Joe Hunt and his group of fast-lane friends start out with a social and investment club, but end up with murderous schemes to maintain their luxurious lifestyles.

In 1983, Joe Hunt, then 23 years old, and a smart and charismatic natural leader, founded a social club for young men from affluent and influential Los Angeles families. Their goal was not only to have a good time but to get rich through various aggressive investment schemes. The social side involved expensive clothes, cars and nights on the town. But within a year, the investment schemes were foundering. Hunt and several members turned to other ploys.

Joe Hunt knew, and disliked, a scam artist named Ron Levin. Levin had conned money out of Hunt and also embarrassed him. "Levin was the first person ever to make Joe look like a fool in front of the rest of the guys," James Pittman, Hunt's former bodyguard, recalled years later. Hunt decided on a lucrative revenge. On June 6, 1984, Hunt and Pittman went to Levin's home. While Pittman held a gun on Levin, Hunt forced Levin to write Hunt a check for $1.3 million. Then when Hunt nodded at Pittman, Pittman shot Levin in the back of the head. The two hauled Levin's body out to Soledad Canyon, used shotguns in an attempt to make it unrecognizable, then buried the corpse. It has never been found.

Nonetheless, Hunt and Pittman were prosecuted for Levin's death. After two juries deadlocked over his case, Pittman pleaded guilty in 1987 to being an accessory to murder after the fact, and helped police in a fruitless attempt to find Levin's body. He was sentenced to three and a half years, which he had already spent in jail awaiting trial.

Hunt, maintaining that Levin had disappeared to avoid arrest on one of his fraudulent deals, was prosecuted by Deputy District Attorney Fred Wapner, later a Superior Court judge and the son of the television jurist. Hunt was convicted of Levin's murder on April 22, 1987, and sentenced to life without parole. In 1996, an appellate court ruled that Hunt could have a hearing to determine whether a new trial was appropriate in the Levin case. Hunt produced witnesses who claimed to have seen Levin alive in Greece, Westwood, West Los Angeles and Florida. Hunt also argued that his attorney in the first trial had been incompetent and failed to use alleged sightings of Levin. The California Supreme Court rejected Hunt's petition for a new trial.

Another Billionaire Boys Club scheme involved extorting money from the father of one of the club members, Reza Eslaminia. His father, Hedayat Eslaminia, a high-level Iranian official during the Shah's reign, had moved to Los Angeles after the fall of the regime, and his son erroneously believed that he had brought a $30-million fortune with him. The Billionaire Boys Club kidnapped Hedayat Eslaminia in July 1984. But before they could get any money out of him, he died of suffocation in a steamer trunk as they were transporting him to Los Angeles.

Joe Hunt defended himself in that trial, and after a hung jury, the prosecutor declined to retry him. Reza Eslaminia and Arben Dosti were convicted of taking part in the murder and sentenced to life without parole. Their convictions were overturned in 1998, however, pending a retrial in 2000.

Joe Hunt.

Charles Keating

Thousands of individual investors lose their life savings in the disastrous collapse of American Continental Corporation and its subsidiary, Lincoln Savings and Loan, whose executives are accused of securities fraud.

Irvine, California-based Lincoln Savings and Loan, and its parent, American Continental Corporation, based in Arizona, went belly up in 1989. The parent company filed for bankruptcy. Federal regulators declared Lincoln Savings insolvent and took over its operations. It would cost U.S. taxpayers $3.4 billion to shut down the savings and loan company, the most costly U.S. savings and loan failure ever. But the big victims were more than seventeen thousand mostly retirement-age investors who lost a total of a quarter billion dollars from their life savings. One distraught investor, an 89-year-old Burbank man who lost two hundred thousand dollars, committed suicide with a razor blade in his bathtub.

American Continental bond sellers, working in Lincoln Savings branch offices, had persuaded investors to take their money from federally insured and protected accounts to buy American Continental's high-risk corporate junk bonds. American Continental bond sellers specifically targeted senior citizens.

"The sales pitch for the junk bonds was deceptive because investors were led to believe that the bonds were just as safe as their insured savings accounts," said Deputy District Attorney Paul Turley of the prosecution team. "Keating personally was privy to the precarious position of his companies, but knowingly failed to tell the bond sellers and investors." Under securities laws, investors are entitled to complete and honest disclosure of the risk level of investments. Keating's bond sellers made material omissions about the safety of the bonds—omissions that became disastrous for investors.

Charles Keating in court.

In April 1989, federal regulators seized Lincoln Savings. Locked doors at Lincoln branches were the first signal to investors that their money was gone.

As the dimensions of the catastrophe became clear, investigations, litigation and hearings were launched. Congress focused on the savings and loan scandal. Because most of the bilked investors lived in Los Angeles County, where Lincoln Savings had more than a hundred branch offices, District Attorney Ira Reiner exercised a rarely used procedure, convening a special grand jury. In September 1990, Reiner announced the first criminal indictments against Charles H. Keating Jr., chairman of American Continental; Judy Elizabeth Wischer, president of American Continental; Robin Scott Symes, chief executive officer of Lincoln Savings and Ray Charles Fidel, president of Lincoln Savings. All were charged with forty-two violations of the California Corporations Code.

Keating's indictment was a special embarrassment for some politicians because he was a big campaign contributor who often lavishly entertained at his Phoenix home. He offered use of his vacation estate and corporate jet to public figures—including Mother Teresa. He was a prominent industry advocate in the congressional debate over savings and loan deregulation.

"Very simply, this case is about tens of thousands of individuals who lost everything because people in government were more concerned about protecting Mr. Keating's business than they were about ordinary people's life savings," Reiner said at the time.

The Senate Ethics Committee held hearings in 1990 to determine whether five U.S. senators—the so-called "Keating Five"—had pressured regulators to go easy on Keating. The five senators were: Alan Cranston of California, Donald W. Riegle Jr. of Michigan, John Glenn of Ohio and Dennis DeConcini and John McCain of Arizona. Keating and his associates had contributed $1.3 million to the senators' campaigns. Senators McCain and Glenn were later dropped from the investigation, and McCain voluntarily testified against Keating at trial.

Keating retained the resource-rich Chicago-based law firm of Kirkland & Ellis for his defense. Many legal observers considered the team from the District Attorney's Office to be fatally out-gunned. But lead prosecutor Bill Hodgman and Deputy District Attorneys Turley, Terry Bork and Patrick Moran would surprise the experts. Lieutenant Jack Horvath and his team from the Bureau of Investigation would play a decisive role, plowing through boxes full of Lincoln Savings documents in an effort to organize thousands of pieces of evidence to make the fraud absolutely clear. Superior Court Judge Lance Ito presided over the trial.

A major boost for the prosecution also came when two of the four defendants—Robin Symes and Ray Fidel—pleaded guilty to reduced charges in exchange for their testimony against Keating and Wischer. In a strategic move that proved advantageous to the prosecution, Hodgman agreed to a defense request to sever Wischer's case from Keating's. Wischer pleaded guilty to lesser charges.

Keating was now in front of the jury alone. A long line of victims testified to being duped into losing their financial independence and dignity. Bond sellers testified that Keating had personally assured them that the junk bonds they were selling were safe. Symes and Fidel, who were now cooperating with the prosecution, testified that Keating had never told them that American Continental was teetering on the brink of bankruptcy.

On December 4, 1991, Keating was convicted of seventeen counts of securities fraud. Victims in the courtroom had tears streaming down their faces. "They felt vindicated," Hodgman said later.

Keating received the maximum sentence of ten years in state prison. Later convicted by a federal court jury, he received an additional twelve-year sentence. With credit for good conduct, he would have served five years. Just months before the five years were up, in 1996, Keating's convictions were overturned and he was freed on a writ of *habeas corpus*. He was still liable for $5.2-billion in civil judgments, however. Most investors have since recovered about seventy cents on the dollar for their bonds. Litigation in the appeals courts continued into the new century. Keating has never admitted that what he did was wrong, or showed any remorse.

Deputy District Attorney Curt Hazell with seized cocaine.

Hector Tapia Anchondo

After the world's largest cocaine seizure, the head of a major drug-transporting operation in Los Angeles is convicted and sentenced to life in prison in 1992.

Investigators estimated that the more than twenty-one tons of cocaine, worth $2 billion wholesale, captured in the world's largest drug bust, would have been enough to get a quarter of the world's population high. On September 29, 1989, Drug Enforcement Administration agents found the cocaine in an unguarded rental warehouse in Sylmar, after neighbors became suspicious about expensively dressed people in their otherwise ordinary light-industrial district. The warehouse was the final stop of a smuggler's trail called "The Trampoline," running from Colombia, through Mexico and into the United States. Along with the cocaine, investigators also seized a computer and a set of carefully kept ledgers that described the operation in detail. A host of traffickers were arrested and prosecuted after the raid, but the prize catch was drug kingpin Hector Tapia Anchondo, who was arrested in Las Vegas the day after the bust. "This guy was the head of the department of transportation for the cocaine cartels," said Ralph Lochridge, a Los Angeles DEA spokesman.

Tapia and a co-defendant—Hugo Fernando Castillon-Alvarez—were prosecuted by Deputy District Attorney Susan Bryant-Deason, who was cross-designated as a federal prosecutor, and Assistant United States Attorney James Walsh. The prosecutors said that the big cocaine seizure was "just the tip of the iceberg" of the Tapia transportation system, and that beginning in 1987, Tapia had been shipping five thousand pounds of cocaine a week to Los Angeles. Over an eight-week trial, Walsh and Bryant-Deason called fifty witnesses, including DEA agents, who described the big shipments, which were taken to the warehouse and broken down into more manageable size.

Both men were convicted of conspiracy to distribute cocaine. Tapia was also convicted of being the principal administrator of a continuing criminal enterprise. He was sentenced to life in prison.

Alco Pacifico de Mexico

Deputy District Attorney David Eng successfully prosecutes two U.S. companies responsible for a controversial hazardous waste site across the Mexican border, in a landmark environmental case.

After awhile, when another cow died, Daniel Muno Garay simply sent an employee over to the nearby lead-recycling plant to pick up the replacement money. It was clear to everyone that waste at the badly managed Alco Pacifico de Mexico plant, which extracted lead from old car batteries, was killing cows at two nearby dairies. The dairies were the major suppliers of milk products in metropolitan Tijuana, Mexico. Mexican environmental regulators had made attempts to force a cleanup, but the plant managers evaded them, sometimes operating only at night. Then, after a 1991 labor strike, the plant was abandoned.

The hazardous-waste mess at the plant became a rallying point for U.S. opponents of the North America Free Trade Agreement, NAFTA, during congressional debate over the trade pact. Anti-NAFTA activists conducted at least a dozen tours for U.S. legislators, including House Majority Leader Richard Gephardt, to see at first hand the immense piles of lead ash and slag. NAFTA, said opponents, would only encourage an exodus of polluters across the border, considering Mexico's more lax environmental regulation. Proponents of NAFTA held that increased trade cooperation between the two countries would actually improve Mexico's environmental controls.

The plant was a *maquiladora*—a foreign-owned Mexican manufacturing plant that operates duty-free. Alco Pacifico was owned by Los Angeles businessman Morris P. Kirk, chief executive

Deputy District Attorney David Eng; hazardous waste site in Mexico.

officer of Gardena-based Alco Pacific Inc. Deputy District Attorney David Eng, an environmental-crime prosecutor, learned about the plant when U.S. customs inspectors found lead waste in a truck re-entering the United States from Tijuana. Investigators tracked the lead to a recycling facility in the City of Industry, near Los Angeles. A Dallas, Texas-based lead recycling firm, the largest in the country, RSR-Quemetco, owned that Los Angeles plant.

Prosecuting environmental crimes in Mexico by U.S. prosecutors is extremely difficult. But Eng decided that because RSR-Quemetco had transported the lead, a hazardous material, through California to Mexico, the crime could be prosecuted under state law. Eng obtained a search warrant for the Dallas offices of RSR-Quemetco, where investigators found records showing that the company had an agreement with Alco Pacifico de Mexico, and that it had known that the lead slag had been shipped to the Tijuana plant and abandoned.

It had been a simple business decision. RSR-Quemetco had decided that it could not profitably get more lead out of a thirty-million-ton mountain of slag at its City of Industry facility. But Alco Pacifico, on the other side of the border, could. Yet once Alco Pacifico got

the lead slag to its Tijuana plant, Kirk discovered that he couldn't get enough lead out of the heap to make any money on it either. When a labor dispute arose, he closed down the plant, left the slag mountain, and left town. Workers hadn't even received severance pay.

Eng charged RSR-Quemetco with unlawful transport of toxic waste. At first, he had little cooperation from Mexican environmental officials. "They made it clear," Eng recalled, "'We don't need you here. This is Mexico. You can't come down here and tell us what to do.'" But Eng persisted, because unless Mexico cooperated, any money from fines wouldn't be used to clean up the Tijuana site. Then Santiago Onate, Mexico's highest-ranking federal environmental prosecutor, learned of Eng's effort. Onate, who understood the implications for the NAFTA pact, cut through local resistance and Eng got the collaboration that he needed.

Just before the RSR-Quemetco case went to trial, Albert Lospinoso, president of the company, decided to settle. He estimated that the legal costs of fighting the charge would be as much or more than the cost of the fine. "We felt we could best meet our goal," he told the *Wall Street Journal*, "by helping the people of Mexico clean up a problem." In June 1993, the company agreed to pay a $2.5-million fine—$2 million of that to clean up the Tijuana mess. District Attorney Gil Garcetti also allocated three hundred thousand dollars of the fine for health care along the border. The value of the lead that could be recovered from the site—estimated at one hundred thousand to two hundred thousand dollars—the Mexican government would use to pay the plant workers' back pay.

Eng charged Morris Kirk separately with three counts of unlawful transport of hazardous waste to Mexico. In December 1993, Kirk pleaded no contest. Alco Pacific was fined $2.5 million. Kirk was sentenced to sixteen months in prison. And the case became a powerful argument for pro-NAFTA forces, serving as a blueprint for bi-national environmental enforcement. NAFTA was ratified by the United States, Mexico and Canada in 1994.

Errol Flynn posing for newspaper photographs in court.

In the Limelight

H ollywood is a business description more than a geographic location. The first Los Angeles movie center, from 1908 to 1911, developed in the tiny suburb of Edendale, near Elysian Park. Studios spread out from there to include many areas throughout the county. Over the years, the District Attorney's Office, with its sprawling jurisdiction, has frequently prosecuted highly publicized crimes in the entertainment community. The industry's international influence, capacity to produce stupendous wealth, and appeal to innovative, experimental and often unconventional artists and entrepreneurs has always made fertile ground for both creative and conniving personalities.

The first movie-makers came to Los Angeles from the east to take advantage of the fine weather and varied, easily accessible scenery—and to avoid the Patent Trust, a cartel organized by ten early movie producers, distributors and their licensees, which monopolized motion picture production in New York and Chicago. As historian Carey McWilliams, author of *Southern California: An Island on the Land*, noted, "the first producers who came to Los Angeles were fugitives—from process servers and the patent trust. Seeking to evade injunctions, they wanted to be as far from New York and as close to the Mexican border as possible."

During this early period, established Los Angelenos referred to the studios of the invading movie-makers as "camps." The term "the movie colony" was a pejorative. And the actors themselves were considered more nuisances than celebrities. Cowboy stars whooped and hollered through town, both on and off the set. Mabel Normand, a beautiful and talented comedienne who starred in Mack Sennett comedies and directed Charlie Chaplin, recalled in a 1930 interview, that "We were a feverish, groping, guessing, suddenly enriched throng of youthful people who didn't know what to do while we were working and didn't know or care what we did while we were playing." Normand herself became entangled in a grim, deadly tragedy as a key figure in a still-unsolved murder.

In later years, many entertainers have suffered the personal torment of stalking—from the fatal encounter of actress Rebecca Schaeffer to incidents involving Madonna, Steven Spielberg, Jackson Browne, Michael J. Fox and the case that brought worldwide attention, Theresa Saldana. In 1990, California passed the first U.S. law to control stalking, in response to the attacks on Saldana and Schaeffer. The law was toughened in 1994 to enhance the ability of police and prosecutors to intervene as soon as possible in a stalker's obsessive campaign. Every state has since passed similar laws and federal laws now also apply. In 1997, the Los Angeles County District Attorney's Office established what became the most comprehensive anti-stalking intervention and prevention program in the country.

William Desmond Taylor

A popular Hollywood film director is killed in his home. Despite an intense investigation, and speculation that continues to this day, no one is ever charged with the crime.

At 7:00 a.m. on February 2, 1922, "Bill" Taylor's valet arrived at the luxurious Alvarado Court Apartments, on South Alvarado Street, to make Taylor's breakfast. The valet picked up a bottle of milk from the front step, opened the front door and screamed, "Mr. Taylor is dead! Mr. Taylor is dead!" Taylor was stretched out, fully clothed, on the living room floor. When police and neighbors came in, a doctor in the crowd said that it looked as though Taylor had had a heart attack. But when the body was turned over, a puddle of blood was discovered under his chest and the coroner later found a bullet in his back. Discovered in a search of his home was a woman's pink silk nightgown and lace handkerchief.

Taylor had been a popular actor turned director in the old Hollywood film industry. He had made more than forty films and was known for a gracious, charitable personality. Ten thousand Los Angelenos showed up for Taylor's funeral. World-savvy, well-read and handsome at age 50, he was also highly attractive to film-industry women. Mabel Normand, the young comedienne and director, was a close friend and frequent companion. Well-known actress Mary Miles Minter, another young beauty, was abjectly in love with him. And there were others. In the confusion that followed his body's discovery, before investigators cleared the murder scene, a male neighbor and close friend went to Taylor's bedroom, removing scores of love letters addressed to the director. The neighbor later explained to investigators that he wanted to spare the writers, some of them married women, from unnecessary scandal.

The morning after Taylor's body was discovered, District Attorney Thomas Woolwine assigned his office's accomplished investigator Ed. C. King to the inquiry into the crime. King coordinated closely with LAPD Lieutenant Jesse Winn.

King and the other investigators developed, and were offered, many theories but little evidence. Mabel Normand was suspected. She had been the last person to admit to seeing Taylor alive. She had dropped by to pick up a book only moments before his death. Normand also apparently spent more than two thousand dollars a week on cocaine, and by some reports Taylor had gone to the authorities to see what he could do to help apprehend her suppliers. Under that theory, Taylor was killed by the suppliers to stop his meddling. Another theory held that the mother of 19-year-old millionaire actress Mary Miles Minter, a strong-willed stage

Mary Miles Minter.

Officials view the Taylor murder scene.

mother named Charlotte Shelby, killed Taylor to remove the object of her daughter's infatuation and potential impediment to the young girl's career. Another suspect, Taylor's former assistant, Edward Sands, disappeared. The investigation languished.

In 1930, District Attorney Buron Fitts had King renew his hunt. King investigated many of the hundreds of people who had confessed to the crime, but came up with nothing. King never agreed with a prevailing theory, that Normand was the murderer. Years later, King wrote an article for a crime magazine in which he said that he had known from the beginning of the investigation who the murderer was. He hinted that it was a woman. But King never could find enough evidence to be comfortable naming the person, and he never did.

Mabel Normand; William Desmond Taylor (background).

Alexander and Lois Pantages

The theatrical mogul and his wife have a tough time in the courts in 1929. Alexander Pantages's case changes the way rape charges are prosecuted in California.

Greek immigrant Pericles Pantages switched his first name to Alexander after reading about Alexander the Great. He got started in show business in the late 1890s, at age 18, during the Alaskan gold rush. He bought a vaudeville theater in Nome that was in financial trouble, and he turned it around by catering to the lusty tastes of the miners. Moving to Seattle in 1902, he combined vaudeville and movies in the first of what would become a nationwide chain of theaters. In 1910, he moved to Los Angeles, where he opened an impressive theater with second-floor offices on Seventh and Hill Streets, downtown.

In August 1929, a 17-year-old Garden Grove vaudeville performer named Eunice Pringle began hanging around Pantages' office, asking for an audition. Her act was a mildly lewd song-and-dance routine that involved barbells. On August 9, she got her audition with Pantages, in his private office. But within moments of walking in, she yelled, "The beast! The beast! Someone save me!" and ran out of the office. The telephone switchboard operators noted that as Pringle ran past she was ripping her clothes off, not putting them on. Nevertheless, Pantages was charged with raping Pringle. The newspapers referred to his "violation of the girlhood" of the young performer.

The case was prosecuted by District Attorney Buron Fitts and Chief Deputy District Attorney Robert Stewart. At the preliminary hearing, defense attorneys W. I. Gilbert and W. Joseph Ford produced witnesses who described a seamy side to Pringle and suspicious reports of a financial windfall to Pringle's agent and lover—which the agent boasted was connected to the Pantages rape charge.

But when the case went to trial, Fitts was able to suppress any testimony about Pringle's background—except that she no longer lived with her parents and had dropped out as a student at the University of Southern California. Then the defense released electrifying affidavits. They were signed by three star witnesses, who declined to testify because they said they had been told they would be beaten, firebombed or killed if they did. The threats, they said, had been delivered by two men from the District Attorney's Office.

Rabble-rousing reverends P.R. "Bob" Shuler and Gustav Briegleb.

At about the same time, Pantages's wife, Lois, had been involved in a drunken traffic accident. Numerous witnesses said that she was driving wildly through town in her expensive Stutz automobile, sideswiping other vehicles, and that she was on the wrong side of the road when she hit a car driven by Japanese-American gardener Juro Rokomoto. Drivers who had been forced off the road, police officers and medical personnel involved after the accident—all swore they could smell liquor on Lois Pantages's breath. When she was taken to the closest hospital for examination, she kicked at police officers and demanded a phone call to her husband. Several family members in the Rokomoto car were injured. Rokomoto himself had a broken pelvis and collarbone. He died in surgery to repair his pelvis a few days after the accident. Mrs. Pantages was charged with first-degree murder.

Now Fitts could describe to jurors a range of depravity for the wealthy couple—he a rapist, she a murderer. The defense team split up. Gilbert and Ford were switched to defending Lois Pantages. A lesser-known lawyer, Jerry Giesler, who would become a popular defense attorney for Hollywood celebrities, took over the rape case. But sympathy for Alexander Pantages had evaporated. The jury convicted

Pantages courtroom scene (left to right): Deputy District Attorney W.I. Gilbert, Pantages, Chief Deputy District Attorney Robert Stewart, District Attorney Fitts.

Pantages of rape, and he received a stiff sentence of fifty years in prison without parole.

Giesler appealed. He argued that Eunice Pringle's shady background was relevant, and should have come out in the trial. The California Supreme Court eventually ordered a new trial, in the process setting a judicial precedent that a rape victim's personal character could be admitted in testimony. In November 1931, after Pantages had spent three years in prison, he was retried. Giesler argued that Pringle had tried to force Pantages to book her act into his far-flung theater circuit, threatening to put him in a compromising situation if he didn't.

This time on the witness stand, Pringle admitted that she had lived with her agent and lover for two years before the alleged rape, moving in with him at age 15. He had promised to find acting jobs for her and to put her through college at USC. Giesler insisted that Pringle appear in court in clothes like those she had worn to her audition with Pantages. In the first trial, she had dressed conservatively, with a demure lace collar. In the retrial, she wore red lipstick, a red dress and high heels. The jury voted not guilty and Pantages was released from prison.

As for Lois Pantages, she continued to deny that she had been intoxicated when the collision took place. More persuasively, her attorneys were able to show that Rokomoto died from receiving too much anesthetic before the surgery—not from the injured pelvis by itself. The charge was reduced to manslaughter. She was convicted and put on ten years' probation. Eighteen months later, in part so that she could accompany her son on his honeymoon, Lois Pantages petitioned to be released from the restrictions of probation. Superior Court Judge Carlos Hardy complied. He terminated her probation, put the case briefly back on the calendar, entered a not-guilty plea on her behalf, then dismissed the case entirely. Fitts called it "a disgusting episode, a travesty on justice in Los Angeles County."

Pringle died in 1933 of "unknown causes," after telling Giesler that she wanted to reveal the truth about the Pantages rape charge. She also reportedly told her mother and a friend, on her deathbed, that she had set up Pantages for a fee, paid by Joseph P. Kennedy, father of

the future U.S. president. Kennedy was then not only a legendary Wall Street manipulator and bootlegger, but also a theater magnate and bitter rival of Pantages. Pringle said that Joseph Kennedy and Buron Fitts had set up the phony rape, promising ten thousand dollars to Pringle and her agent-boyfriend, as well as acting work at a major movie studio. Pringle said that she never got her share of the money, and never got the promised movie-studio part.

Clockwise from top: Eunice Pringle, newspaper headline, Pantages (second from left) in the courtroom.

Pedro Gonzalez

In 1934, a talented and candid Mexican-American broadcaster runs up against District Attorney Buron Fitts, a charge of rape, and ends up in San Quentin.

Radio singer Gonzalez.

Pedro J. Gonzalez had an astonishingly romantic and vivid youth, beginning with his forced enlistment in the Mexican Revolution in 1910. He was then a young telegrapher in Chihuahua, Mexico, reporting rebel movements to the government in Mexico City. When Pancho Villa's soldiers captured him, he was given a choice, at gunpoint: join Villa or die. When later captured by government troops, Gonzalez was about to be shot by firing squad when a village teacher told several children to stand in front of him, to protect him. The soldiers relented. One of those children later became his enduring wife, Maria. And in 1923, he and his family moved to Los Angeles.

Gonzalez was a singer with a deep tenor voice. He was also a social progressive—an influence of his time with Villa, whom he came to admire. When radio station KMPC rejected Gonzalez's bid to sing on its variety hour, because he sang only in Spanish, he began to do voice-overs for Spanish commercials on the same station. He also composed ballads and sang them with his new band, Los Madrugadores (the Early Risers), at 4:00 a.m., on the radio. And he commented on the issues of the day. Gonzalez became an immensely popular figure with Latinos in Los Angeles, and the first Spanish-language broadcaster in the United States.

But in the early 1930s, in the shock of the Depression, the U.S. Department of Labor and the Immigration and Naturalization Service ended decades of unfettered border crossings between the United States and Mexico and began a sweep of Spanish-speaking residents throughout the Southwest, called Operation Deportation. Law-enforcement agencies repatriated some one thousand five hundred people from Los Angeles County alone, and an unknown number were assisted by local charities helping people to return voluntarily before they were rounded up by the INS. Many were U.S. citizens who were simply picked up on the streets of Los Angeles and expelled at the Mexican border. Singer Woody Guthrie and others decried the sweeps. So did Pedro Gonzalez on his radio programs. "It's nothing more than a racist attack against all Mexicans," Gonzalez told listeners. "We are neither illegals nor undesirables."

District Attorney Buron Fitts was running for reelection in 1932, and he needed Mexican-American votes. He bought political ads that ran on Gonzalez's radio show. And at first Gonzalez supported Fitts. But Fitts also campaigned for support among anti-Mexican elements. No matter the financial support the Fitts campaign had provided his program, Gonzalez turned against Fitts in the election.

In 1934, Fitts charged Gonzalez with statutory rape. Dora Versus,

age 15, testified that Gonzalez had taken her to a hotel room and given her liquor, then attacked her sexually. Gonzalez strongly denied the charge. And Versus soon recanted her testimony to Anna Zacsek, the attorney for Gonzalez. Saying that "my conscience is bothering me," Versus said that she had been threatened by two policewomen, who told her that unless she testified to being raped by Gonzalez, she would be sent to a correctional institution. But one of the police-women then announced that Versus, then confined to the Home of the Good Shepherd, a Catholic institution, had changed her mind again and stuck to the story that she was raped. Though it was widely believed that Gonzalez was being framed, Superior Court Judge Robert A. Scott denied Zacsek's petition for a new trial and recommended that Gonzalez—still a Mexican citizen—be deported as soon as he completed his prison time.

Pedro Gonzalez was sentenced to from one to fifty years and was sent to San Quentin, where he agitated for improved conditions for prisoners. Protests were raised on his behalf, many of them spearheaded by his wife. Two Mexican presidents pleaded his cause. Ricardo G. Hill, Mexican consulate in Los Angeles, petitioned the governor's office for a full pardon.

After six years in prison, Gonzalez was paroled and deported to Mexico in 1940. He went back on the radio in Tijuana and formed another band to play his ballads. In 1971, Gonzalez was readmitted to the United States and moved to San Diego, where most of his U.S.-born family remained. He became a citizen and, in 1995, died at age 99.

Gonzalez at 89.

Errol Flynn

A dashing actor is accused of statutory rape by two young women in a sensational 1942 Los Angeles trial.

It all started when Los Angeles police officers were asked to find a missing Nebraska teenager, Betty Hansen. When she was tracked down in a Santa Monica hotel, she described her experiences since arriving in Los Angeles, which included Hollywood parties. She supported her story by producing Errol Flynn's unlisted phone number, and the accusation that they had had sex. She was then 17, which made the seduction, if it happened, statutory rape in California. But the grand jury declined to indict Flynn when the District Attorney's Office brought the case before it.

District Attorney's investigators continued their probing, however, and they came across another complaint filed with the Los Angeles

Flynn with attorneys Jerry Giesler and Robert Ford; (below) Peggy Satterlee and Betty Hansen with attorney Thomas Cochrane; (background) the Sirocco.

County Sheriff's Department. The mother of Peggy Satterlee, who had been 15 years old at the time, had reported that her daughter had been seduced, twice, on Flynn's yacht, the *Sirocco*. The sheriff's office hadn't considered the charges to be serious at the time. And Peggy Satterlee had gone on to become a nightclub dancer. But now the District Attorney's Office combined the two cases into a single complaint. Deputy District Attorneys Thomas W. Cochran and John Hopkins prosecuted for the people. Jerry Giesler, by now termed by newspaper reporters "The Great Mouthpiece," defended Flynn. Flynn denied having had sex with either young woman. He well knew the consequences of sexual relations with minors and well knew, and used, the phrases "jail bait" and "San Quentin quail."

Cochran and Hopkins had only to convince jurors that intercourse had taken place, since no mitigating circumstances changed the charge

of statutory rape. Giesler believed that the two women were testifying in hopes of avoiding criminal charges on other matters. So he attacked their credibility, to sow seeds of doubt about their fundamental stories.

Giesler was prevented from bringing up many details of Hansen's previous sexual experiences with men. But Hansen had also admitted to the grand jury that she had been caught engaging in what Giesler later described as "some rather unusual sexual practices," and that a young man had been prosecuted for the crime. Giesler was eventually allowed to present this information to the jury. Hansen also admitted that she had come to the party where she met Flynn precisely because she was told he would be there. She planned to ask for help finding work in the movie business. And she admitted that the young man who brought her to the party had given her advice about how to "play up" to Flynn.

As for Satterlee, she alleged that Flynn had used force with her both times he raped her. This clearly allowed Giesler to cross-examine Satterlee about her "previous sexual adventures," as he later put it—in a legal precedent that Giesler had set himself, defending the Alexander Pantages rape case. Though Cochran and Hopkins strongly objected, Giesler got Peggy Satterlee to admit that she, her mother and her sister often hitchhiked around the country. Satterlee also admitted that she had had an abortion. Then Giesler received an anonymous phone call that gave him more background to convince jurors that Satterlee was anything but an innocent maid.

Satterlee and a 42-year-old boyfriend, a Canadian pilot named Owen Cathcart-Jones, had been caught cavorting in a funeral parlor, tearing the sheets off corpses. To establish this, however, Giesler had to induce the prosecution to call Cathcart-Jones to the stand. Giesler began to introduce the pilot's name into his cross-examination of Satterlee, in a way that suggested they were lovers.

Cochran eventually took the bait and called Cathcart-Jones to the stand to establish that the two had never been alone and didn't have a romantic relationship. In his cross-examination, Giesler asked about various places Cathcart-Jones and Satterlee had visited together, ending up at the mortuary. The transcript reads:

Q: And she was kind of playing hide-and-seek around the corpses, wasn't she? Do you remember that?

A: Yes.

Q: Do you remember she showed you—opened it up and showed you—the body of an elderly lady?'

A: Yes.

The jury, and the audience, were aghast and had to be quieted by the court bailiff.

Finally, Giesler cast great doubt on Satterlee's claim that Flynn had lured her below decks to his stateroom with the promise of a beautiful view of the moon from the porthole. She clearly stated that she saw the moon. Cochran and Hopkins, the prosecutors, called to the stand an astronomy professor, who testified that the moon had been out and able to be seen that night. But Giesler brought in a local harbormaster and two ship captains who said that from the position of the *Sirocco* at anchor that night, the moon would have been on the other side of the boat, unable to be seen through Flynn's porthole.

In his charge to the jury, Superior Court Judge Leslie E. Still noted to jurors that since Hansen had admitted to an illegal sexual act, but had not yet been prosecuted for it, and since Satterlee's admitted abortion was illegal, "You may consider that both girls were hoping for leniency."

Still congratulated the jury when it returned with an acquittal. "I think you have arrived at a proper verdict," he told them.

Busby Berkeley

A Hollywood director noted for his extravagant musicals is put on trial for murder after an auto accident.

For years, Busby Berkeley was the most courted movie director in Hollywood. He was known in his early years in film for never having made a motion picture that lost money. And he introduced novel camera techniques and huge production numbers that revolutionized the industry, bringing lavish escapism to movies of the Depression years.

But he also had been arrested often for being drunk and for driving while drunk. On September 8, 1935, again intoxicated, he was driving home from a party along what is now the Pacific Coast Highway, near Santa Monica Canyon, when he caused a head-on collision with two other cars. Three people in one of the oncoming cars died of their injuries and a fourth was badly hurt. Berkeley was tried for three counts of second-degree murder.

Los Angeles and Hollywood moguls worried about the bad publicity his trial could bring to the film business, which already had a tarnished image. In 1921, Fatty Arbuckle had been charged with the rape and murder of a young actress during a drunken party in a San Francisco hotel room. The day Berkeley went to trial, actress Thelma Todd, another hard-drinking Hollywood star, had been found dead in her automobile after a night of party-going.

Deputy District Attorney David Coleman prosecuted the case.

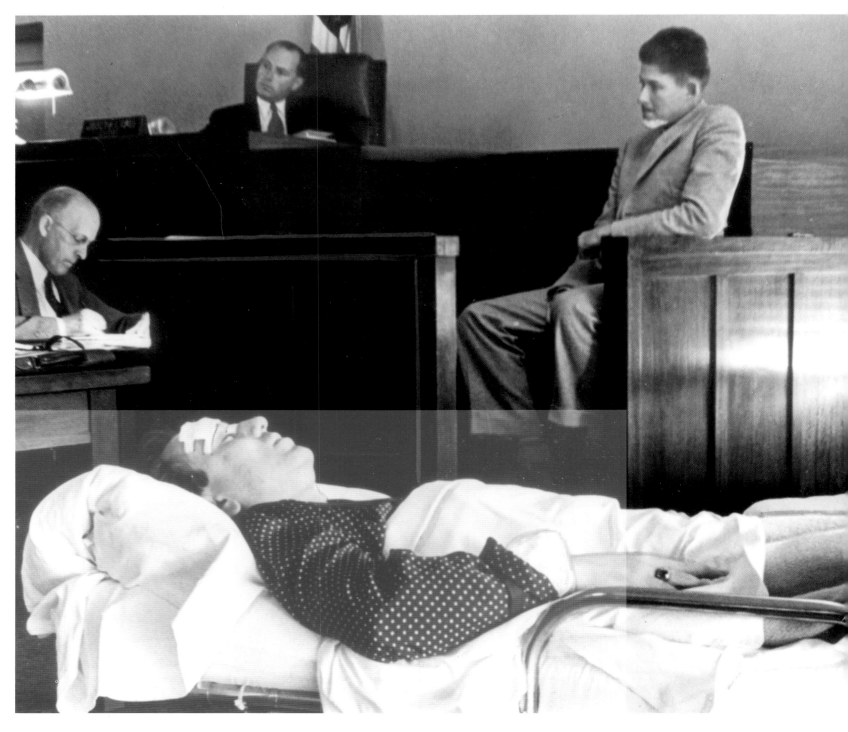

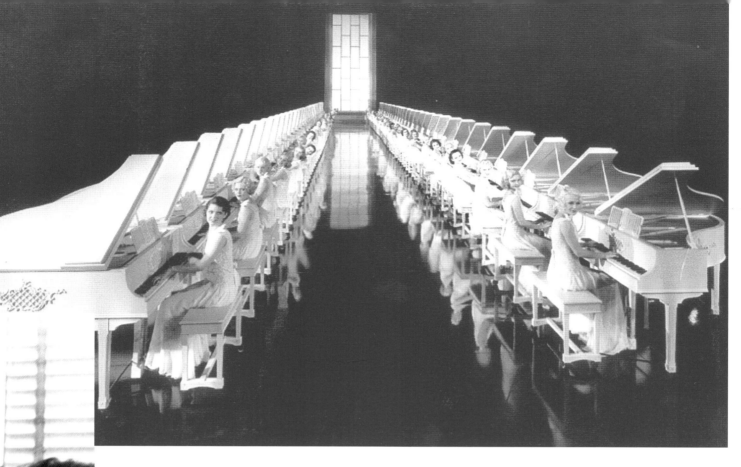

Since Berkeley had suffered head and leg injuries in the crash, Berkeley was defended by attorney Jerry Giesler, who had him appear in his first trial lying on his back in a hospital bed. Giesler also brought a damaged auto tire into court, claiming that the accident had been caused when the tire blew. Berkeley had a contract with Warner Brothers. A line-up of Hollywood stars who also worked for Warner Brothers, including actor Pat O'Brien, claimed at the trial that Berkeley had left the party sober.

The first two trials ended with hung juries. In a third, in 1936, Berkeley was acquitted. Berkeley continued to maintain his innocence, saying that the crash was an accident, although at the behest of an insurance company he did pay ninety-five thousand dollars to settle associated damage suits. In the end, the trials marked the downturn of his career. He directed his last movie in 1962 and died in Palm Springs in 1976.

Clockwise from left, Busby Berkeley appears in court on a hospital bed, 1935; production shot from Berkeley's *Gold Diggers of 1935*: Berkeley watches his attorney Jerry Giesler during the second trial.

Robert Mitchum

The young actor is convicted of conspiracy to possess marijuana and is incarcerated for two months with no ill effect on his career or his teenage fans.

Robert Mitchum and his wife had been separated for a time, but in September 1948, she was driving back from the East Coast to California to reconcile with the actor. She had accused him of "going Hollywood," saying that she no longer approved of his friends. Hollywood rumors also circulated that he frequently smoked marijuana.

A joint LAPD and federal narcotics task force was investigating the use of drugs by entertainers. Mitchum, 30 years old, had been under surveillance since December 1947. One night at a party in Laurel Canyon, Mitchum and three others—two lesser-known actresses and a real estate salesman—were arrested in a well-planned police raid. Someone had just handed Mitchum a marijuana cigarette; there were others still smoldering in ashtrays. Mitchum was charged with marijuana possession and conspiracy to possess the drug. All four were released on $1,000 bail each.

Reporters quoted Mitchum lamenting, as he was being booked, "I'm ruined... I'm afraid this is the bitter end of my career." He also predicted that his wife would now not return to him.

In fact, his wife stood by him, and so did the motion picture studios. Mitchum was contracted to RKO and the David O. Selznick organization. "It is our belief Bob will come out of his trouble a finer man," Selznick announced, "and will go on to even greater success than he enjoyed prior to this unfortunate situation." Selznick noted that millions of Mitchum's fans "have demonstrated their eagerness that he should have a second chance." But letters also deluged authorities and others in Los Angeles saying that letting Mitchum off too easily would set a bad example for the nation's young people.

Keeping the scandal short-lived was at the heart of Mitchum's defense by lawyer Jerry Giesler. The District Attorney's Office invited Mitchum to defend himself before the grand jury, but on Giesler's advice, the actor declined. Then Mitchum agreed to, as Giesler recalled, take "his medicine like a man," and asked the judge to decide the case based on police and other testimony before the grand jury. This avoided a drawn-out trial by jury, which Giesler predicted could seriously harm the actor's career. He was convicted on the conspiracy-to-possess charge and sentenced to two years, all but sixty days of which were suspended.

Mitchum, a strapping roustabout in his early years, began his short sentence at the downtown county jail. When he was told he would be transferred to the sheriff's honor farm at Castaic, Mitchum mildly protested. "I would rather stay here," he announced. "I was pretty happy down there in the tank. The men have made me tank trusty." And when he was released, he genially concluded, "Jail is like Palm Springs without the riffraff. A great place to get in shape, only you meet a better class of people."

Mitchum with actress co-defendant and defense attorneys; (background) Mitchum upon his release from jail.

Lili St. Cyr

The noted ecdysiast is arrested in 1951 and tried for indecent exposure for stripping at Ciro's in Hollywood.

The act that got Lili St. Cyr arrested on the Sunset Strip, in 1951, was almost sedate. She appeared on stage fully dressed, then gradually took her clothes off down to a bra and G-string. While she hid behind a bath towel, held by a maid, St. Cyr climbed into a translucent bathtub. The audience was treated to a view in outline of St. Cyr's splendidly curvy frame as she took a "bubble bath." The towel came out again as St. Cyr exited the tub. The maid wrapped it around her and she walked off the stage. Lili St. Cyr, born Willis Marie Van Schaack, in Minneapolis, made it clear that both words in "striptease" were important—the tease as much as the strip. Indeed, she had always been noted for stripping only so far, then telling the audience, "That's it, boys. You're not gettin' any more from me."

Two women in the audience whom St. Cyr's lawyer, Jerry Giesler, described as "matronly," didn't have as benign a view of her performance, however. On the second night, the two women returned with a retinue of Los Angeles County deputy sheriffs, who arrested St. Cyr for indecent exposure. Deputy District Attorney Bernard Gross prosecuted the case.

Defense attorney Giesler suggested trying the case at Ciro's, where St. Cyr had performed, so that jurors could judge for themselves whether the stripper had shown too much. But the judge demurred. The prosecutor called as witnesses two beefy deputy sheriffs. Giesler suggested a certain hypocrisy in these mature men's claims, as one testified, that "Miss St. Cyr's show was terrible. I couldn't help noticing that at one point she was in the nude. I was horrified." The deputy sheriffs also complained of having to watch St. Cyr's "bump and grinds."

Giesler called to the stand a no-nonsense female newspaper reporter named Florabel Muir who said that she had seen nothing wrong with the act. He also called Herman Hover, the overweight owner of Ciro's, and cajoled him into demonstrating a hilarious version of a stripper's bump and grind, thrusting his hips back and forth until everyone in the courtroom was convulsed with laughter.

Gross sought to recover the seriousness of the proceedings. One prosecution witness said that he had been able to see St. Cyr nude, through the towel. Giesler produced the towel, the bra and the G-string. St. Cyr, fully clothed, wrapped the towel around herself in front of the jury. Clearly, she had never been nude. She was acquitted.

St. Cyr in court; (inset) glamour shot.

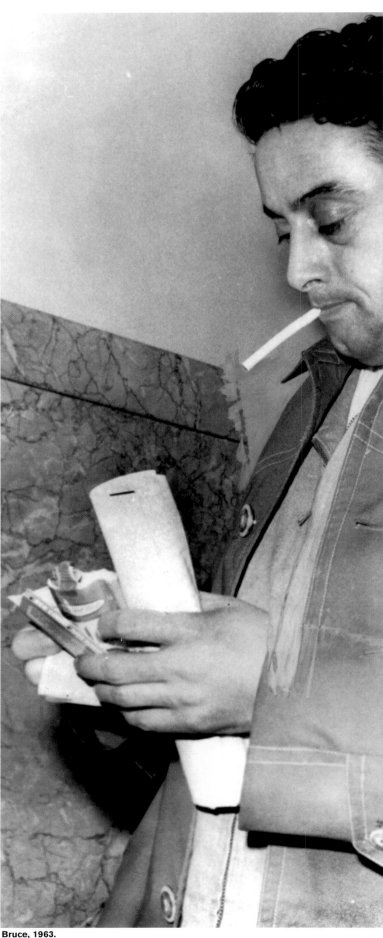

Lenny Bruce

In 1962, the controversial comic is charged with obscenity for a performance at the popular Troubadour night club.

Lenny Bruce, a standup comedian whose gritty humor and social commentary became a rallying point for free-speech advocates, was born Leonard Alfred Schneider in 1925. As his career grew, he had been arrested in several U.S. cities, for narcotics violations and obscenity, before he began a twelve-day booking at the Troubadour night club in West Hollywood in October 1962.

Deputy District Attorney Richard Hecht took in the show, along with a friend and colleague, Sherman Block, then a vice-squad officer with the Los Angeles County Sheriff's Department (Block would later serve many years as county sheriff). But on this night, he served as a translator of Yiddish for his friend Hecht. At the time, it was a misdemeanor offense to speak or sing lewdly in public. One of the tamer words that Bruce used was "schmuck"—mildly obscene Yiddish slang for penis as well as for a jerk or a fool. There were plenty of other sexual references in his show.

Bruce was first arrested for obscenity on October 17 at the Troubadour. Two more arrests followed, and the three were combined in the same trial, which began in February 1963. Over Christmas and New Year's, Bruce had bought copies of the U.S. Constitution and *Black's Law Dictionary*, deciding that it was about time for him to study the law himself, instead of relying on his attorneys to keep him out of court.

Deputy District Attorney Ronald Ross tried the case in Beverly Hills Municipal Court. Burton Marks was the defense attorney. Though Marks had implored Bruce to get a haircut and dress up a little, Bruce declined the haircut and took the stand in an old blue chambray shirt and Levi jacket. He also refused to take the standard oath. He said he'd tell the truth, but wouldn't raise his hand or swear to it. When Ross cross-examined him, Bruce wouldn't directly answer his questions. He wanted to make other, broader points instead.

When Ross asked him, for instance, what he wanted his audiences to experience, Bruce said, "I want them to stop punishing each other, and I want them to open up the jails...." But the prosecution also played taped excerpts from his performances, filled with four-letter words. They laughed at the jokes, but the contrast with the un-funny side of Bruce as he sat on the witness chair split the jury down the middle. On February 15, the trial ended with a hung jury, and Bruce was not retried. He died of a drug overdose in 1966.

Bruce, 1963.

Roman Polanski

The director of *Chinatown* flees the country after pleading guilty to unlawful sex with a minor in 1977.

Roman Polanski had made his peace and pleaded guilty to the least serious of six charges stemming from an incident at actor Jack Nicholson's home in March 1977. According to Deputy District Attorney Roger Gunson, who was responsible for the case, while Nicholson was away, Polanski had taken photographs of a 13-year-old girl from Woodland Hills, served her champagne laced with the powerful sedative methaqualone, or Quaaludes, and then he had sex with her in a Jacuzzi and in the house. The victim's family had insisted that the District Attorney's Office accept Polanski's plea to avoid exposing the child to the frenzy of the news media.

When Polanski claimed to the probation department that the incident naturally evolved from the circumstances at Nicholson's house, Gunson used Polanski's own films to dispute the assertion. The prosecutor pointed out that Polanski's movies portrayed a theme of innocence encountering corruption, in the personas of a young woman and a lecherous older man. Also, water was always involved. The prosecutor argued that the alleged crime closely paralleled the plot of *Rosemary's Baby*, in

Polanski in the spotlight, 1977.

which Mia Farrow, numbed with alcohol and drugs, is raped on a ship.

Polanski pleaded guilty to unlawful sex with a minor on August 8. To avoid the dangers that Polanski, as a celebrity and child molester, could face in the county jail, Superior Court Judge Laurence Rittenband sent him to the more-secure mental ward of the state Department of Correction's Chino facility, to do his custodial time under the pretext of a diagnostic study. When Polanski was released from Chino after doing half the expected time, Judge Rittenband told Polanski's attorney that he was going to sentence Polanski, who had expected probation, to state prison. Polanski got on an airplane for London, and then moved to France, where he remains.

In 1997, Polanski, who has said that he misses working in Hollywood, prompted a meeting of Gunson, Polanski's attorney and Superior Court Judge Larry Fidler to press Polanski's case for a negotiated return to the United States. The victim, then age 33 and living in Hawaii, had said that she would have no objection. But after widespread opposition developed over Polanski's potential return, particularly in Hollywood, the director remained in France.

John Belushi

An erstwhile rock singer is charged with second-degree murder and furnishing drugs to comedian John Belushi, who died of a drug overdose in 1983.

A heroin addict and former backup singer for Canadian singer Gordon Lightfoot came to the attention of the District Attorney's Office when she told a reporter for the *National Enquirer* that she had mixed and injected the "speedball"—a mix of cocaine and heroin—that killed comedian John Belushi on March 5, 1983.

Cathy Evelyn Smith told the tabloid reporter that she had spent the previous five days with Belushi, a regular on the television production *Saturday Night Live* and a movie actor, in a bungalow at the Chateau Marmont hotel on the Sunset Strip. "John supplied the coke, I supplied the heroin," the *Enquirer* quoted Smith. "I was Florence Nightingale with the hypodermic."

The Los Angeles County Grand Jury indicted Smith for murder and furnishing Belushi drugs on March 15. She was then in Canada. Based on a Los Angeles warrant for her arrest, Canadian authorities issued their own warrant. Smith surrendered in Toronto and was eventually extradited to Los Angeles for trial. She was charged with one count of second-degree murder and thirteen felony counts of furnishing or administering heroin and cocaine to Belushi. Prosecutors never contended that Smith tried to kill Belushi, but they argued that second-degree murder is the appropriate charge for anyone committing a dangerous felony—in this case, providing drugs—when death occurs. District Attorney Robert H. Philibosian said that despite the massive publicity over Belushi's death, he expected that Smith would receive a fair trial in Los Angeles.

As soon as she was returned to Los Angeles, however, attempts to plea-bargain the case intensified. Philibosian had said that he wouldn't consider reducing the major charge from murder to manslaughter. But after new District Attorney Ira Reiner took office in January 1984, Assistant District Attorney Curt Livesay said that the office felt that the case was "ripe for disposition," and that uncertainties about evidence that could be used in a trial were a concern.

Represented by defense attorney Howard L. Weitzman, Smith pleaded no contest on June 11, 1986, to involuntary manslaughter and three counts of furnishing a controlled substance. Had she stood trial, she could have faced a ten-year sentence if convicted of the more serious charges. Deputy District Attorney Elden S. Fox asked for and obtained a sentence of three years in state prison for Smith.

Twilight Zone

A military helicopter is blown out of the sky by special-effects explosions during filming, and veteran actor Vic Morrow and two first-time child actors are killed.

It was 2:30 a.m., July 23, 1982, on a shallow stretch of the Santa Clara River, near Saugus, when the Huey military helicopter began its attack on the replica of a Vietnamese village. This was to be the final location shoot for the Steven Spielberg movie *Twilight Zone*, directed by John Landis. Below in the river veteran actor Vic Morrow was carrying two Vietnamese-immigrant child actors. He held 6-year-old Renee Chen, of Pasadena, and 7-year-old Myca Dinh Lee, of Cerritos, one in each arm, as they escaped the doomed mock village. Special-effects explosions were set to blow up harmlessly along the helicopter's flight path.

A camera assistant in the helicopter described the fireballs they actually experienced. "The first one was so bad, we turned to leave," said Randall Robinson. "The second knocked us on our side, and the third blast that hit us was under the tail rotor... We got blown out of the sky." Only twenty-four feet below, Morrow and the children were cut down by the main rotor blades as the helicopter crashed on top of them. Morrow and Lee were decapitated. Abdon Llorente, a National Transportation Safety Board investigator at the crash site, estimated that the third fireball, which had been set off underneath a hut, had subjected the tail section to a "substantial amount of heat"—at least six hundred degrees—and that "something" had hit the helicopter,

separating the tail rotor from its shaft. Later the investigator said he thought that a glue-pot lid left unintentionally on the hut roof, as well as shards of bamboo from the hut structure, had damaged the tail.

From the first, director John Landis was criticized for ordering the pilot to fly too low during the scene, as well as for other violations of regulations covering film production. The federal Occupational Safety and Health Administration cited the production for thirty-six safety code violations, assessing fines of more than sixty-two thousand dollars. Three executives on the picture were fined five thousand dollars each by the California Labor Commission for allowing the child actors to work past 6:30 p.m. without the permits and supervision required by state labor law. Numerous civil suits were also filed, beginning with a $200-million wrongful-death suit filed by the parents of one of the children.

The grand jury indicted Landis, special-effects chief Paul Stewart and the helicopter pilot, Dorcey Wingo, on three counts of involuntary manslaughter each. George Folsey Jr., the associate producer, and Dan Allingham, unit production manager, were indicted for involuntary manslaughter and child endangerment only in the deaths of the two child actors, because they were hired illegally. Landis was also indicted for two manslaughter counts involving child endangerment, for allegedly conspiring with Folsey and Allingham to employ the children at night without a permit.

In July 1986, the case went to trial, prosecuted by Deputy District Attorney Lea Purwin D'Agostino. She was confronted by seven defense lawyers representing the five defendants. From the start, the trial was marked by bitter exchanges between prosecution and

During the filming of *Twilight Zone*, moments before chopper crashes amid *special-effects explosions*.

defense. D'Agostino said that had she been in charge of the case at the preliminary hearing, she would have pressed District Attorney Ira Reiner to ask for second-degree murder charges against Landis, as well as child-endangerment and labor-code violations.

D'Agostino felt that a murder charge was appropriate because after a scene shot more than two hours before the fatal crash, the pilot had told Landis he was worried about the size of the fireballs—that the helicopter had almost crashed then. "That is just a warm up for

during the preliminary hearing—that she had overheard Landis say, "We're all going to jail" for hiring the two children illegally. When Folsey's attorney, Harland Braun, cross-examined her about why she was only now saying this in court, Schuman said that she had told Kesselman, the prosecutor who Reiner had removed from the case after the preliminary hearing in 1985.

Braun put Kesselman on the stand. He wanted to know why, if this was now material information, Kesselman had not told the

Parties assembled in court.

what's coming," Landis had been quoted as replying. Then, instead of closing down the set—as directors Richard Brooks and Jackie Cooper would testify should have been done—Landis added explosives and brought the helicopter even lower for the fatal scene.

Attorney James Neal, Landis's attorney, shot back, "absurd and outrageous... but nothing surprises me about statements she makes." Film workers from the production testified for both the defense and prosecution.

D'Agostino's basic argument was that the defendants were grossly negligent about safety on the set. Just before the cameras rolled, Landis had ordered Wingo, the pilot, to fly in lower than Wingo had planned. Wingo had argued with the director that this was unsafe, but in the end complied. The helicopter scene, D'Agostino told the jury, "could have been done without sacrificing any artistic reality... without sacrificing any human life." D'Agostino's predecessor on the case, Deputy District Attorney Gary Kesselman, had already given immunity to the man who set off the fatal charge, James Camomile, who admitted in court that he started the explosion before the helicopter was at a safe distance, but contended that at all times he was under the direction of Landis.

Defense attorneys argued that the deaths resulted from an accident that could not have been foreseen. If anything, Camomile was at fault, they contended. Neal, in his opening remarks, complained of "Monday-morning quarterbacking," noting that had the helicopter gone out of control in a slightly different direction, "it would have been the defendants here who would have been dead." The helicopter crashed no more than six feet away from Landis and others on the set.

A key prosecution witness was production secretary Donna Schuman, who told the trial jury—but not the grand jury or the court

defense about Schuman's quotation. Kesselman said that Schuman had never told him about the alleged conversation. If true, this meant that Schuman had lied to the court.

D'Agostino surprised the courtroom by voluntarily taking the stand to impugn Kesselman's own credibility, and to support the truthfulness of her star witness. Braun and the other defense attorneys called for dismissal of the case, citing prosecutorial misconduct. They argued that one or the other of the two feuding prosecutors hadn't told the truth about the witness. Superior Court Judge Roger W. Boren, who presided over the case, denied the motion for dismissal.

The defense also argued that the true cause of the damage to the helicopter's tail rotor was now a central issue in the case. The attorneys contended that heat alone peeled off the skin of the tail rotor blades, an event that had never occurred before in a helicopter— and therefore was an unforeseeable accident, not negligence.

D'Agostino called Llorente, the National Transportation Safety Board investigator to the stand. In a 1984 report from the board, debris and heat from the explosion had been blamed as probable causes of the damage. But Llorente, following federal policies, and supported by Judge Boren, testified only to what he saw at the scene, not his conclusions about the cause. Llorente, Boren noted, "is not the board himself." In any case, the judge instructed the jury, before it began deliberations, that the prosecution did not have to prove the precise cause of the crash—just that an accident was reasonably foreseeable.

The trial, predicted to last four months, lasted ten. The jury in a single round of balloting, voted to acquit all five defendants. "You don't prosecute people for unforeseeable accidents," said jury foreman Lois Rogers. D'Agostino said that she was "shocked," but hoped that "if nothing else... this prosecution has made other directors more cautious."

The Cotton Club Murder

Eight years after New York impresario Roy Radin disappears on his way to dinner, four people are convicted of his murder.

In the early summer of 1983, Roy Radin was 33 years old and already a millionaire—as a producer of East Coast vaudeville revivals and police benefits. His ambition now was to get into the movie business. In 1982, on a trip to California, he met another aspiring entrepreneur looking to make an entrée into the film industry. Karen Greenberger was also an attractive, 25-year-old dealer connected to Latin American drug interests. She and Radin regularly snorted cocaine together. But Greenberger was also romantically involved with Robert Evans, once head of Paramount Pictures, who had produced *The Godfather* and *Chinatown*. Greenberger introduced Radin and Evans and the two agreed to fund a movie Evans wanted to make, *The Cotton Club,* about a famous Prohibition-era speakeasy in New York's Harlem. Greenberger expected to collect a finder's fee in

disagreement over her finder's fee. Actually, the plan was to kidnap Radin in order to find out what he knew about the stolen money and cocaine.

Radin had been nervous and had asked actor and friend Demond Wilson, a co-star of the *Sanford & Son* television series, to follow the limousine. But Wilson got lost. Radin was never seen alive again. A month later, a beekeeper found his decomposed body, still dressed in his dinner clothes, in a dry wash near the town of Gorman. He had numerous gunshot wounds to the head; part of his face had been blown away by a stick of dynamite that had been exploded in his mouth.

The sheriff's department investigators had little luck trying to crack the complex case for the next four years. Then in a conversation with William Rider, brother-in-law of *Hustler* magazine publisher

Larry Flynt, investigators learned that William Mentzer and Alex Marti had told him in a poker game that they had killed Radin. Mentzer, Marti and Robert Lowe had met Greenberger when the three men were working as bodyguards for Rider, who was then in charge of security for Flynt. Rider made secret recordings of conversations with Lowe and Mentzer, in which they admitted killing Radin in concert with Marti. All four were charged with murder. Robert Evans was not charged with a crime, and he declined to testify, citing his Fifth Amendment rights against self-incrimination, when he was called to the witness stand.

Deputy District Attorneys Sally Thomas and David Conn prosecuted the complex case of drug and movie deals. The prosecutors argued that Greenberger had Radin killed when he refused to provide information about the drug and money theft and she began to suspect that she was being eased out of the potential profits from *The Cotton Club*. In her defense, Greenberger claimed that Mentzer, another former lover, had ordered her out of the limousine the night she and Radin went to dinner, and that she never saw

Defendants in court; (inset) Robert Evans testifying.

the deal. But she became disappointed when she learned it would only be fifty thousand dollars.

After a stash of three hundred thousand dollars and eleven pounds of cocaine was stolen from a San Fernando Valley house that Greenberger had thought was secure, she suspected Radin's involvement, and that he knew where the loot was. On May 13, 1983, Greenberger picked up Radin in a limousine in front of the Plaza Suite Hotel in Hollywood on the pretext that the two would discuss their

Radin again. She claimed that Mentzer killed Radin at the behest of yet another of her ex-lovers, Miami drug dealer Milan Bellechesses, in a dispute over drugs.

In late July 1991, Greenberger and Lowe were convicted of second-degree murder and kidnapping, which brought an automatic sentence of life without parole. Mentzer and Marti were convicted of first-degree murder and kidnapping for financial gain. Mentzer and Marti were sentenced as well to life without parole.

Theresa Saldana

A schizophrenic Scottish admirer stabs actress Theresa Saldana in his compulsion to send her "into eternity" in 1982. The case becomes a landmark in anti-stalking law.

A Scottish-born drifter, Arthur Jackson was mentally ill all of his life. He had been first hospitalized at age 17. As he grew older, he came to America illegally several times and even served in the U.S. Army until he attempted suicide and became a psychiatric patient. He was treated at various army hospitals—and consistently diagnosed with chronic paranoid schizophrenia. He was obsessed with palaces, prisons and a dead U.S. bank robber named Joseph Cretzer, who had been killed by guards in 1946 while leading a prisoners' riot at Alcatraz. Jackson had learned about Cretzer in a newsreel at the movies when he was 11 years old.

In 1961, living illegally in the United States, Jackson wrote an aggressive, bizarre letter about architectural preservation to the new U.S. president, John F. Kennedy. The White House passed the letter to the Secret Service, where it was judged to be threatening. Jackson was found and deported. He returned, again illegally, in 1966. He was deported again when he was caught in San Francisco, trespassing in an office building to use a typewriter. He went back to Scotland, where he lived for most of the next two decades with his mother in a welfare apartment, spending all of his free time at the movies. His mother died in the late fall of 1980, when Jackson was 45 years old. Three months later, Jackson happened to see the American film *Defiance,* co-starring Jan-Michael Vincent and a beautiful young actress who was just becoming well known, Theresa Saldana.

Though *Defiance* was a simple street-gang morality tale, Jackson was powerfully affected. He imagined deep connections to his personal life in the characters and their actions. And he developed an uncontrollable, if weirdly spiritual passion for Saldana. Within two days of seeing the film, Jackson had formed a plan. He would kill Saldana. The U.S. judicial system would in turn execute him for her murder. (He specifically wanted to be shot in the back of the head.) Then he and Saldana and other people with whom he had been obsessed at one time or another—including Cretzer, his "soul mate"—would be together in the hereafter. A compulsive writer, Jackson described in his diary the vision of his life with the actress: "Theresa Saldana is the countess of Heaven in my heart... I have psychedelic fantasies of romance about her in springtime—enchanting visions of our walking together through the gardens of magnificent palaces of Heaven."

He also wrote various documents that he felt necessary to his plan, including "A Solemn Petition to the Government of the United States," which stated his demands about how he wanted to be executed for Saldana's murder: "An indoor execution conveys an atmosphere of spiritual warmth... Each of the six shots should be fired at intervals of five seconds and in accordance with my religious principles... "

Jackson flew to New York on New Year's Day of 1982, planning to find Saldana and kill her on January 24, exactly one year after he first saw *Defiance.* He entered the country openly this time and had his passport stamped at the airport. Sixteen years after his last deportation, his name was no longer on immigration officers' lists. He wanted to use a gun, considering it the most "humane" weapon with which to kill Saldana. But without a U.S. driver's license or other domestic identification, he couldn't buy one at any of the stores he encountered. He would eventually settle on a knife instead.

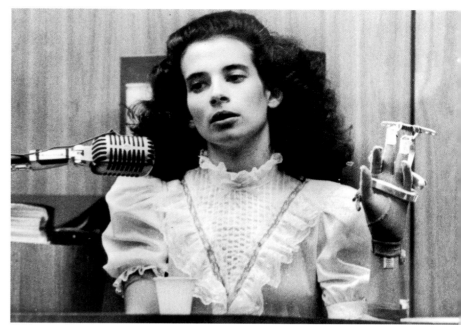
Saldana on the witness stand.

He also had trouble finding Saldana. She wasn't at her New York apartment. And her theatrical agent would only tell him that Saldana was living for the next few months in Los Angeles. When Jackson called the agent three more times, giving a different name each time, she got worried and warned Saldana that a "nut" was looking for her. Saldana's mother also started to receive strange phone calls. Saldana became fearful and cautious, but relaxed when nothing more happened during the next week.

Meanwhile, Jackson had boarded a Greyhound bus, taking a rambling tour of the country on his way to California. In Los Angeles, when he still couldn't find Saldana's home address, he hired a private detective. Jackson had the apartment address by the end of the day. Saldana was living in West Hollywood with her husband.

At 10:00 a.m. on a Monday morning, March 15, Saldana left her apartment, on her way to a piano class at Los Angeles City College. Jackson walked up behind her as she was unlocking her car, asked if she were Theresa Saldana, then grabbed her tightly and began to stab her repeatedly in the chest. The neighbors heard her screams for help and called the police. Jeffrey Fenn, a 28-year-old Sparkletts Water Company delivery man, was a hundred feet away. He ran over, pulled Jackson off Saldana and kicked and wrestled him to the ground. Waiting for the police to arrive, Jackson kept asking how long it had been since his attack, so that he could later note the details in his diary. When Jackson was later questioned by detectives, he was disturbed to learn that Saldana would likely live—all his planning had been for nothing. In fact, Saldana nearly died from loss of blood. But a crack cardiac team at nearby Cedars-Sinai Medical Center closed her wounds, using twenty-six pints of blood, and, miraculously, she survived.

Jackson was tried for first-degree attempted murder and assault with a deadly weapon. Deputy Public Defender Steven Moyer wanted to plead not guilty by reason of insanity. But Jackson refused, saying that he was not crazy—and that he didn't trust a mental institution to ever let him out to continue his "mission." Deputy District Attorney Michael Knight, who thought that Jackson would be kept longest behind bars with criminal convictions, agreed that he was disturbed but contended that his detailed written plan constituted a premeditated and deliberate attempt to murder. The first trial of Jackson began on September 30, 1982.

The public was at the time particularly skeptical of insanity defenses, having in mind the controversial 1978 "Twinkie Defense" of former San Francisco supervisor Dan White, who had killed the mayor and a fellow supervisor. White's lawyer had successfully argued for conviction for manslaughter, not murder, based on White's diminished mental capacity from a junk-food diet that the lawyer contended made him depressed. Reacting to wide public outrage at the White trial, the State of California had banned the diminished-capacity defense in 1981.

Even so, in the Arthur Jackson trial, Moyer heavily relied on two psychiatrists as expert witnesses. One, Dr. Ronald Markman, a forensic psychiatrist, testified that Jackson's severe schizophrenia was obvious. "I think if you got a hundred psychiatrists examining Mr. Jackson," Markman testified, "I doubt you would get any more than one or two of them disagreeing with that diagnosis." Markman also told jurors that Jackson's actions were directly caused by his mental illness. "His entire waking existence is a product of his disease," Markman said. The other defense psychiatrist was blunter: "The fact is, the man is crazy." Meanwhile, Theresa Saldana and her surgeon gave a horrifying portrait of the attack and her injuries. There was little sympathy for Jackson, crazy or not.

Prosecutor Knight, in his closing argument, called on jurors to ignore the question of Jackson's mental illness—to judge him on the simple fact of whether they believed that he intended to kill Saldana. "I'm asking you to use your common sense," he told the jury. "The only way this system can ever work is that people keep in the back of their minds that when things look like a duck, and walk like a duck and quack like a duck, they are probably a duck... Schizophrenia is not a defense to murder... You are responsible for the acts that you understand you are doing and you understand that you shouldn't be doing, and if you do them anyway, you are responsible."

The jury quickly and unanimously returned guilty verdicts on both charges. Though the trial judge said that he would have preferred sentencing Jackson to life in a high-security mental institution, he was limited to the maximum sentence of sixteen years, which could amount to much less considering time served and the state's parole statutes—as little as six more years in prison.

In fact, Jackson became eligible and was scheduled for parole on June 15, 1989. Saldana and her supporters sought a way to keep Jackson incarcerated. It turned out that he had continued to threaten Saldana, as well as Jeffrey Fenn, her rescuer, through letters written from his prison cell. Saldana brought a complaint to the District Attorney's Office and Knight and Senior Investigator Dennis Stults moved quickly to use the new threats to prolong Jackson's time in prison. The new state law they invoked had been passed largely due to lobbying from Victims for Victims, an advocacy group founded by Saldana after the attack. Then the District Attorney's Office found itself with unexpected extra time to consider these new charges when the Board of Prison Terms, as punishment for breaking the windows in his cell, added another 270 days to Jackson's prison time.

Meanwhile, in 1987 Jackson had also written a letter to the British consulate in Los Angeles which was forwarded to Scotland Yard. In this letter, Jackson confessed to several previous crimes in Great Britain, including the unsolved 1967 murder, during a bank robbery, of a brave young passerby who had given chase and confronted him in an alley. As British detectives looked at the details of Jackson's meticulous letter, they began to take him seriously. They filed a murder charge and requested extradition. Now, for the L.A. prosecutors, one issue was whether the British or American prosecutors had the stronger case, and should have precedence in trying Jackson.

Veteran Deputy District Attorney William Hodgman was assigned to assess the two cases. He reported to District Attorney Ira Reiner that the Los Angeles charges for Jackson's threatening letters constituted a winnable case—but that the British murder case was stronger. Hodgman recommended that Los Angeles defer, allowing Jackson to be extradited to stand trial in England. But Saldana and her security consultant, Gavin de Becker, argued that Jackson would ultimately be more likely to spend the rest of his life behind bars—and unable to harm Saldana or others—if he first served additional time in a California prison, and was only extradited to England for trial on the murder charge after that. Reiner decided to try Jackson first in Los Angeles.

Jackson went on trial again on December 3, 1990. By then, Hodgman had been assigned to the Keating prosecution and Deputy District Attorney Susan Gruber took over the case. Gruber, who had earlier and successfully prosecuted a woman for stalking actor Michael J. Fox, called Saldana to the stand. Saldana testified that the first threatening letter that she had received after the attack, eighty-nine pages long, had included the ominous vow that "on the ashes of his dead mother and the scars of Theresa Saldana that he would complete his divine mission of killing me." But "the most frightening aspect about them," said Saldana of the letters, "was that for the first time since this happened, he stated that he had other people who were in place to murder me."

Saldana, Sheriff Block (left) and Fenn, who became a deputy sheriff.

Jackson demanded to be put on the stand, which was his right. He then explained the letters as a way to compel the government to execute him, as he had always wanted. Though the letters referred to Saldana as an "Assassination target," Jackson now claimed that this was a "red herring," to get the federal authorities to take his death wishes seriously. On December 14, Jackson was convicted on all counts. Before sentencing, Saldana addressed Jackson directly. "Arthur Jackson, I ask you to please leave me and my family alone." He was sentenced to the maximum of five years and eight months.

In 1996, Jackson, now 61 years of age, was released from prison and promptly extradited to England, where he pleaded guilty to manslaughter and other charges from the 1967 killing. The charge was reduced from murder because of his reduced mental capacity. He was confined indefinitely in a Scottish mental hospital, where British authorities told the California Board of Prison Terms that he is expected to remain for the rest of his life.

As for Saldana, the stress of her recovery from the attack destroyed her first marriage, though she later married again. She wrote a book, *Beyond Survival*, and appeared in the television movie *Victims for Victims*, both of which depict her stalking.

Madonna

Though many in the entertainment press took the matter lightly, a stalker seriously threatened to slit pop singer Madonna's throat in 1995.

Madonna at Academy Awards; notes left by stalker (below and background).

At first, the intrusion didn't seem extraordinary. When an obsessed fan, Robert Dewey Hoskins, age 37, first crawled over the wall into singer Madonna Ciccone's Hollywood Hills compound, on April 7, 1995, bodyguard Basil Stephens simply ran him off the property. When Hoskins returned to the front gate the next day, Madonna's personal assistant, Caresse Henry, refused to let him in.

But on this second visit, Hoskins became enraged, threatening to kill both the entertainer and Henry. He stuffed a note into the intercom box at the gate, with drawings of hearts and various messages— "kiss, kiss, kiss, kiss"—written over a religious tract entitled "Defiled." The note included the question, more a demand than a plea: "Will you be my wife for keeps?" And this time, Hoskins didn't leave. Henry called Stephens, who was away from the compound. Stephens came back to the house. Hoskins told Stephens that he would kill him if he didn't give the note to Madonna, and that if she didn't marry him that very night, he would "slice her throat from ear to ear." Stephens ran him off again. As this was happening, Madonna was on a bike, riding with her personal trainer, pedaling up the road to her house. Hoskins passed her, stared at her in a way that she remembered "chilled" her, but kept walking. Apparently he hadn't recognized the singer, who was wearing sunglasses, a cap and baggy clothing. When she got home, Stephens and Henry showed her the note, which scared her, and they called the police. Officers searched the area but couldn't find Hoskins.

Hoskins came in over the wall again seven weeks later, wearing a cowboy hat and carrying a backpack and a duffel bag. He had also brought a wooden heart, with the inscription, "Love to my wife Madnna [sic]." Madonna, as it happened, was in Florida. Stephens saw Hoskins on a television monitor, recognized him and called another security guard, as well as the Los Angeles Police Department. When the other guard arrived, he and Stephens tracked Hoskins to the pool area, where they found him soaking wet and wearing only shorts. Hoskins threatened Stephens again, yelling, "I'm going to kill you! This is my property and Madonna is my wife." While the other guard went to let the LAPD officers through the front gate, Stephens tried to calm Hoskins down and to get him to get dressed. Instead, Hoskins tried to grab Stephens's .45-caliber pistol. They wrestled. Stephens kept control of his gun

and told Hoskins several times to lie down on his stomach and surrender. But Hoskins lunged at him again and kept trying to seize the gun. Stephens fired, hitting Hoskins in the left arm and lower abdomen.

Hoskins survived and was charged with stalking, two counts of making terrorist threats and misdemeanor assault on Stephens. The case was prosecuted by Deputy District Attorney Rhonda Saunders, who worried that massive pretrial publicity would make it difficult to find an impartial jury. The international entertainment press, in particular, had often treated the matter lightly, sometimes referring to Hoskins as "Mr. Madonna."

Though cameras were banned at the trial, Madonna fought having to appear personally to testify, saying that she didn't consider herself to be a material witness to Hoskins's crimes. A detective caught up with her jogging and tucked a subpoena under her arm, ordering her to be in court the next day. Her lawyer appeared, but she didn't. Saunders told the court that her case couldn't be presented without Madonna testifying that the acts of Hoskins made her fear for her safety. Madonna's attorney tried to arrange for her to testify on videotape, saying that Madonna didn't want to grant Hoskins the face-to-face encounter that he had long sought. He also said that Madonna had to travel to Argentina to begin filming the movie *Evita*.

But as Saunders pointed out, the primary target of a stalker isn't always the only one at risk. In this case, the bodyguard and Madonna's personal assistant had been threatened. "The issue is stalking," Saunders told reporters outside the court, "not who Madonna is." Saunders asked the court for a body attachment, equivalent to an arrest warrant for witnesses who won't obey a subpoena. The witness is held in custody, or posts bail, until called to the witness stand. Though Saunders was granted the body attachment, with a $5-million bail, the judge would only issue it to the prosecutor on the day Madonna was scheduled to testify.

In fact, Madonna did appear at the downtown criminal courts building as ordered. Saunders was now concerned that the jury would question her credibility as a witness because it had been widely reported that she had to be forced to testify. But Saunders took the edge off this by asking the singer how she felt being in the same court with Hoskins. "Sick to my stomach," Madonna responded from the witness stand. "... I feel incredibly disturbed that the man who repeatedly threatened my life is sitting across the room from me. I feel we are making his fantasies come true." Hoskins hummed music to himself as she testified for ninety minutes.

The jury convicted Hoskins, who didn't stop his threats even while waiting to be sentenced. He repeated his vow to slice Madonna's throat "from ear to ear" to a sheriff's deputy at the jail, who testified at the sentencing proceeding. And later, he told the judge that he planned to come back when he was released from prison to "take care of" everyone in court. He was given the maximum allowable sentence on the charges, ten years. Madonna sold her house and has since suffered from nightmares about the incident. Her lawyer, after the verdicts, said that Madonna was now glad that she had testified. Madonna herself released a statement saying that she hoped that "the outcome of this case lets other stalking victims know that the system can, and does, work."

National guardsman on night patrol, Watts riots, 1965.

Turmoil in the Streets

"People have a right to protest, to demonstrate, to use their freedom of speech to air grievances—and we support this," affirmed Robert P. Heflin, who was appointed chief deputy district attorney in 1998. "We only become involved when the criminal law is violated. But that can involve serious violence."

Since the early years, Los Angeles, like other cities, has experienced the devastation and tragedy of unforgiving mobs. And in a city that has been multi-ethnic for more than two centuries, the most vicious riots and group mayhem have been rooted in racial antagonism. That doesn't mean, of course, that race has been the prime motive for every rioter at every moment.

Some mobs have certainly come together in anger after longstanding injustice. But precisely why each person joins the crowd can be a lot more complicated. Once lawlessness presents opportunity, however, criminals often join in force. According to various post-riot assessments, many of the most destructive rioters were drawn by the chance to directly injure a perceived enemy; the chance to steal; the chance to see destruction at first hand; the chance to indulge a sadistic fascination in other peoples' loss, or the excitement of breaking society's boundaries in a big, anonymous and seemingly invulnerable group.

A few years after one of the ugliest episodes in L.A. history, the 1871 Chinese massacre, the local poet and historian A. J. Wilson recalled the mob that savaged Chinatown's residents: "American 'hoodlum' and Mexican 'greaser,' Irish 'tramp' and French 'communist'—all joined to murder and dispatch the foe. He who did not shoot, could shout; he who feared to stab, could steal; there was work for all."

Once the destruction begins, a riot becomes a criminal matter and usually a significant strain on the criminal justice system. After the fires were controlled in Watts in 1965, the event was examined for lessons to be learned. In the necessarily limited purview of the District Attorney's Office, better methods were developed to handle large numbers of criminal cases filed after mass arrests.

"Out of our experience with the Watts riots," Heflin said, "we created emergency procedures, a very formalized structure to react quickly—to set up command posts, to get our lawyers in position, to cooperate with law enforcement officers." The district attorney's staff must rapidly review arrest reports and decide on charges to meet the forty-eight-hour deadline for arraigning a defendant. And at each progressive step in the judicial process, this bulge of cases has to be accommodated. "Riots create a great dislocation for the criminal justice system," added Heflin. "And then afterwards we'll be second-guessed by journalists and society. Did we prosecute the right people? Did we prosecute them for the right charges?"

The Chinese Massacre

In a climate of racial suspicion, a shooting in L.A.'s tiny Chinatown escalates into an ugly bloodbath in 1871.

Chinese immigrants to Los Angeles in the early years generally maintained their deeply rooted traditional ways, some of which seemed mysterious or sinister to those unfamiliar with the several thousand years of Chinese history and culture. Common gossip had it, for example, that all Chinese gambled, smoked opium, patronized and traded in prostitutes and ate such strange foods as abalone. On July 19, 1871, just four months before the massacre in Chinatown, the *Los Angeles Star* editorialized: "We venture the assertion that many a dark and terrible deed has been perpetrated by these heathen in their secret dens, which will never come to the knowledge of the Christians whose places they are usurping." In fact, most of the fewer than two hundred Chinese residents in Los Angeles were honest and hard-working. Some, of course, were not.

On the afternoon of October, 24, 1871, a long-running feud between two Chinese tongs—fraternal organizations that often acted like gangs—set off an attack on the city's Chinese immigrant population that brought national and even international condemnation. In fact, many Americans on the East Coast first heard of Los Angeles as the scene of an appalling race riot.

The Hong Chow and Nin Yung tongs were battling over control of a beautiful young woman named Ya Hit. Treated as mere property for prostitution in the trade among the tongs, she was valued at twenty-five hundred dollars, a substantial sum at the time. It remains unclear whether Ya Hit had been stolen from, or had run away from, the Nin Yung Tong. In any case, she was now in the hands of a rival, the Hong Chow. The Hong Chow Tong was led by Yo Hing, a prominent merchant well known by the entire Los Angeles community as the Los Angeles agent of a powerful Chinese company.

The Nin Yung Tong got Ya Hit back by filing a complaint with the authorities, claiming that she had stolen jewelry. When police officers dutifully arrested her and brought her in on the complaint, the Nin Yung paid her bail and carted her back to their quarters. At the time, this was a common ploy used by the tongs to enlist the mechanisms of U.S. justice for their own ends.

But Yo Hing now added a new twist. He counter-attacked by

convincing the woman to secretly marry him, which returned her to him under U.S. law. The angry Nin Yung Tong countered that move by putting a thousand-dollar price on Yo Hing's head. And three days later, on the morning of October 23, several shots were fired at Yo Hing as he walked down a Chinatown street. In the charges and countercharges over the attempted murder of Yo Hing, Ah Choy, the woman's brother, and another Hong Chow member were arrested. Meanwhile, Yo Hing was also brought in. Ah Choy had filed a complaint against him, alleging assault with intent to murder—claiming that Yo Hing had pulled a gun on him too. All were released when their respective tongs paid their bail. But when they returned to Chinatown, both sides prepared for war.

About 5:30 p.m. the next day, gunshots were heard again in Calle de los Negros, the rough street of saloons, brothels, opium dens and gambling emporiums in the heart of L.A.'s Chinatown. At the sound, Deputy Sheriff Jesus Bilderrain finished his whiskey in Higby's Saloon and went to investigate. He found Ah Choy, the woman's brother, shot fatally in the neck after having fired wildly into a crowd of bystanders. Other tong members cut loose with their pistols. Bilderrain was wounded in the shoulder and wrist, by an unseen attacker. He called for help and other officers came running. But one of the first arrivals was a civilian, a popular old rancher and former bar owner, Robert Thompson. Thompson mounted the porch of a long, L-shaped, adobe building of interconnected apartments called the Coronel Block. As he strode up to one front door, he was shot squarely in the chest. Several other bystanders were wounded as well by gunfire from the building. Thompson, carried a couple of blocks away to Wollweber's drug store, died an hour later.

Word spread quickly through town that the Chinese were "killing whites wholesale" in Calle de los Negros. A mob of more than five hundred Los Angelenos of various ethnicities and backgrounds—from an enraged city councilman to well-known thieves and troublemakers—descended on Chinatown. Many were drunk. Many recognized the opportunity to loot Chinese merchants and private homes said to be filled with gold and other valuables. Others simply wanted to take the opportunity to persecute the "heathens." But previously respectable citizens took part as well. The owners of Broderick & Reilly's bookstore donated a rope. A housewife in the neighborhood gave her clothesline to be used to hang the Chinese. At its height, the mob constituted more than eight percent of the entire Los Angeles population.

Calle de los Negros, the mob-killing scene; newspaper headline on massacre.

Traditional Chinese New Year celebration; indictment in massacre (left).

By this time, the tong leaders and most of their followers had slipped away. The horrific attack fell on the innocent Chinese left barricaded in the Coronel Block building. The cat-calling mob cut holes in the roof, firing their guns down into the interior apartments. Attempts were made to burn the building. Any Chinese falling into the mob's hands were beaten and summarily lynched. When conscientious police officers or appalled citizens tried to stop the rioters, they too were threatened with lynching.

Finally, the mob broke into the Coronel Block building and dragged out most of the remaining occupants, including two teenage boys and a well-respected doctor, Chien Lee Tong, known among many non-Chinese as Gene Tung—the Chinese community's sole physician. All were beaten or shot, then hanged. One rioter wrenched the lynched doctor's finger off, to steal his rings. Every Chinese store and home was sacked

Some law officers and civic leaders were able to extricate a few Chinese men and women from the mob and to get them to the city jail for protection. Three-time District Attorney Cameron E. Thom, Sheriff James F. Burns and other fair-minded citizens gathered a group of men who eventually took control of the Coronel Block from the mob. But by then it was too late. Most of the rioters had already returned to the saloons to celebrate their deeds.

In all, nineteen Chinese men and boys were murdered, amounting to roughly ten percent of the Los Angeles Chinese population. The only victim who had anything to do with the warring tongs was Ah Choy, Ya Hit's brother, who had been killed early in the afternoon—apparently by a tong rival, not by the mob. Yo Hing and the other members of the two rival tongs had fled early in the fighting, and were safe.

In November after a grand jury was convened, Judge Ygnacio Sepulveda, descendant of a pioneer California family, gave the jurors a backbone-stiffening order: "Shall law stand for naught, and immorality and crime have high carnival in our community?... Set an example of true courage in the performance of your duty... In this way only can you satisfy an offended God, violated law, and outraged humanity."

Yet many officials and witnesses called before the grand jury protected the rioters, claiming faulty memories. In the end, thirty-seven of the mob were indicted. District Attorney Thom prosecuted fifteen, with eight convicted—all for manslaughter. These included Louis Menelle, G.R. Johnston, Charles Austin, P.M. McDonald, Jesus Martinez, Refugio Botello and Estevan A. Alvarado. All were released within a year of beginning their sentences, however, when their defense attorney, former District Attorney Edward J.C. Kewen, appealed successfully to the California Supreme Court, which ruled on a technicality that the original indictments hadn't established that physician Chien Lee Tong had, in fact, been murdered.

But the grand jury also declared that "...the officers of this county as well as of this city, whose duty it is to preserve the peace and to arrest those who are violating the law, were deplorably inefficient in the performance of their duty during the scenes of confusion and bloodshed which disgraced our city, and has cast a reproach upon the people of Los Angeles County."

The years that followed saw improvements in law enforcement and in the entire Los Angeles criminal-justice system. As an early step in this direction, the office of district attorney was elevated to a full-time paid position in 1878.

The Sleepy Lagoon Murder and the Zoot Suit Riots

The controversial conviction of a dozen young men for murder, later overturned, sets the stage for a vicious five-day rampage.

Sleepy Lagoon, near an area in East Los Angeles known as the Williams Ranch, was the name coined by a reporter for a modest pond in a gravel pit, shaded by willow trees. The area was popular among young Mexican-Americans for swimming and as a lover's lane. Today, the name is a reminder of a particularly rancorous period in Los Angeles race relations.

In the early evening of August 1, 1942, Henry Leyvas, a 20-year-old ranch hand who worked for his father, had taken his girlfriend for an automobile ride to Sleepy Lagoon. Leyvas and his friends were described by the police as the 38th Street Gang, though that was a name they never applied to themselves. In any case, Leyvas was attacked and beaten at Sleepy Lagoon by another young group known as the Downey Boys. After the fight, Leyvas went off and returned with several carloads of his 38th Street friends—men and women ranging in age from 14 to 22—intending to even the score.

No one was at Sleepy Lagoon when they returned, but they found a birthday party going on at the home of Mrs. Amelia Delgadillo, about a half mile east of the pond. A live orchestra was playing dance music. Apparently, some of the Downey Boys had already crashed the party and there had been fighting earlier with the Delgadillo family. When Leyvas and his friends arrived, another free-for-all broke out among the young men and women.

Sometime after midnight, a young man named Jose Diaz was found beaten insensible on a dirt road near the Delgadillo home. Taken to a hospital, he died without regaining consciousness. Two other men had been stabbed at some point in the off-and-on clashes.

Already prodded by the press to see any altercation as gang violence, police responded with a massive roundup of young Mexican-Americans, equating any who adhered to currently popular teenage fashions—exaggerated hairstyles and particularly the flamboyant zoot suit—with criminality.

The police, newspapers and the Anglo public had taken little notice of a study by Karl Holton of the Los Angeles Probation Department which flatly stated that "there is no wave of lawlessness" among Mexican-American youth.

Most Los Angeles newspapers followed the manhunt with headlines that announced: "Baby Gangsters," "New Zoot Gangster Attacks Result in Arrest of 100," "Hair Style Used in Identification of Hoodlums" and "More Zoot Suits in Jail." In all, three hundred suspects were rounded up after the Sleepy Lagoon death. Twenty-two members of the 38th Street group, including Henry Leyvas and an Anglo-American,

Court arraignment of Sleepy Lagoon defendants; motion on defendants' release (inset).

Victor Thompson, were put on trial on charges of murder and assault with a deadly weapon with the intent to commit murder. Besides Leyvas, the ranch hand, they included an aspiring professional baseball player, a defense-plant worker, a Navy volunteer awaiting induction, another Navy volunteer who had already been sworn into the service, four woodworkers and furniture makers and a former employee of the U.S. Engineering Department in Alaska. The case was prosecuted by Deputy District Attorney John Barnes. Superior Court Judge Charles W. Fricke presided.

The trial was a long, bitter battle, conducted in an inadequate courtroom setting. George E. Shibley, one of the defense lawyers, particularly contested his inability to confer with his half-dozen clients—either in the courtroom during the proceedings or outside during recesses. In session, the defendants were seated together but well apart from their attorneys. During recesses, Fricke ordered the defendants taken en masse to the prisoners' room. "And I do not want anybody to stop those prisoners and try to talk to them," he told the defense. He pronounced that if the defense attorneys "want to talk to their clients they will have to do it at some other time." Judge Fricke also wouldn't allow defendants to walk up to speak to their attorneys while court was in session. "I am not going to tolerate defendants walking around the courtroom of their own sweet desire."

Meanwhile, even some prosecution witnesses testified that Diaz, the victim, had left the Delgadillo house before the defendants arrived. The autopsy doctor testified that Diaz's hands were injured in a way consistent with fighting with his fists. And three and a half hours after his death, Diaz's blood contained .12 percent alcohol, though the doctor couldn't swear whether he had been drunk at the time he died. Some witnesses testified that Diaz had been hit by an automobile before the suspects arrived; others, that he could well have been killed in an earlier fight.

Despite the conflicting evidence, twelve defendants were convicted—three, including Henry Leyvas, of first-degree murder; nine of second-degree murder. They were sentenced to terms of from eighteen months to life and packed away to San Quentin and Chino state prisons.

Many Los Angelenos were outraged. The Sleepy Lagoon Defense Committee was formed, with historian Carey McWilliams as chairman and Harry Braverman as treasurer. Braverman, a member of the grand jury, had argued against the original indictment of the 38th Street juveniles. The Citizens' Committee for the Defense of Mexican-American Youth, formed by renowned L.A. civil-rights leader Alice McGrath, issued a report, "The Sleepy Lagoon Case," with a foreword by writer and actor Orson Welles.

The next year, 1943, racial tension in Los Angeles only got worse. While many local leaders dismissed as Communist propaganda any charge that Latinos and blacks were being discriminated against, skating rinks still posted signs saying "Wednesdays reserved for Negroes and Mexicans," upscale theaters and ballrooms routinely refused them admission, and casual groups that among Anglos would be considered normal teenage pals were being rounded up as "*pachuco* gangsters." Then on the evening of June 3, 1943, eleven sailors on leave from their Los Angeles base were walking through an East Los Angeles barrio when they were attacked, they said, by a group of young *pachucos*. The next night, two hundred sailors from the naval armory near Chinatown hired a fleet of taxis to take them through downtown Los Angeles and to the predominately Mexican-American east side of town.

They stopped and assaulted every juvenile in a zoot suit that they ran across. Sometimes they also stripped the youths naked. Sometimes they burned or ripped-up their suits. And police essentially stood back—saying that it was a matter for the military police. Sometimes,

the police arrested the victims. In a few cases, police stations provided safe havens for zoot-suiters.

Night after night the sailors formed their self-appointed "task force" to, as one sailor put it, complete "what the police have failed to do." By June 5, U.S. Marines had joined the sailors in their attacks. And soon any Mexican-American youth, zoot suit or no, was fair game. In fact, in the end, more than half the victims beaten weren't even wearing a zoot suit. Civilians joined the marauding servicemen. The mobs turned on the lights in movie theaters and roamed the aisles looking for zoot-suiters. They halted and searched streetcars. A black war worker, wearing his defense-plant badge but no zoot suit, was pulled from a streetcar and lost an eye to the mob. Finally, military commanders decided that the Los Angeles authorities were unable to stop the mayhem. They put an end to most of the rioting by declaring downtown Los Angeles off-limits to naval personnel, and by sending in the Military Police and Shore Patrol to enforce the ban.

The riots had brought condemnation on an international scale. First Lady Eleanor Roosevelt criticized "the attitude toward Mexicans in California." The Mexican ambassador to the United States brought the matter up with the U.S. Secretary of State.

On June 10, District Attorney Fred N. Howser also declared that the situation could no longer be tolerated and that he would ask for a grand jury investigation. Federal and state investigations were conducted. Still, in Los Angeles, many continued to believe that the riots had a useful "cleansing" effect. And what Howser considered intolerable didn't seem to include the attacks on young Mexican-Americans. Instead, Howser said, "It is manifest to the citizens of the county of Los Angeles that a state of near anarchy has existed in this county for the past several weeks. This condition has been brought about by the growth of gang life in our community. We are faced with the humiliating fact that the Navy has found it necessary to declare certain portions of the city of Los Angeles 'out of bounds' for sailors."

The Los Angeles City Council blamed the zoot suit itself for causing all the trouble, and made it a misdemeanor to wear one. The *Los Angeles Times*, in an editorial published a week after the attacks ended, condemned historian McWilliams and others who termed the riots racially motivated. "When trouble arose through the depredations of the young gangs attired in zoot suits," the *Times* editorial writer declared, "it was their weird dress and not their race which resulted in difficulties. That is a simple truth that no amount of propaganda will change."

As to the Sleepy Lagoon case, more than a year after the Zoot Suit Riots, the convictions were overturned when the District Court of Appeals ruled on thirty-four points of an appeal for a new trial. After reviewing more than six thousand pages of trial transcript, and fourteen hundred pages of briefs, the court found insufficient evidence to tie any of the defendants to the Diaz death, and no conclusive evidence that any of them had used a deadly weapon—only their fists. Judge Fricke, the court ruled, had accepted inadmissable and immaterial evidence, had shown prejudicial conduct in wrongly criticizing defense lawyers in front of the jury, and should have allowed all defendants to communicate with their attorneys at all times. Deputy District Attorney Barnes then announced that because there was no new evidence to justify a new trial, all charges would be dropped.

After almost two years in prison, the released men were met with shrieks of delight by more than a hundred fifty relatives, sweethearts and supporters when they walked out the front door of the Hall of Justice. "The air was electric with excitement," the *Times* reported, "as the liberated men were besieged by well-wishers who enthusiastically pumped their hands and slapped their backs. Tears flowed unashamedly."

1,000 RIOT IN L.A.
Police and Motorists Attacked

Routine Arrest of 3 Sparks Watts Melee; 8 Blocks Sealed Off

An estimated 1,000 persons rioted in the Watts district Wednesday night and attacked police and motorists with bricks and bottles before some 100 officers...

The Watts Riots

In 1965 a traffic stop for suspicion of drunk driving sparks a still-controversial outburst of looting and rebellion, as well as a new expression—"Burn, baby, burn."

One of the pivotal crises in race relations in the United States began on the warm early evening of Wednesday, August 11, 1965. Cruising through central Los Angeles, white California Highway Patrol officer Lee W. Minikus was told by a passing black motorist that he had just encountered a reckless driver. Minikus spotted the car, turned on his red light and pulled over 21-year-old Marquette Frye and his passenger, and brother, Ronald Frye, 22, both African-American. The routine stop was made at 116th Street and Avalon Boulevard, two blocks from the Frye brothers' home and at the edge of the predominately black Watts district. When Marquette Frye failed a field sobriety test, Minikus arrested him as a suspected drunk driver, radioed for his partner who was also on a motorcycle, and called for a patrol car to take Frye into custody, and for a tow truck for the car—since Ronald Frye also appeared to have been drinking. Watching all this was a small but growing crowd—perhaps twenty-five to fifty people at first—who had been out enjoying the summer air.

Ronald Frye quickly walked the two blocks to get their mother, Rena Frye, so she could claim the car. Otherwise, with neither brother able to drive, it would be towed. When they got back to the scene, Rena Frye first criticized her son, Marquette, for getting drunk. To this point, Marquette Frye had been quiet and cooperative. But now, in front of a crowd that had grown to about three hundred people, Frye began yelling at the officers that they would have to kill him to take him in. Three more Highway Patrol officers arrived in response to a call for backup. She had by now become hostile herself, and so was the crowd. Rena Frye jumped on the back of one of the officers, tearing his shirt. In a struggle to get Marquette Frye to stay put in the patrol car, one officer, apparently inadvertently, hit his forehead with a nightstick, drawing blood. As the officers got the Fryes under control and were starting to drive away, someone in the crowd spat on one officer. The procession halted and two patrolmen pulled a young woman, and then a man, out of the crowd, arresting both. The angry crowd threw rocks at the patrol cars as they finally left the scene.

Throughout that first night, small mobs formed. Several white motorists in the Watts area were pulled from their cars and beaten, and localized vandalism brought almost thirty new arrests.

Clockwise from top: riot headline; a young Daryl Gates, future police chief; police holding suspects in "Operation Mop Up."

The next afternoon, the Los Angeles County Human Relations Commission held a turbulent meeting in an auditorium near the arrest site, attended by community leaders, black civil-rights advocates, elected local officials and the media. Most speakers, including Rena Frye, called on the people of Watts to stay home and stay calm, so that, as she said, "we will not have a riot tonight." But the meeting ultimately "misfired," in the words of the controversial McCone Commission report ordered by Governor Edmund G. "Pat" Brown. Instead of sticking with a call for law and order, the report noted, the focus shifted to "a discussion of the grievances felt by the Negro." In fact, to many, this wasn't a diversion but exactly the point— the complaints of Watts residents were at the core of their anger and key to the opening events of the rioting.

But little of this discussion made the evening television news after a black high-school student grabbed a microphone at the meeting and announced that later that night the attacks would move to nearby white neighborhoods—an incendiary threat which was widely and dramatically reported by the press.

That Thursday night, as many as eight thousand rioters faced five hundred police officers, deputy sheriffs and highway patrol officers. The mob overturned cars, broke into businesses and set cars and buildings afire. When firemen came in to put out the blazes, the mob threw rocks, cement, bricks and bottles. Snipers shot at the firemen. Rioters broke through the police perimeter. Still, by 6:45 a.m. Friday, the violence had calmed to the point that the Los Angeles Police Department's emergency control center told state officials that the rioting seemed to be under control.

L.A. police Chief William Parker (left) conferring with Gov. Edmund G. Brown before news conference; aerial view of riot zone.

Marquette Frye (right); mother, Rena; attorney Al Wirin (far left);
Frye's brother (behind).

Fires had destroyed more than two hundred buildings, of the more than six hundred that were burned or looted.

The courts and prosecutors, working day and night, were able to process all the 3,438 arrests—seventy-one percent of which were for burglary and theft. More than fifty thousand pieces of stolen property were recovered. In the end, 2,278 adult felony cases were filed and, in rough numbers, three hundred fifty defendants were found guilty; eight hundred were convicted of misdemeanors, seven hundred cases were dismissed, and another three hundred fifty defendants were found not guilty.

The Frye family filed suit charging police brutality. Mayor Yorty asked the District Attorney's Office to investigate the Frye arrests, which had set off the violence. In a report to Yorty, District Attorney Evelle J. Younger noted that it wasn't within the authority of his office to investigate police conduct that might be "unprofessional, inefficient or rude." He considered only whether officers used criminal levels of unreasonable or excessive force. And within those boundaries, Younger concluded that the force used while arresting the Frye family was necessary under the circumstances. He added that the U.S. Attorney had decided that no investigation or charges against the arresting officers were appropriate on the federal level either.

In the larger assessment of the riots, several conclusions of the McCone Commission were hotly contested by many observers. One was that only two percent of Watts residents had been rioters, and that these had been "marginal" people. In fact, most rioters had jobs and were slightly better educated than others living in Watts. Many Commission critics considered the rioting to be largely a genuine protest, not just an excuse to steal and destroy. Thomas Reddin, for instance, a future LAPD chief, testified to the Commission that the pattern of looting showed that rioters focused on white merchants who had taken advantage of Watts residents in the past. In contrast, white merchants who had extended credit and otherwise been sensitive to the community, were generally spared—as were virtually all residences, libraries, schools, public buildings and gas stations. The mob, agreed historian Robert M. Fogelson of the Harvard-MIT Joint Center for Urban Studies, "made a point of looting and destroying stores that were notorious for their high prices and hostile manners."

But the mob reformed less than two hours later and soon three thousand rioters were looting stores in the Watts business district. Firemen and ambulance drivers now refused to enter the area without armed escorts. The National Guard had been alerted the previous afternoon. At 9:15 a.m., Los Angeles Police Chief William H. Parker and Mayor Sam Yorty decided to call out the guard. Parker made the formal request to the Governor's office at 10:50 a.m. But Lieutenant Governor Glenn Anderson, acting on behalf of Governor Brown, "wished to consider the matter further" before committing the guardsmen, according to the McCone Commission. With this and other delays, all later criticized by the commission, the first guardsmen weren't on the streets until after 10:00 p.m. Friday. By then, the first riot-related death had already occurred, when a black bystander was killed in a crossfire between the mob and the police.

Friday night and Saturday morning saw the heaviest looting and arson—one thousand fire alarms in the twenty-four hour period between Friday morning and Saturday morning—with sniper fire at police and firemen and expansion of the destruction to other neighborhoods. But by then, guardsmen were pouring into the area. An 8:00 p.m. curfew imposed on a 46.5 square-mile sector Saturday night was largely effective, though some destruction continued into Sunday. The last of almost fourteen thousand guardsmen deployed for riot control were removed from Watts a week later.

Thirty-four people had been killed, including thirty-one local residents and rioters, a deputy sheriff, a fireman and a Long Beach policeman. More than a thousand people were injured, including one hundred thirty-six firemen, ninety LAPD officers, ten guardsmen and another twenty-three officials from various government agencies.

Officer David Hudson with recovered stolen property.

Ruben Salazar

A Mexican-American journalist is killed by a tear-gas projectile during a 1970 anti-Vietnam War protest that turned into a riot.

On a smoggy Saturday afternoon, August 29, 1970, a protest rally by Mexican-American groups opposed to U.S. involvement in the Vietnam War—part of the National Chicano Moratorium—had turned into a rampage in East Los Angeles, with looting and arson by some of the twenty thousand protesters. One of the reporters covering the story was Ruben Salazar, 42, a former foreign correspondent who had

Ruben Salazar, 1970.

become a widely followed columnist writing about Chicano affairs for the *Los Angeles Times*. He was also news director of KMEX-TV, a Spanish-language television station, for which he was working that day.

Salazar, KMEX reporter William Restrepo and photographer Octavio Gomez had been reporting on the demonstration at Laguna Park since 7:00 a.m. When the rally became violent after the sheriff's department received reports of a liquor-store looting, riot-helmeted deputy sheriffs using batons and tear gas cleared the center of the rally. Before the park was emptied, dancers had been performing on a stage and most demonstrators were sprawled on the grass, resting after their march. Some demonstrators threw rocks and bottles at the deputies as they swept the park. Others ran down Whittier Boulevard, breaking windows and torching businesses. It was a "self-fueling fire," as *Los Angeles Times* reporter Frank del Olmo described the scene. "Every action triggered a bigger reaction...."

During the riot, sheriff's deputies received a citizen's report that one or more armed men had entered the Silver Dollar Café, an East Los Angeles tavern near the center of the disturbance. Salazar and Restrepo were inside at the time, among a dozen patrons, having

stopped to use the restroom and then lingering to drink a beer. Standing on the sidewalk, Sheriff's Deputy Thomas H. Wilson fired two heavy-duty Federal Flite-Rite tear-gas projectiles through the curtained bar entrance. The high-velocity, pointed-tip, tear-gas shell, ten inches long and an inch and a half in diameter, is designed to penetrate walls in barricade situations. Its manufacturer specifically warned that it was "Not to be used in crowd control."

Restrepo and others in the bar crawled out the back door of the Silver Dollar Café on hands and knees, choking on the tear gas. Deputies collected them at the back door and searched, unsuccessfully, for the reported weapons. Restrepo was taken a block away and detained. Restrepo later told the *Los Angeles Times* that his shirt had been splattered with blood, which he had assumed was Salazar's. "I told [the deputies] I wanted to go back to the bar because my boss was still there," said Restrepo, "but they didn't let me go back."

Almost two hours passed because deputies had no gas masks that would allow them to reenter the bar. Salazar's body was eventually pulled out of the bar by a civilian. The first projectile fired had passed completely through his skull, killing him instantly.

City councilman and future mayor Tom Bradley, U.S. Representative Edward Roybal and twenty other elected officials called for an investigation of Salazar's death. Sixty-one witnesses testified at the coroner's inquest—including those in the bar, who declared that they had not been ordered by deputies to clear the room before tear gas was fired. Deputies testified that they had given prior warning. Deputy Wilson said that he hadn't been aware at the time whether he had a Flite-Rite or a less-deadly cardboard tear-gas cannister loaded when he fired. "I wanted to get it inside quick," he told the inquest jurors. It was not established at the inquest that anyone in the bar actually had been armed.

The inquest jurors ended up in disagreement. Three of the seven voted to declare that Salazar had been killed by accident, though at least one of these later regretted that decision and said that the two others had also been confused by their instructions. Four voted for stronger language, that Salazar had died "at the hands of another"— which, had it been unanimous, would have prompted prosecution of the deputy who fired the fatal projectile.

In October 1970, District Attorney Evelle J. Younger announced that he wouldn't press charges. He had considered only one possible criminal charge that might have been brought against Wilson, he said—involuntary manslaughter. But that would have required, he said, "aggravated, culpable, gross or reckless" negligence. And "it is my conclusion that negligence, if any, was not of that caliber and that no criminal charge is justified." Younger also told reporters that from his experience as a prosecutor, he predicted that if three of seven inquest jurors thought the death was an accident, he would expect that at least one in twelve criminal-trial jurors would have voted the same, which made prosecution unrealistic. Federal prosecutors similarly declined to bring charges against the deputy. Sheriff Peter J. Pitchess added that he saw no misconduct in using the wall-piercing projectile because the curtain over the front door created a "barricaded situation."

Salazar's widow and three children sued the County, charging that the sheriff's department had been negligent in not following "proper and lawful guidelines for the use of deadly force." A unanimous Board of Supervisors agreed to settle the civil suit with a payment of seven hundred thousand dollars, then a record for the County. As for the sheriff's department, it discontinued use of Federal Flite-Rite tear-gas projectiles after Salazar's death. And Laguna Park was renamed Ruben Salazar Park.

Rodney King and the 1992 Riots

When four white Los Angeles police officers are acquitted of the beating of a black motorist—a scene dramatically caught on videotape—arson and looting break out.

Just before 1:00 a.m. on Sunday, March 3, 1991, George Holliday, the manager of the Hollywood branch of a national plumbing firm, was startled awake at his home in Lake View Terrace by the sounds of sirens and a helicopter overhead. Like several of his neighbors, he went out on the balcony of his apartment and saw an arrest taking place less than a hundred feet away. He had just bought a videotape camera. He trained it on the scene. First, a large black man surrounded by police charged at one officer, who was able to club him to the ground. Then several officers kicked the man and beat him repeatedly with their riot batons.

The next morning, Holliday brooded over the beating and his record of it. He called the Foothill station of the Los Angeles Police Department, the station closest to his home. But the officer he spoke to wasn't interested, Holliday said later. He called Cable News Network (CNN), but no one answered the phone in the Los Angeles office. So he took his videotape to the television station that he usually watched himself, KTLA-TV. They were interested. And when the station took a copy to LAPD headquarters for comment, senior police commanders quickly began their own investigation.

That Monday night, KTLA aired the tape of the beating of motorist Rodney King, and now CNN picked up the story. But in editing the tape down from eighty-one seconds to sixty-eight seconds, to get rid of an out-of-focus section, KTLA-TV had deleted the three-second segment in which King rushed one of the officers—and was far from a passive victim. What television viewers worldwide would see for months and years

Los Angeles Times

DAILY 35¢
DESIGNATED AREAS HIGHER

THURSDAY, APRIL 30, 1992
COPYRIGHT 1992/THE TIMES MIRROR COMPANY /CCVV/130 PAGES

CIRCULATION:
1,164,388 DAILY / 1,531,527 SUNDAY

All 4 in King Beating Acquitted
Violence Follows Verdicts; Guard Called Out

■ **Trial:** Governor deploys troops at mayor's request after arson, looting erupt. Ventura County jury apparently was not convinced that videotape told the whole story.

By RICHARD A. SERRANO
and TRACY WILKINSON
TIMES STAFF WRITERS

SIMI VALLEY—Four Los Angeles police officers won acquittals Wednesday in their trial for the beating of black motorist Rodney G. King, igniting renewed outrage over a racially charged case that had triggered a national debate on police brutality.

Hours after the verdicts were announced, angry demonstrators torched buildings, looted stores and assaulted passersby as civic leaders pleaded for calm. Gov. Pete Wilson deployed the National Guard at the request of Mayor Tom Bradley, who warned residents to "stay off the streets."

Bradley, in a late-night televised

Deputy District Attorney Terry White questions Officer Lawrence Powell on use of baton; headline on officers' acquittal and beating video footage (insets).

afterwards was the brutal beating of a lone black man by a circle of white police officers. Few could watch the scene and not feel outrage, including veteran police officers. LAPD Chief Daryl Gates said the tape left him, "sick to my stomach, sick at heart."

Ironically, in the trial that followed, police trainers and martial-arts experts testified that had the first blows been more brutal—or, at least, more effective—King could have been subdued and arrested with far less violence. Most of the officers' blows—fifty-six separate blows by LAPD estimate—went wild and only bruised King, they said, allowing him to continue to move around instead of taking the required prone position and being handcuffed. "In fact, every investigation of the incident revealed appalling deficiencies in the skills, training, and judgment of the officers who arrested Rodney King," Lou Cannon,

declared, in pre-trial questionnaires, that they were strong supporters of the police.

In these circumstances, the videotape that seemed so damning instead became a liability to the prosecutors. Before the trial, the Simi Valley jurors had also seen only the edited TV version. Several jurors later said that they were greatly surprised to see the full videotape, with King charging Officer Powell before the beating began. To them, it showed that King had resisted the officers, at times violently. And defense attorneys added other details that strengthened this different picture—that King was an ex-convict on parole; that before capture he had led California Highway Patrol officers on an eight-mile-long drunken chase at speeds of more than a hundred miles an hour; that he had refused to cooperate with the arresting officers and had

Denny pulled from truck; Williams points at victim (right).

the *Washington Post* Los Angeles bureau chief at the time, summed up in his detailed reconstruction of the case and its consequences, *Official Negligence: How Rodney King and the Riots Changed Los Angeles and the LAPD.*

At the same time, the fact that King could take all this punishment and still resist reinforced the officers' conviction that King—an imposing man at six feet two inches, well over two hundred pounds and with a weight-lifter's upper body—was not only wildly drunk, but "dusted" on the drug phencyclidine, PCP, sometimes called "angel dust." PCP is widely believed by police officers to make users impervious to pain, potentially increasing their violence and aggressiveness.

Yet most people in and out of law enforcement still considered the videotape to be stark proof of police brutality. Deputy District Attorney Terry White made that case to the grand jury, obtaining indictments of the four officers most directly involved: Sergeant Stacey C. Koon and officers Laurence M. Powell, Timothy E. Wind and Theodore J. Briseno. Eleven days after King's beating, the grand jury indicted the officers for assault with a deadly weapon and assault by force likely to produce great bodily injury. District Attorney Ira Reiner grimly described the case as a "terrible moment" for law enforcement.

White and Deputy District Attorney Alan Yochelson prosecuted the case, and their first big setback came when the trial was moved from multi-ethnic Los Angeles to predominantly white, conservative Simi Valley. They also ended up with an all-white jury, most of whom

been physically strong enough to literally throw two of them simultaneously off his back when they first tried to handcuff him; that he was so strong and belligerent that he continued to resist despite two 50,000-volt shocks from a non-lethal Taser gun; that he had spat blood at a female paramedic and a female police officer and was otherwise irrational, obscene and unpredictable, and that the officers had reason to fear for their own safety until he was finally subdued—because they hadn't been able to search him for a weapon.

In the trial, Sergeant Koon, who had been in charge, also argued forcefully on his own behalf that his big fear was that unless King were overpowered quickly, the violence might escalate to the point that someone—most likely King himself—would be killed. Indeed, Koon told the jury that he had taken control of the arrest when a Highway Patrol officer had pulled her gun, creating a potentially dangerous escalation of the tension. To a jury already sympathetic to police officers, these revelations put a new light on the complete videotape.

While the news media continued to report about the trial as if the videotape assured conviction, White and Yochelson knew that their prosecution was in trouble. They decided that they couldn't risk putting King on the stand. King had told inconsistent versions of the beating and had been drunk at the time. Since then, in conversations with the prosecutors, he had also been unpredictable and sometimes antagonistic.

Meanwhile, the defense brought in witnesses, some from the LAPD,

Denny's smashed-up truck; Williams and Watson gesturing for media cameras (inset).

who were expert in the police use of force. Especially impressive to jurors was Sergeant Charles Duke, a Special Weapons and Tactics (SWAT) team legend and former instructor at the Police Academy. Duke went through the videotape frame-by-frame, telling jurors why each blow and kick to Rodney King was justified. Duke also told jurors that it was certainly LAPD policy to use batons on a suspect if that suspect was combative and hadn't been searched.

White and Yochelson recruited their own LAPD experts, but their testimony was overshadowed by Duke's, with his long experience in the field. The prosecutors wanted LAPD Chief Gates to testify that this use of force was outside LAPD policy. Gates had condemned the beating when he had first seen the videotape. But Gates declined to appear—and the prosecutors were understandably reluctant to bring an angry Chief Gates into the courtroom under subpoena. In the end, White concentrated again on the videotape. He urged jurors, "Now, who are you going to believe, the defendants or your own eyes?"

One of the defense lawyers, Michael Stone, a former police officer himself, countered by reminding jurors that police officers risk their lives in such situations to protect the public, and he referred to a sign he had seen in a police gym: "There are no second-place ribbons in a street fight."

White, in his closing remarks, argued that, "Men and women across this country do their job every day as law enforcement officers without resorting to the violence and brutality...that you have seen on this screen over the last six weeks. What these officers say in here implicitly, if not explicitly, is that they are immune from prosecution... They treated [King] like an animal."

Public opinion polls throughout Los Angeles and Ventura counties showed that the majority of residents of all ethnic backgrounds agreed with that assessment, since the edited videotape seemed to be open-and-shut proof of excessive force. Chief Gates, Mayor Bradley and most LAPD officers predicted convictions of at least some of the officers.

But after a tense week of deliberation, the Simi Valley jurors acquitted all four officers on all counts—with the sole exception of a deadlock on the count against Laurence Powell for assault under color of authority. One juror explained later to *The American Lawyer* magazine that most of the jury felt that Rodney King "is the only criminal, and he's free. And these four men have lost their careers." Dorothy Bailey, the jury forewoman, told author Lou Cannon that the big issue for jurors was whether the prolonged beating of King was within LAPD policy. She and the other jurors decided that it was, based largely on the testimony of Sergeant Charles Duke, the much-decorated LAPD expert.

"In my opinion," Bailey told Cannon, "it's not right or morally acceptable to beat any human being, but if LAPD policy has determined it's right in certain circumstances, we had to go with that and we did."

In Los Angeles, the acquittals, announced mid-afternoon of April 29, created an explosion of shock and anger throughout the city. An all-white jury had acquitted four white officers of beating a black man in an incident that seemed unequivocal on the edited videotape.

The mayor and LAPD top brass, in particular, had been so sure of the guilty verdicts that they had made almost no serious attempt to mobilize officers before the verdicts came down. Indeed, Gates and many top officers were variously away, or off duty, or at a training seminar when the verdicts were read. In a much-criticized incident, Chief Gates himself set out for a fund-raising event on the west side despite early reports of trouble. Many police planners, recalling the pattern of the 1965 Watts Riots, also didn't expect any disturbance, if it came at all, until dark.

But just five minutes after the last "not guilty" echoed in the Simi Valley courtroom, angry crowds began to form at 55th Street and Normandie Avenue. Less than an hour later, rioting had begun with the looting of a Korean-American liquor store, the first of many in what has been termed the worst riot in U.S. history. Over the next five days of destruction, fifty-four people would die, more than twenty-three hundred would be injured, almost nine hundred buildings would be destroyed and property losses would run more than nine hundred million dollars. In the aftermath, 3,294 adults and 333 juveniles would be charged with riot-related felonies. And again, the most widely known incident would be one that was recorded on videotape.

In the first hours of rioting, Reginald Oliver Denny, a 36-year-old truck driver hauling a load of sand, entered the intersection of Florence and Normandie Avenues. He had been listening to music, not the news, and the first he realized something was wrong was when he saw looters stealing from a truck in front of him. He also had no way of knowing that just an hour before, a skirmish line of about thirty police officers, faced with several hundred angry rioters, had retreated from this flashpoint—

and would abandon the intersection to the mob for the next two hours.

A small group of black gang members had taken over the intersection. They waved African-American drivers through untouched. But white, Latino and Asian drivers were dragged from their vehicles, beaten and robbed. Television-news and police helicopters circled overhead, but for three hours there was no authority on the ground.

Antoine "Twan" Miller pulled open Denny's door as he drove slowly through the intersection, to avoid hitting anyone. Others dragged the slightly built Denny out of his truck. Henry Keith "Kiki" Watson kept Denny's head on the pavement with his foot. Denny was kicked, beaten with a claw hammer and struck by various thrown objects. But the attack that would horrify television viewers watching the assault live came from Damian "Football" Williams, a member of the 71 Hustlers, part of the Eight Tray Gangster Crips, a powerful South Los Angeles street gang. Williams, standing close to Denny, smashed him in the right temple with a heavy chunk of concrete. After Denny crumpled, Williams did a victory dance over his unconscious body— like the end-zone dance of a touchdown-making football player, which he had once aspired to be.

Four African-American friends watching the live television coverage saw Denny attacked. And they became the ones who saved his life. No matter their anger at the Rodney King verdicts, they decided, as one of them put it, "Somebody's got to get that guy out of there." The local residents—Titus Murphy, an aerospace engineer, Bobby Green, a trucker, Lei Yuille, a nutritionist, and Terri Barnett, a store-window display designer—drove to the intersection, picked Denny up off the street and drove him in his truck the three miles to Daniel Freeman Memorial Hospital. He was within moments of death, with more than ninety fractures of his skull, when the Good Samaritans brought him in. And they weren't the only black Los Angelenos to brave the mob to save lives. Actor and writer Gregory Alan-Williams hauled badly beaten Japanese-American Takao Hirata to safety through a hail of rocks, bottles and threats. And there were many others.

After order was restored, three of Denny's assailants—Antoine

Henry Keith Watson (left) and Damian Williams face Judge John Ouderkirk in court.

Miller, Henry Watson and Damian Williams—were arrested. LAPD Chief Gates went in person to arrest Williams. They were charged, variously, with attempted murder, aggravated mayhem, torture and robbery. More charges were later added for attacks on other victims, including Takao Hirata. Another Denny attacker, Gary Anthony Williams, who had gone through the victim's pockets after he was beaten unconscious, turned himself in to police the same day. He later pleaded guilty to attempted robbery and received a sentence of three years in prison.

Miller's case was also separated from the others in mid-July, and in a negotiated settlement, Miller pleaded guilty to a felony—assault with a deadly weapon—and two misdemeanors, receiving stolen property and grand theft. He was sentenced in December to twenty-seven months probation, considering time already served while awaiting trial.

The high-profile trial of Watson and Williams, presided over by Superior Court Judge John Ouderkirk in the downtown Criminal Courts Building, began jury selection on August 5, 1993. Deputy District Attorneys Janet Moore and Lawrence Morrison faced difficult challenges. Many South Central residents had begun to rally to the defense of the two gang members. A Free the L.A. 4 Defense Committee, referring to the original four defendants charged with beating Denny, had been formed. One reason that Williams and Watson were attracting support was that District Attorney Ira Reiner had seemed to black residents to have piled-on charges unfairly, including an unusual application of the crime of torture (a count that was later dropped). Reiner had also used his one peremptory challenge to remove the only black judge in line to try the case, Superior Court Judge Roosevelt F. Dorn.

Meanwhile, on August 4, the day before Watson and Williams went on trial, Sergeant Stacy Koon and Officer Laurence Powell had been sentenced for their convictions on federal charges of violating the civil rights of Rodney King, in a much-watched second trial that had been launched after the Simi Valley state-court acquittals. The African-American community had generally felt relief when the two had been convicted. But now, their sentences—drastically reduced from normal guidelines by the federal trial judge, for "mitigating circumstances"—had enraged many Los Angeles blacks all over again. The mitigating circumstances, according to U.S. District Judge John G. Davies, included the fact that King had provoked the actions of Koon and Powell; that Koon and Powell would face more proceedings and punishment as they lost their jobs with the LAPD; that they weren't likely to commit more crimes; that their notoriety would make them targets for abuse in prison, and that they had already essentially been tried for the same crime in state court. Davies reduced what would otherwise have been sentences of from five to seven years in prison, at the least, to thirty months and a fifty-dollar fine. Koon and Powell would be released from prison in 1996.

All this made picking a jury extremely difficult since the jurors came from the downtown, South Central and Koreatown areas most damaged by the rioting, and home to the rioters. Judge Ouderkirk allowed almost any potential juror from the still-tense area to be excused from the trial. And many of the prospective jurors that the prosecutors expected to be most likely to convict didn't want to have anything to do with another highly controversial, highly publicized trial. "We had a tremendous flight of jurors in this case," Moore told Lou Cannon after the trial. "Just hordes of them refused to stay."

The jury finally seated was praised by District Attorney Gil Garcetti, however, for its racial diversity: three Latinos, five Anglos, three African-Americans and one Asian-American. Nine of the twelve original jurors were women. Six alternates were also chosen.

In pre-trial hearings, charges had been added and thrown out. Williams now faced charges of attempted murder, aggravated mayhem, two counts of robbery and six counts of assault with a deadly weapon. Watson was now charged with attempted murder, two robbery counts and two counts of assault with a deadly weapon.

The prosecutors attempted to keep racial tensions to a minimum, in part by reminding jurors that many riot victims were saved by African-Americans, some of whom testified during the trial. There was also little dispute over identifying Williams and Watson as the attackers seen in the videotape of the Denny assault. But Denny himself, on the witness stand, was so kind-hearted towards his recent assailants and their relatives that Moore began to worry that he had done more harm than good with the jury. As she told Cannon later, "He took a lot of guilt off their shoulders and basically said to them, 'Hey, it's okay if you let [Williams and Watson] go."

Williams's attorney, Edi M.O. Faal, contended that events at Florence and Normandie had been too random for Williams to have premeditated an attempt at murder. If Williams had wanted to kill Denny, he easily could have, Faal argued. Faal also regularly signaled to jurors that they should not forget that in this court two white prosecutors were trying Williams and Watson, who were black, before a white judge. "I never lost sight of the racial division in the courtroom," Faal, who is black, later told Lou Cannon. "... Many of the jurors told me afterwards that they got the point."

Meanwhile, supporters of the defendants demonstrated every day outside the courthouse, as well as attending the trial. Outside, demonstrators chanted a simple threat: "No justice, no peace." And one sign read: "The rebellion was justified."

Moore argued to jurors in her closing remarks that Williams and Watson weren't being charged for an angry reaction to the Simi Valley acquittals. "They are here because they acted in a violent and unconscionable way," Moore said. "They are not here because we are holding them responsible for the Los Angeles riot."

So many jurors had fallen by the wayside during the trial that all but one alternate would be on the final panel deciding the verdicts. In the end, ten of the twelve jurors were women, and these were comprised of four Latinos, four African-Americans, two Asian-Americans and two Anglos. In comments made after the verdicts, jurors made it clear that they thought that Williams and Watson had been charged with more crimes than they had committed. Many jurors also thought of them as basically two human beings who had got caught up in the riots, at the wrong place at the wrong time. Whatever their motivations, the jurors returned unexpectedly light verdicts. Watson was convicted of misdemeanor assault on Denny. He later pleaded guilty to a felony charge on which the jury had brought in a hung verdict. He also later violated parole and was sentenced to seven years in prison.

Williams was convicted only of simple mayhem for beating Denny, and of misdemeanor assault against four other victims. Judge Ouderkirk sentenced Williams to the maximum penalty, ten years in prison. With time already spent incarcerated, he would be eligible for parole in fewer than four years.

District Attorney Garcetti described the light verdicts as "incomprehensible." A poll by the Los Angeles Times found that three-quarters of L.A. Latinos, two-thirds of Anglos and more than half of all African-Americans agreed with the proposition that the verdicts were "motivated more by fear for [the jurors'] own safety and of civil unrest" than by "fair and sensible consideration of the evidence." Deputy District Attorney Moore said afterwards that, "We really were up against...a community perception that the justice system is not fair to the African-American."

In 1994, Rodney King won $3.8 million in compensatory damages in a civil lawsuit filed against the City of Los Angeles.

District Attorney Asa Keyes's booking photo.

Public Corruption

os Angeles is the home of the recall—a brisk way of removing a dishonest or incapable public official when no one wants to wait for the next election. In the late 1800s and early years of the new century, an unusual mix of forces came together in Los Angeles to fight corruption with far-reaching reforms. The Progressive movement was active in other cities and states, but nowhere were reformers more dogged in their labors than in Los Angeles.

Los Angeles became a hotbed of political groups, all growing under the Progressive tent—the Citizen's League, the Voter's League, the Municipal Reform Association, the League for Better City Government and the Republican Lincoln-Roosevelt League. The Municipal League of Los Angeles, formed in 1902, a federation of the Progressive groups, believed that charter reform was the first need. In 1902 city voters agreed. The next year, the Los Angeles "Home Rule" charter became the first governmental body in the country to contain the recall provision. In 1904, Los Angeles City Councilman James P. Davenport was ousted in the nation's first recall election—for conniving to award City advertising to the *Los Angeles Times*, though the newspaper's bid was ten thousand dollars higher than its competitor.

Meanwhile, the corruption of individual police officers has been a plague on Los Angeles over the decades, as in most major cities. In 1899, a Committee of Safety hired Pinkerton detectives to investigate the bribery of police officers, whom many believed allowed vice to thrive. The committee's suspicions were confirmed.

In recent years, dangerous rogue cops have been a problem. Two of the most vicious were Richard Von Villas and Richard Ford, who were charged in 1983 for conspiracy to commit murder. They were arrested within moments of killing a Granada Hills nude dancer in a particularly brutal fashion, to make the murder look like the crime of a sexual psychopath. The officers expected to collect one hundred thousand dollars from an insurance policy on her that listed Von Villas as the beneficiary. The two officers were also charged with murder in a separate murder-for-hire scheme. The two offered to mutilate a woman's ex-husband for seventy-five hundred dollars, kill him for fifteen thousand dollars. In the end, they received twenty thousand dollars—and the husband's body has never been found. Ford and Von Villas were convicted in both cases.

Another officer, William Ernest Leasure, said that he was bored writing traffic tickets when he went on a murder-for-hire and theft spree in the 1980s. He killed two people, shooting one woman in the back. He stole yachts, cars and vintage military airplanes, including an F-86 Sabre fighter jet. Over time, he dragged other officers into his exploits. In 1991, Leasure was sentenced to two prison terms of fifteen years to life.

Most public corruption is less dramatic yet spurred by a common motive—greed.

Frank Shaw

Corrupt Los Angeles Mayor Frank Shaw becomes one of the first big-city U.S. mayors to be recalled under laws passed by Progressive reformers. His brother and most of the LAPD leadership come down with him in 1938.

Frank Shaw was elected mayor in 1933 and quickly outdid all predecessors in political and police corruption. Shaw brought in his old friend James E. Davis as chief of police. Joe Shaw, his brother, became his secretary and aide—blatantly selling favors from his City Hall office. Joe Shaw peddled city civil-service jobs, including jobs on the Los Angeles Police Department and the Fire Department, as well as the answers to promotion exams and the promotions themselves, for ambitious workers already on the city payroll. Advancement from fireman to fire captain could be had for two hundred fifty dollars to four hundred dollars; for another four hundred dollars or more,

Left to right: Joe Shaw; Lt. Lynne Kynette; Joe Shaw in court with attorneys Roland Swaffield and Richard Cantillon.

there were jobs as battalion chief. No competitive bids were needed for city contracts—just a suitable bribe. For large industries this might typically run five thousand dollars as a down payment, with five hundred dollars expected every month thereafter.

The Central Vice Squad was riddled with men in Shaw's organization who gave madams and gambling dens plenty of warning when a raid was planned. One well-known brothel owner, Lee Francis, took pride in having Russian caviar and chilled champagne on hand when the officers showed up at the door.

As Frank Shaw headed for a second term, in 1937, honest Los Angelenos were fed up. Restaurant owner and grand jury member Clifford Clinton—of the city's legendary Clifton's Cafeterias—led the reform effort, supported by a group of wealthy Progressives known as the Minute Men. Harry Raymond, a former LAPD detective now working as a private eye, joined the brave crusade as its chief investigator. Superior Court Judge Fletcher Bowron, who would later become mayor himself, served the cause by keeping his reputation for honesty intact as the battle royal developed.

Clinton formed the Citizens Independent Vice Investigating Committee, or CIVIC, a group of five hundred businesses, church and civic clubs. Clinton and two fellow reformers on the grand jury presented a provocative report to the grand jury that same year. "A portion of the underworld profits have been used in financing campaigns [of]...city and county officials in vital positions," the report summed up, "...[While] the district attorney's office, sheriff's office, and Los Angeles Police Department work in complete harmony and never interfere with...important figures in the underworld." The report estimated that at the time, Los Angeles was home to six hundred brothels and three hundred gambling houses, sporting twenty-three thousand slot machines.

Howls of outrage assailed Clinton and his group—from the Shaws, Police Chief Davis, District Attorney Buron Fitts and others in the city establishment. The grand jury foreman called Clinton "public enemy number one" and "the Cafeteria Kid." In physical and financial attacks, Clinton's cafeterias were stink-bombed and hounded by health inspectors, his taxes were raised and his family threatened. Clinton's Los Feliz home was bombed. He and his family were luckily asleep on the undamaged side of the house. Then, only two months later, Lieutenant Lynne Kynette, head of the LAPD's Intelligence Squad, better known as the "red squad," bombed Raymond in his car. Raymond was thought to have damaging information on a police commissioner. Badly hurt, Raymond survived. Kynette called the hospital after the blast, and when he learned that Raymond was going to live, he grumbled, "That's too bad. Next time we will do a better job."

Raymond recovered and testified to the grand jury, which had been ordered by Judge Bowron to investigate the corruption charges. And when the town learned that their own police officers were bombing private citizens, the recall effort was launched. Frank Shaw fell to one of the first mayoral recalls in a major U.S. city, losing in September 1938, to Fletcher Bowron.

District Attorney Fitts seemed not so much part of the Shaw machine as using the grand jury to "settle old scores and to protect old and new friends," according to historian Kevin Starr. Fitts, a bitter political enemy of Judge Bowron, had blamed him when Fitts was questioned by the grand jury about a real-estate deal. Then in 1934, the grand jury had indicted Fitts for perjury for lying in his previous testimony. He was acquitted in 1936.

But as details of the Shaw scandal continued to unfold, Fitts changed his tune. In late 1938, Fitts obtained statements from fire department officers that directly linked Joe Shaw, the brother, to the sale of test answers to firemen taking promotion exams. Fitts generously credited his Chief Deputy Eugene Williams as well as Deputy District Attorneys Vernon Ferguson, Orville Emerson and Tom O'Brien with obtaining the crucial statements.

Fitts also obtained indictments of Kynette and two other police officers for the Raymond bombing. In 1938, Kynette was sentenced to two years to life. Police Chief Davis, who had once bragged that he had ordered his officers to shoot first and ask questions later, was forced to resign, along with twenty-three other top LAPD officers.

Ex-mayor Shaw was never indicted. Joe Shaw was convicted in 1939 of sixty-three counts of selling city jobs and promotions, but he never went to prison.

District Attorney's office 1926; District Attorney Buron Fitts, seated fourth from left.

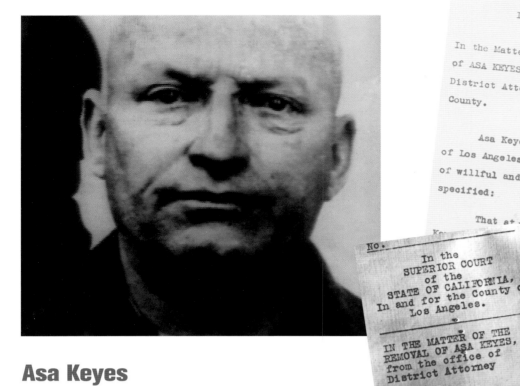

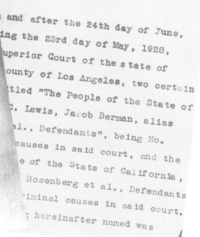

Asa Keyes

A district attorney's reluctant prosecution in the Julian Petroleum scandal brings suspicions of bribery that prove to be true in 1928.

Court observers were puzzled at first when District Attorney Asa "Ace" Keyes, seemed to be unconcerned about the complex prosecution of ten executives of Julian Pete—the high-flying Los Angeles oil company that had collapsed in 1927, leaving forty thousand investors with worthless stock. Keyes had appointed relatively inexperienced Chief Deputy District Attorney Harold "Buddy" Davis as the lead trial attorney. Keyes offered little help himself. A disgusted Superior Court Judge William Duran at one point told the courtroom, "I want the record to show that District Attorney Keyes was present in this court while Davis was arguing with a difficult legal problem without once offering to give him the benefit of his knowledge or assistance."

Keyes did, however, from time to time arrive in court to make surprising motions. In one, Keyes asked the judge to dismiss charges against several of the defendants, including Ed Rosenberg, a major defendant in the Julian Pete case. The judge said no. Keyes also delivered the prosecution's final argument. In it, he laid the blame on only one of the ten defendants and directly contradicted many of the arguments of his two assisting prosecutors, Deputy District Attorneys Julian Richardson and A.H. Van Cott.

The strange behavior was explained after the trial. Two disgruntled employees of a downtown tailor shop hatched a plan to make a little money, by selling a hot scandal to a newspaper. Their former boss, Ben Getzoff, spent most of his time in a back room, drinking bootleg liquor with politicians. One of the disgruntled employees, while still employed at the tailor shop, had kept a diary of the comings and goings of Getzoff's well-known visitors after he noticed that two Julian Pete defendants—Rosenberg and Jacob Berman—had dropped by. Asa Keyes was already a routine guest and beneficiary of Getzoff's "medicinal" liquor cabinet. Keyes's visits during the time of the trial went into the diary as well. When the grand jury learned that this diary was being

offered to the newspapers, it began secret hearings and brought Getzoff's former employees in to testify. In October, the grand jury charged Keyes with accepting thousands of dollars in bribes, with Getzoff as the go-between, to assure acquittals in the Julian trial for Jacob Berman and Ed Rosenberg.

Former Chief Deputy District Attorney Buron Fitts, who had been appointed to that job by Keyes, and who was also the district attorney-elect, became the special prosecutor in the Keyes bribery trial. Early in 1929, Keyes was convicted of accepting golf clubs, a new Lincoln automobile, a chaise lounge and as much as one hundred fifty

thousand dollars from the defendants. With part of the money he had bought a home in Beverly Hills. Davis was convicted of taking a seventy-five-hundred-dollar bribe, though his conviction would later be overturned on a technicality. Ed Rosenberg and Getzoff were convicted of bribery, receiving a sentence of from one to fourteen years each.

Keyes was also sentenced to from one to fourteen years in state prison. But after serving two years in San Quentin, Keyes received a governor's pardon in 1932. He returned to Los Angeles and died in his Beverly Hills home in 1934.

Clockwise from opposite top left: Asa Keyes; accusation documents; Keyes, Deputy District Attorneys Julian Richardson and A.H. Van Cott; prosecutors Buron Fitts (left) and William E. Simpson; Keyes (center) and defense team, including William B. Bierne (far right).

Buron Fitts

A feisty district attorney during the Depression falls under suspicion when a prostitution ring is exposed.

Buron Fitts was a proud veteran of two world wars, returning from World War I with a knee injured from a gunshot wound that would require a score of operations over his life to avoid amputation. He became a leader in the American Legion, which always gave him a strong base of political support. During World War II, Fitts went back into the military, joining the Army Air Force. He commanded combat operations in Europe and North Africa.

Fitts became a deputy district attorney under Thomas Woolwine years and chief deputy under District Attorney Asa Keyes. In 1926, Fitts was elected California lieutenant governor. Two years later, when

Fitts testifies at his perjury trial; (top) with defense attorneys Jerry Giesler and Joseph Scott.

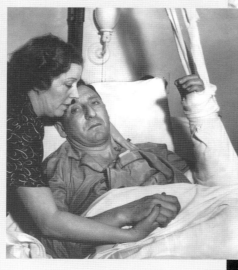

Keyes was indicted for bribery, Fitts was appointed special prosecutor to take charge of the case. Fitts ran for district attorney as well, and won, serving from 1928 to 1940.

In office, Fitts concentrated enforcement efforts on gambling and other vice charges. But in 1930, he ran into trouble himself—in a vice scandal.

A well-known District Attorney's Office investigator, Leslie T. White, had come upon a prostitution ring specializing in underage girls. The ring's madam said that she had supplied young women to several wealthy businessmen, including John P. Mills, a real-estate developer and friend of Fitts. The madam claimed that she had delivered a young virgin every week to Mills. A sixteen-year-old girl was willing to testify against Mills and he was charged with statutory rape. But eventually the other businessmen charged in the case were acquitted. Fitts took the occasion to drop the remaining charge against Mills, saying he lacked sufficient evidence to take Mills to court and that the complaining witness had disappeared.

Political rival Superior Court Judge Fletcher Bowen, a future reform mayor, urged the grand jury to take a close look at Fitts and several other politicians. The grand jury responded with an indictment of Fitts—and his sister, who worked as his secretary—for bribery and perjury. The grand jury charged that Fitts and his sister had sold Mills a low-value orange grove that the Fitts family had owned, receiving much more than it was worth in the trade—essentially a bribe to Fitts to drop the rape charge against Mills. After two years of legal wrangling, Fitts was acquitted at trial. His sister's charges were dismissed.

Clockwise from top: Special Prosecutor Clyde C. Shoemaker in final argument before jury; Fitts, striking forceful pose; shown with wife, Fitts was hospitalized after unknown assailants shot him in the arm near his house.

Arthur C. Harper

In 1909, amid widespread corruption in Los Angeles government, a mayor resigns when he is threatened with recall.

As the story goes, when Mayor Arthur C. Harper and water-department superintendent William Mulholland drove to Owens Valley on Mulholland's initial survey to find a route for the Los Angeles Aqueduct, it would have been easy to track them. Their path was strewn with empty bourbon bottles.

Mayor Harper, a frequent visitor to saloons and brothels around town, was long acquainted with imperfection. Harper was elected in 1906, backed by the considerable and corrupting resources of the Southern Pacific Railroad. Soon after taking office, Deputy District Attorney Thomas Woolwine accused Harper of conspiring with a well-known hoodlum and with his own chief of police to gain control of prostitution and illegal liquor sales in Los Angeles. Harper responded by naming the police chief to the Board of Public Works, which was then in charge of building the aqueduct.

Edwin T. Earl, a reformer and publisher of the *Los Angeles Express*, was another Harper critic, and his newspaper conducted its own investigation, headed by attorney Earl Rogers. Rogers found that gamblers, saloon-keepers and madams were buying stock in such companies as the Los Angeles-Utah Stock Company, Pacific Securities and the Pacific Sugar Company. These existed on paper only—and Harper and some of his police-commission appointees owned most of the stock. The gamblers, bartenders and madams who bought stock were left untroubled in their business by the police. It was a clever protection racket.

District Attorney J. D. Fredericks, who had been elected in 1902, didn't share Woolwine's enthusiasm for the investigation, however. Still, with Rogers's information, the evidence went before the grand jury.

The grand jury declined to indict Harper, announcing that it could find no direct evidence of graft. It did mildly rebuke the mayor for allowing liquor-law infractions to occur. Progressive movement leaders decided on another method to remove Harper— the new charter's recall provision.

Support grew for a recall when the mayor's name turned up in another corrupt scheme. Southern Pacific's Los Angeles land agent and lobbyist, Walter Parker, who also controlled the Southern California Republican Party, bribed City Clerk Harry J. Lelande. For a thousand dollars, Lelande agreed to speed up a city ordinance that would give Southern Pacific a right-of-way through the dry Los Angeles River bed. Despite an outpouring of anger when the bribe became public, the council voted to pass the ordinance.

In the end, a scheme that directly involved Harper brought his downfall. Rogers gathered evidence, including the statement of one of the gangsters involved, that Harper, a police commissioner and the police chief were receiving five hundred dollars a month in protection money from brothel owners. Publisher Earl told Harper that he would hold off printing the story if the mayor stepped down. Only days before the recall election, Harper resigned.

Baldo M. Kristovich

A Los Angeles County public administrator and public guardian is accused of mishandling the estates in his care. He is convicted of perjury in 1972.

Baldo Kristovich was a veteran County employee who started out as a legal research bailiff at $125 a month in 1938. He became a County department head in charge of the Public Administrator and Public Guardian's Office in 1960. This County officer and his staff act as the executor of estates in which there are no heirs. The public administrator's office typically sells at public auction assets ranging from automobiles and personal property to trust deeds and securities. But Kristovich was allegedly doing a little trading on the side, without public bids, and giving family members, friends and prominent acquaintances, as well as himself, some attractive deals.

Kristovich was indicted on October 6, 1971, for a total of twenty felony counts of conspiracy, conflict of interest, preparing false evidence, perjury and grand theft embezzlement. Deputy District Attorneys Donald Eastman and Timothy Flynn prosecuted the case.

Specifically, in half of the case, Kristovich was tried for selling three trust deed notes from one of the estates under his supervision to a nephew, Joseph L. Vicelja, at a big discount over their true values. Vicelja then sold the deeds to Zella P. Dodd, the 79-year-old widow of a construction-company executive. Kristovich, outside his county duties, happened to be Dodd's personal attorney. And Dodd, it was later shown, was senile. In one of the transactions, Vicelja, a supervising engineer with the country road department, bought a note with an unpaid balance of $17,129 for $14,600. In fact, he didn't even pay that. All Vicelja had to pay out of pocket was ten percent of the bid amount ($1,460) and $100 in escrow costs, because he turned around and sold it to Dodd, who paid the difference to the public administrator. Vicelja and Kristovich pocketed $2,529.

The other charges against Kristovich were based on the illegal sale—at below-market prices and with no competitive bidding— of automobiles and other belongings from the estates. A long line of high-level public officials in Los Angeles, from judges to County officers, had gotten good deals on cars from Kristovich. The prosecutors also called more than fifty witnesses, including public officials from Northern California and friends from all over, who had obtained big discounts on television sets, refrigerators, watches and other household furnishings.

Vicelja was charged with four felonies. He was tried along with Kristovich. But the jury acquitted him of grand theft. A juror fell ill after eleven days of deliberations. The prosecutors decided not to use an alternate juror to continue the jury's considerations of the verdicts. Vicelja was free.

Kristovich was convicted on two counts of perjury and two of preparing false evidence. He was sentenced to five years of unsupervised probation and a twenty-five-hundred-dollar fine. Removed from his position, he was never to return to public service again. "The point of that case was to get him out of office," Eastman said. Kristovich was also suspended from practicing law for several years.

Peter F. Schabarum

In a rare use of state campaign-fund laws, a former
Los Angeles County supervisor, state assemblyman and former
grand jury foreman pleads no contest to three counts
of felony tax evasion in 1997.

Pete Schabarum, a nationally known figure because of his leadership in the campaign to impose term limits on politicians, retired from the Los Angeles County Board of Supervisors after two decades, in 1991, at age 62. Under California law, politicians are allowed to keep existing campaign funds if they turn them over to non-profit charitable foundations, which they can create themselves. But the money must be used to further the aims of the foundation—it can't be drawn for the politician's personal use. Schabarum's case was considered the first application of new state laws controlling the use of retired politicians' campaign war chests.

In retirement, Schabarum founded the Foundation for Citizen Representation, dedicated to political education on issues the veteran politician had espoused over the years. But he also took fifty thousand dollars in foundation money and transferred it into and out of another foundation associated with the Los Angeles County Museum of Natural History. Then he used the money to travel to Europe, South America, Africa and other tourist destinations, in some cases accompanied by his wife.

Schabarum was prosecuted by Deputy District Attorneys Susan Steinfeld and Thomas Krag, both with the District Attorney's Special Investigations Division. They had directed a two-year investigation of Schabarum and his foundation. He was charged by the grand jury, in 1997, with three felony tax counts, two counts of grand theft and one count of perjury.

When Schabarum pleaded no contest to the tax charges, just before the case went to trial, lead prosecutor Steinfeld dropped the grand theft and perjury counts. He was sentenced to three years probation, three years of community service and to pay more than sixty-five thousand dollars in restitution, back taxes and other penalties. Schabarum also agreed to dissolve his foundation.

Schabarum's defense attorney, John Barnett, said that the former supervisor wanted to avoid a trial over "accounting problems."

Steinfeld begged to differ. "This is a man who ran the County budget and its billions and billions of dollars for twenty years," she said. "And now he says he doesn't understand finances and that he was going on the advice of others? He's not accepting personal responsibility, when of course, he should be. He's the one who did this, knowingly, intentionally." Schabarum, after his sentencing in a near-empty courtroom, said quietly, "I have no reputation."

In 1998, Superior Court Judge Charles Horan reduced Schabarum's felony tax-evasion convictions to misdemeanors. "I made a mistake," Schabarum admitted in the hearing that resulted in the sentence reduction. Deputy District Attorney Krag had strongly opposed the reduction, and was disappointed with the outcome. Nevertheless, he said afterwards, "He is a convicted felon and the fact will remain that he is a convicted felon. It doesn't change history."

Los Angeles County Supervisor Pete Schabarum.

Art Snyder

Former Los Angeles City Councilman-turned-political lobbyist Art Snyder finds himself, his wife, other relatives and his law firm's staff in trouble over campaign funds laundering.

When Art Snyder left the Los Angeles City Council in 1985, after eighteen years in office, he didn't leave politics. He became one of the most influential political lobbyists in Los Angeles. Snyder had been controversial throughout his nearly three decades of political life. But early in 1995, Snyder, his wife Delia Wu Snyder and five others in his law firm, as well as the firm itself, were indicted on charges of campaign money laundering. These were the first criminal indictments developed from a three-year investigation by the state Fair Political Practices Commission and the Los Angeles City Ethics Commission.

Specifically, Snyder and the others were charged with conspiring to make contributions to local and state politicians in someone else's name—a way of illegally circumventing contribution limits. The city council members, county supervisors and state and federal elected officials who received the funds apparently didn't know they were illegal.

The funds listed in the indictments totaled sixty thousand dollars. But companies that had done business with Snyder and his law firm were ensnared in the probe as well. The Evergreen shipping firm, based in Taiwan, paid an $895,000 fine for laundering $170,000 in campaign money. Snyder's brother-in-law, William Wang, was the Los Angeles manager of Evergreen.

At first, Snyder snubbed the charges. "You'd think there wasn't any crime in Los Angeles anymore—there weren't burglars and robbers running around," Snyder told the *Los Angeles Times*. Snyder also argued that because he was a lobbyist and not a candidate, he should have been punished only with an administrative fine.

Deputy District Attorneys Gail Ehrlich and Katherine Mader described Snyder's argument as a "legal absurdity." The Supreme Court would ultimately agree, rejecting Snyder's claim that lobbyists are immune from prosecution.

On September 5, 1996, more than a year and a half after the indictments were filed, Snyder pleaded guilty to nine misdemeanors—one conspiracy charge and eight counts of violating the ban on making campaign contributions in someone else's name. His six-month jail sentence was postponed pending appeals.

Los Angeles City Councilman Art Snyder (left).

Charles E. Sebastian

A popular mayor and former police chief ends up mired in a personal scandal and resigns in 1916.

He was a hero as a police chief, once helping to capture a crazed railroad worker who showed up at a police station with more than fifty sticks of dynamite, threatening to blow up the building. Charles Sebastian was also a handsome man, and though married, drew the attention of many women around town. His friends prodded him to run for mayor, and in the 1915 election, he did.

His campaign rallies were standing-room-only, while his opponents' drew only handfuls of supporters. But Sebastian's political enemies played rough. They discovered that Sebastian had a long-time mistress, Lillian Pratt. Two months before the election,

Charles Sebastian

Sebastian was arrested for contributing to the delinquency of a minor. Edith Serkin, Pratt's 16-year-old sister, told the District Attorney's Office that she was always present when the two lovers spent time together at the Arizona Hotel. She testified at a three-week trial that she had seen them "dally sexually." Despite this, the jury acquitted Sebastian and he remained the front-runner by a wide margin.

The night before the election, persons unknown fired two pistol shots at him. On election day, Sebastian was arrested on another trumped-up charge—that he had faked the attempt to murder him, to gain sympathy in the election. He was elected and the charges were dropped.

Sebastian's relationship with Pratt continued. But Sebastian's wife, Elsie, discovered letters from her husband to Pratt, which hadn't been mailed. One said, referring to an official trip, on which his wife had accompanied him, "I wish you could have been along instead of the Old Haybag." Elsie Sebastian took them to the *Los Angeles Record*, which had loudly opposed Sebastian. The newspaper printed the lot under the headline, "The Haybag Letters!" Now the public turned against Sebastian. He resigned in September 1916, after just a year in office, citing ill health. He worked at various jobs after that, including a stint as an investigator in the District Attorney's Office—a job given him by District Attorney Thomas Lee Woolwine, the same man who had tried to put him in jail. His last job was running a gasoline service station. His wife divorced him and he moved with the loyal Lillian Pratt to a cottage in Venice, where he died in 1929.

Rampart

An LAPD officer in an elite anti-gang unit is prosecuted for stealing cocaine from a police evidence lockup. He reveals a pattern of lawlessness among fellow officers that results in a wide-reaching scandal.

The Rampart Division of the Los Angeles Police Department serves a geographically small but densely populated inner-city district between downtown Los Angeles and Hollywood. Its predominately Latino and Korean-American population of 375,000 residents has long been plagued with street gangs. The area was particularly hard hit during the 1992 riots, especially in Koreatown. The Rampart Division is literally one of the most active police stations in the country and it made aggressive use of an LAPD program called Community Resources Against Street Hoodlums, or CRASH, meant to focus an elite group of officers on gang crime.

In early March 1998, six pounds of cocaine were checked out from the central property room of Parker Center, LAPD headquarters, supposedly as evidence in a drug trial. By the end of the month, with the cocaine not returned, an internal LAPD investigation was begun. In August, Officer Rafael Perez, a member of the Rampart Division's CRASH unit, was arrested on suspicion of stealing the cocaine, intending to sell it. In December, his first trial ended with a hung jury.

Former Rampart Division Officer Rafael Perez.

Nine months later, during jury selection for his second trial, Perez pleaded guilty to the cocaine theft. In return for a sentence of five years in prison, Perez agreed to name other officers in the Rampart Division who had planted evidence to obtain arrests, who had beaten suspects, who had covered-up unjustified shootings, who had routinely indulged in perjury and who had committed other criminal offenses.

No matter that many of the defendants had long criminal histories, in all cases in which these tainted officers had been the primary link to the evidence that obtained a conviction, the District Attorney's Office had no choice but to move to set those convictions aside.

As the dimensions of the corruption became clear, District Attorney Gil Garcetti estimated that hundreds—and potentially thousands—of cases would have to be reviewed in a process that could take years. Agreeing with Garcetti, Los Angeles County Public Defender Michael Judge noted that more than eight hundred cases were potentially tainted by some involvement with Perez alone and would have to be reviewed. Another two thousand five hundred cases involved CRASH officers who had either been fired or who were under investigation. Of highest importance were those cases in which defendants were still incarcerated.

The scandal widened. CRASH units from other districts, including the 77th Street Division, also came under scrutiny. The City of Los Angeles began paying out hundreds of thousands of dollars in civil settlements to residents who asserted that LAPD officers brutalized

them and lied about incidents that led to arrests and criminal trials. Though city attorneys often stated that in particular incidents police actions were correct, the Rampart scandal engendered such widespread suspicion of police credibility that the City became leery of risking enormous judgments if they allowed these civil cases to go to trial. Mayor Richard Riordan estimated that the scandal would cost the City alone more than $40 million—including civil-case settlements, legal costs and the price of reforms at the LAPD.

For the District Attorney's Office, the cost to review the County's criminal convictions hit $4.3 million by July 1, 2000, with no quick end in sight. Prosecutors had to review each criminal case in detail, since in trials involving several defendants, only some of the convictions may have had to be set aside. In one case, for instance, prosecutors moved to set aside a 27-year-old woman's guilty plea to one count of selling a controlled substance. Perez admitted that he and another officer had lied when they stated that the woman had sold rock cocaine in person to the other officer, fabricating the detail that she spat the cocaine out of her mouth. But a co-defendant, convicted in the same case, had been convicted with other, untainted evidence. That conviction was left intact.

By late July 2000, with more than forty prosecutors, investigators and clerical staff assigned to the district attorney's Rampart team, close to a hundred convictions had been overturned. The LAPD's CRASH units had been disbanded. And criminal complaints ranging from perjury to attempted murder had been filed against the first four officers to face charges arising from the scandal.

Los Angeles Police Chief Daryl Gates (far right) comforting family of slain detective Thomas Williams: daughter Susie and son Ryan.

In the Line of Duty

etired District Attorney's Office investigator Leslie Turner White, in his 1936 memoir, *Me, Detective*, described how he and his colleagues reacted to the shooting of a police officer during the height of a war among organized gangsters in 1931. White was then part of District Attorney Buron Fitts's Gang Squad. Five gang members had just shot and paralyzed a Long Beach police officer, W.H. Waggoner, and White would be making a raid along with officers from the LAPD and other agencies. "It was one thing for gangsters to shoot a gangster, but Waggoner was a cop," White recalled, "...and we had only one treatment for cop-killers! The public's indifference only increased our enthusiasm. To the public a cop was just a mugg paid to die for about a hundred and fifty bucks a month... We were grimly determined to break up this organization as soon as possible—for our own protection... It was tacitly understood that once this mob was cornered, no prisoner would be taken. They were cop-killers!"

Seven decades later, the prospects for police officers were more encouraging. By the end of the century, murders of officers on their jobs were in a substantial downtrend. In fact, FBI figures for 1999 showed that, nationwide, forty-two were killed, the lowest number of feloniously slain officers in thirty-five years. The use of handguns against officers also declined substantially.

Most—sixteen percent—were killed on disturbance calls. Ten percent were killed in ambushes, like that of LAPD investigator Thomas Williams in 1985. In about a third of cases, again as in the Williams case, the ambushed officers are attacked off-duty.

Support for the families of slain officers has improved as well. Police departments now prepare in advance to help families of men and women in these high-risk jobs. Concerns of Police Survivors, or COPS, a non-profit organization, offers help to both families and police departments. Like D.A. Investigator White, the group is determined to see that justice is done, sooner or later.

The Death of Thomas C. Williams

In 1985 a veteran LAPD officer is gunned down in front of his child by an armed robber he testified against.

When he saw it coming, he yelled to his son, "Duck!" Off-duty LAPD detective Thomas C. Williams, 42 years old, was a thirteen-year veteran of the Los Angeles Police Department. He was picking up his 6-year-old son, Ryan, at the Faith Baptist Church day-care center in Canoga Park, after work. His son was getting into the passenger side of Williams's truck when the detective caught a glimpse of a man in a car across the street. He warned his son, and as the boy quickly crouched, the masked shooter sprayed bullets into the detective, the truck and the crowded building behind. Williams, hit eight times, fell dead. Miraculously, no one else was injured.

Earlier in the day, Williams, the investigating officer on an armed robbery case, had appeared at the trial of Daniel Steven Jenkins, age 30, but had gone back to the North Hollywood station because he was not needed in court. The case had gone to the jury that afternoon. Deputy District Attorney Maureen Duffy-Lewis, who had prosecuted the case, was, like Williams, apprehensive because Jenkins and his accomplices were violent—and Jenkins was free on sixteen-thousand-dollars bail.

In 1979, Jenkins, a limousine-service owner, had pleaded guilty to assault with a deadly weapon after shooting the father of a boy who had filed a police report about him. The previous July, George Carpenter, theater manager and star witness in the current robbery case, had been shot five times and nearly killed as he was eating in a restaurant—in what turned out to be an attempt to keep him from testifying against Jenkins.

Jenkins and four others were charged with murder and conspiracy to commit murder for the ambush slaying of Williams. Jenkins was also charged with the attempted murder of Carpenter. Three of the five cases were severed from those of Jenkins, the primary suspect, and co-defendant Ruben Antonio Moss. Deputy District Attorney Richard L. Jenkins, no relation to the defendant, was assisted by Deputy District Attorney E. William Gravlin in prosecuting the police-slaying case in 1988. The prosecutor put three witnesses on the stand who testified that the defendant had offered them as much as ten thousand dollars to help him kill Williams before he could testify in the robbery trial. All had refused. After Williams testified, Jenkins—who had obtained an illegal Mac 10 machine pistol that proved to be the murder weapon—simply killed Williams for revenge, the prosecutor argued. A close friend of Jenkins whose murder-conspiracy charges were dropped when he agreed to testify for the prosecution, said that on the day of the ambush, Jenkins had told him, "I had to take care of it myself."

The day after Williams was killed, the first trial jury convicted Jenkins of the 1984 robbery of George Carpenter. After a five-month trial, the second jury convicted him of conspiracy to commit murder and of murdering Williams in retaliation for the performance of his duties, a special-circumstance charge. The jury also convicted Jenkins of Carpenter's attempted murder.

Deputy District Attorney Jenkins told jurors that the defendant "killed Detective Williams in the shadow of the cross," outside the church day-care center. Daniel Steven Jenkins was given a death sentence. Moss was also convicted of murder and sentenced to life in prison without possibility of parole.

The bail rules under which Jenkins had been set free during his robbery trial were toughened after the Williams murder.

Detective Thomas C. Williams.

The Death of Julie Cross

The first female U.S. Secret Service special agent killed in the line of duty is shot in an attempted robbery in 1980.

Special Agent Julie Cross, 26, a former San Diego police officer, had joined the Secret Service in October 1979. At about 9:15 p.m. on June 4, 1980, less than a year later, and after only three days in her latest assignment, she and partner Lloyd Bulman were in their parked unmarked car on a dark neighborhood street near Los Angeles International Airport. They were on stakeout as a perimeter chase team to prevent the possible escape of suspects being investigated for counterfeiting. The airliners flew so close overhead that they could barely hear anything.

Two armed robbers, unaware that Cross and Bulman were federal agents, approached the car from behind. When Cross saw the gunman coming, she got out and drew her handgun. Bulman tried to get out of the driver's seat but had a gun thrust to his head. He told the men that he and Cross were "police officers." Not believing him, one of the would-be robbers said that he was too. The four struggled, two on each side of the car. The attacker on the passenger side grabbed the agents' twelve-gauge shotgun from the front seat. As Cross dove back into the car for protection, the killer hit her with two shotgun blasts. Then he came around to the driver's side, where his partner was on the ground wrestling with Bulman. He fired another shotgun shell only six inches from Bulman's head, but somehow missed. "I was stunned," Bulman said later, "because I thought that he had just blown the side of my face off." Apparently believing that Bulman was dead, the killers fled.

The Los Angeles law-enforcement community and the public were outraged. But suspects and evidence were elusive. The Cross killing remained unsolved until 1987.

That year, LAPD investigator Richard "Buck" Henry was promoted to homicide detective in the West Los Angeles Pacific Division and assigned a pile of unsolved cases to work on, including a triple murder and the apparently unrelated Cross killing. He developed new evidence to link Andre Stephen Alexander to the 1978 triple slaying. Deputy District Attorney Sterling "Ernie" Norris filed murder charges against Alexander and an accomplice. In 1990, Deputy District Attorney Lester Kuriyama, now assigned to the triple-murder case, won three first-degree murder convictions. Alexander was sentenced to life in prison.

Then a former girlfriend of Alexander approached Kuriyama and Henry with information implicating Alexander in the Cross murder. Two years later, and twelve years after Cross's death, Deputy District Attorney Susan Speer of the Crimes Against Police Officers Section filed charges against Alexander in the Cross slaying—one count of murder, with the special circumstances of murder of a peace officer engaged in the performance of her duty, as well as murder during a robbery. The statute of limitations had run out on any charges that could have been filed for the attempted murder and robbery of Bulman. Kuriyama, assisted by Deputy District Attorney Lorraine "Loni" Petersen, prosecuted again. Alexander was given a death-penalty sentence in 1996. Twenty years after the slaying, his partner in the Cross murder had yet to be publicly identified.

When the death sentence was announced, Kuriyama described Alexander as a "very, very violent career criminal... For two decades he's been committing crimes. He's killed four people and tried to kill two others. Even in jail he attacked and choked a deputy sheriff. He can't even get along in jail, let alone out here in society."

President Bill Clinton congratulates prosecution team; Deputy District Attorneys Petersen and Kuriyama (flanking president); Detective Henry (second from left).

The Death of Ian James Campbell

Two plainclothes police officers are kidnaped in Hollywood in 1963. In a horrific denouement depicted in Joseph Wambaugh's *The Onion Field*, an officer is brutally executed.

On a Saturday night in Hollywood, March 9, 1963, two young plainclothes LAPD officers, Ian Campbell and Karl Hettinger, stopped a car after it made a suspicious U-turn on a side street. In the maroon Ford with Nevada license plates were two ex-convicts out to rob a liquor store—Jimmy Lee Smith and Gregory Ulas Powell. The officers approached the Ford with flashlights, but without their guns drawn. Smith got out from the passenger's side and raised his hands. Powell, who was driving, got out then turned quickly and put a pistol in the face of Campbell. Then he got behind the officer, grabbed him by the back of his coat, and marched him around the back of the car. Hidden behind Campbell, he told Hettinger to give up his gun. Hettinger reluctantly complied when Campbell told his partner, "He's got a gun in my back. Give him your gun." Powell and Smith put the officers in the Ford, with Campbell driving, and headed to Bakersfield.

Ninety miles from Hollywood, they got off the freeway and Powell directed them to an onion field, not far from a lighted farmhouse. As they neared the field, Powell told the officers that they would be let go there, and that they could use a telephone at the farmhouse to call for help. They all got out of the car, the two officers standing side-by-side with their hands raised. Then Powell said to Campbell, "We told you we were going to let you guys go, but have you ever heard of the Little Lindbergh Law?" Powell was referring to a California statute that allowed prosecutors to ask for the death penalty in a case in which a kidnapping victim is harmed. The law didn't apply in this situation, however.

"Yes," Campbell replied, nonetheless. Powell raised his gun and shot the officer in the mouth. Campbell was thrown on his back by the impact. Then either Smith or Powell stood over Campbell and fired four more bullets into his chest, with the officer's own gun. Hettinger yelled and took off after Powell's first horrifying shot. Hettinger clambered over a fence, ripping his clothes, then weaved down the road and across the furrows. Powell and Smith fired into the night but missed him. Then Powell started trailing Hettinger on foot while Smith took the car and went down the road to cut Hettinger off. Hettinger, careening across the fields in terror, came across a farmer, Emmanuel

Defendant Jimmy Lee Smith (far left) directs LAPD investigators in crime reenactment. Arrow shows where Hettinger jumped fence in escape.

McFadden, who had just finished plowing a field by moonlight. Hettinger told him that they were now both in danger from the killers. McFadden's tractor was being overtaken by the approaching lights of the Ford. McFadden and Hettinger abandoned the tractor and ran through the fields, eventually reaching another farmhouse four miles from the killing spot. The farmer and his wife took them in, the farmer and his son got their guns out, and Hettinger called the Bakersfield police. Smith, meanwhile, just kept driving, got on a highway and left Powell searching for Hettinger in the onion field. Smith ran out of gas and was arrested in a Bakersfield rooming house. Powell was arrested later that night in another stolen car, on his way back to Los Angeles. A flashlight marked "Hettinger LAPD" was found in the car.

Deputy District Attorney Marshall Schulman prosecuted the case. Deputy Public Defenders John Moore and Kathryn McDonald defended Powell. Attorney Ray Smith defended Smith. Superior Court Judge Mark Brandler, a former deputy district attorney, presided.

Powell and Smith were charged with one count each of first-degree murder. Though other charges could have been filed, Schulman reasoned that he didn't want jurors to have lesser crimes to choose among. He considered the death penalty the only appropriate sentence for the two killers. Schulman was also intent on proving that Smith,

As for Officer Hettinger, immediately after the shooting he had told detectives as they debriefed him that he was positive that while Powell was shooting at him, Smith had shot down at Campbell. But by the time the trial began, Hettinger was having second thoughts. He told Schulman that he was no longer one hundred percent certain that it had been Smith. He thought so, but was no longer sure.

The trial was bitterly fought, and it was bizarre at times. Powell told the judge that he had been reading legal texts and wanted to represent himself, which was denied. Later, he claimed that he'd tried to commit suicide after the murder, but had jerked his hand away just before firing the gun.

Smith disrupted the proceedings with rambling statements about his family and his diet, as well as repeated requests for a new attorney. "I might as well defend myself as to have him sit here for me," Smith said, referring to his court-appointed attorney, Ray Smith— no relation—"and it don't do any good and I'm goin' to the gas chamber anyway." Jimmy Lee Smith's requests to represent himself were also denied.

But one sharp exchange between the prosecutor and defense attorney Moore would prove to be more important than it first appeared. Moore had objected to the testimony of a detective who had interrogated

Karl Hettinger.

Ian Campbell.

not Powell, had stood over Campbell and fired the four last shots into the officer's chest. That would be necessary for a first-degree murder conviction.

But the matter was complicated. Both Smith and Powell said that the other one had fired those four shots. The five shots had indeed come from two different guns. Powell admitted that he fired the first shot; the four additional shots came from another weapon.

This made Smith the more likely candidate to have fired the last four shots. Smith conceded in court that he remembered seeing Campbell's coat and arm twitching as each shot entered his chest.

Powell shortly after his capture. Powell had been questioned without an attorney present.

"I object on the grounds it is a violation of this defendant's constitutional right to have the presence of an attorney or the advice of an attorney at any time."

"Oh, that is a frivolous objection," Schulman countered.

"I will cite the district attorney for misconduct," said Moore testily.

"And I will cite *you*," Schulman responded.

"And move for a mistrial at this time," continued Moore, in a strategy that he would employ with almost every prosecution witness.

Each time Moore objected to testimony introduced in the trial that had been obtained without a defense attorney present, Judge Brandler overruled the objection. And he denied all Moore's motions for a mistrial on that point.

Despite the trial's many distractions, both defendants were convicted of murder, and on September 12, 1963, both were given the death penalty.

But a series of U.S. and California Supreme Court decisions—strengthening defendants' rights to counsel during questioning, and the right to remain silent until that occurs—culminated in the federal *Miranda* ruling of 1966, which required a specific code of conduct to be followed during police interrogations. Though investigators had indeed told Powell and Smith that they had these rights, in 1969, the California Supreme Court found the warnings insufficient under the new standard and ordered a new trial for the killers. The District Attorney's Office had seen a reversal coming because of the state Supreme Court's 1965 *Dorado* ruling, upon which Miranda was based. Deputy District Attorney Phil Halpin had already been assigned to prosecute the next onion-field trial.

In an even more contentious battle—ultimately split into two trials—Halpin was joined by Deputy District Attorneys Pat McCormack,

Joe Busch, Raymond Byrne, Dino Fulgoni and Sheldon Brown. Deputy Public Defender Charles Maple represented Powell. Irving Kanarek defended Smith. In just one of an unending stream of acrimonious moments, Kanarek accused Halpin of wearing a handgun into the courtroom one day. For the next day and a half, prosecutors and counsel wrangled—until it became clear that Halpin, during a recess, had asked one of the bailiffs his advice about buying a pistol, and had briefly stuck the bailiff's gun into his belt.

Both killers were convicted again, nonetheless. Smith this time was given life imprisonment. Powell again received the death penalty. But Powell's sentence was switched to life in 1972, when the death penalty was abolished in California.

Smith served nineteen years in prison and was paroled in 1982. Since then, however, Smith has been returned to prison several times, on parole violation, drug-use and other convictions, most recently in 1996. Powell has sought parole since his first review date in the early 1980s. But he is expected to spend the rest of his life in prison.

Officer Hettinger, who remained haunted and disturbed by the scene in the onion field, resigned from the police department. He eventually moved to Northern California to manage a commercial nursery. He died in Bakersfield in 1994.

Defendants Jimmy Lee Smith and Gregory Powell.

The Deaths of Kevin Burrell and James MacDonald

The first Compton police officers to be murdered in the line of duty are shot execution-style by a gang member in 1993.

Officer Kevin Michael Burrell, 29 years old, and Reserve Officer James Wayne MacDonald, 24, both in uniform, were driving to investigate a late-night disturbance on a rainy February 22, 1993. On their way, they stopped a red Chevrolet pickup truck for a traffic violation. Regis Deon Thomas, 21, a member of the Bounty Hunters street gang, was behind the wheel. As the officers attempted to arrest Thomas, pulling his arms behind him to attach handcuffs, Thomas broke free and pulled out a nine-millimeter semiautomatic hand gun. He fired rapidly at the officers, who despite their bullet-proof vests were both hit in vulnerable parts of their bodies. Then, with both officers wounded and incapacitated on the ground, and at a point at which Thomas could have escaped, he paced around, methodically

Deputy District Attorney Mark Arnold contended that Thomas had attacked the two officers because he was on parole from a previous perjury conviction. Possessing the gun was a parole violation. "He knew from previous experience that he was going to jail," Arnold told the court.

Defense attorney Jay Jaffe argued that while Thomas resembled bystanders' descriptions of the man who killed the officers, his was a case of mistaken identity. When Thomas's girlfriend and mother of their four children, Dashaunna Cody, revealed that she and Thomas had recently had a jailhouse wedding, Jaffe unsuccessfully argued that this precluded her testimony against her new husband. Part of that testimony was that Thomas often borrowed her red Chevrolet pickup. Detectives had also found a nine-millimeter handgun in Cody's purse. Cody's gun and Thomas's gun had been stolen at the same time from a Las Vegas sporting goods store.

Arnold videotaped the testimony of witnesses at the preliminary hearing, predicting that the trial might be a year away and witnesses could be hard to reassemble. It was a prescient move. When the trial began, only two of the four most important witnesses were available to testify—a mother and her teenage son who had been driving by the scene at the time of the killings. They had been threatened

Officers Kevin Burrell and James MacDonald.

shooting each in the head. Neither officer had a chance to draw his own gun.

The manhunt went on for weeks, failing to turn up the killer. Slowly, from witnesses' accounts, police narrowed the investigation to one suspect, whom the department named to the news media. Thomas learned that he had been identified on a television news report. He quickly surrendered to a television reporter who accompanied him to the police station.

Thomas was charged in the murders of Burrell and MacDonald. He would be tried during the same trial on earlier charges of murder, possession of illegal weapons and perjury, in the downtown Los Angeles Criminal Courts Building.

if they testified and were not identified by the police. A young woman in their car had apparently fled to avoid testifying. A man who testified that he had helped Thomas get rid of the murder weapon, and had heard Thomas boast of the killings, was in Arizona avoiding extradition. He told police that he had been threatened too. And he had sued the City of Compton and Los Angeles County for negligence, alleging that because investigators hadn't relocated his mother as promised, she had been shot to death by the gang in revenge for his testimony. He was also the key witness, since he was the only one who could positively identify Thomas.

Thomas was convicted of the officers' murders and sentenced to death.

The Death of James R. Barton

After the murder of a San Juan Capistrano storekeeper, Sheriff Barton and a volunteer posse chase a gang of *bandidos*. Four of the posse, including Barton, are killed.

In January 1857, word arrived in Los Angeles that a gang of robbers led by Pancho Daniel, a desperate character who had escaped from San Quentin in a bloody outbreak, was headed toward Los Angeles. Another leader of the marauding group was veteran criminal Juan Flores. Their aim, word had it, was to slaughter Yankees. The ladies of the American families in Los Angeles were gathered in the Armory Hall while the men stood guard around them. Then news arrived that George W. Pflugardt, a German-born storekeeper in San Juan Capistrano, had been killed and robbed as he made his dinner. The arrogant bandits had eaten his meal after they killed him.

Sheriff Barton, who was considered brave but reckless, formed a party of volunteers and headed south to find the gang. At the San Joaquin Rancho, eighteen miles from San Juan Capistrano, Don Jose Andres Sepulveda told Barton that the gang had set a trap for him and that they had twice the men that he had in his posse. Sepulveda recommended sending a messenger to round up more volunteers. But Barton plunged ahead the next morning. With only five other men, Barton met the gang in Santiago Canyon. Two posse members escaped alive after the fighting. Daniel himself was said to have killed the sheriff, shooting him in the heart, left arm and right eye.

Now the City declared martial law and organized for its defense. The effort to bring Daniel and his men to justice was expanded. The California Legislature sent money. The U.S. Army sent troops from Fort Tejon and San Diego to help guard the town. Groups of mounted men began to scour the countryside for the gang, which had disbanded. General Andres Pico, brother of the last governor under Mexican rule, Pio Pico, was particularly lauded for his dashing success in tracking down the offending *bandidos* and hanging them on the spot. Juan Flores and fifty-one others from the gang were captured and brought back to Los Angeles.

Then the Vigilance Committee took over, setting up its own court system, with "Judge" Jonathan R. Scott presiding. Scott, a prominent attorney, was said to have brought a keen appreciation of lynching with

The late Murder of Sheriff Barton and Three of his Party.

In our last publication we alluded to the report which had arrived here, at a late hour on Friday evening, of the murder of the Sheriff and three of his party, by a gang of robbers which has infested the county for some ti[...]

him when he immigrated from Missouri. When a suspected murderer was brought in, Scott asked the crowd to determine his fate. Inevitably, someone yelled, "Hang him!" Then, as Harris Newmark remembered in his memoirs, *Sixty Years in Southern California*, Scott intoned, "Gentlemen, you have heard the motion; all those in favor of hanging So-and-So, signify by saying, Aye!" The mob would then head to the jail, shove the jailer aside, and hang the accused. Eleven of the gang, including Flores, met this fate.

In 1858, Daniel was caught and brought to Los Angeles. He was prosecuted by District Attorney Ezra Drown and defended, at one point or another in the extended proceedings, by various attorneys, including Kimball H. Dimmick and Cameron E. Thom. But Los Angelenos got tired of Daniel's time-consuming defense. Claiming bias, he had the court dismiss nearly two hundred prospective jurors, as well as the coroner. Dimmick won a change of venue, to move the trial to Santa Barbara. But before he could be moved, Daniel was lynched. The coroner's jury concluded that, "the deceased came to his death by strangulation, by a crowd of persons unknown."

Top to bottom: headline on Barton's murder; Andres Pico; posse co-leader Tomas Sanchez with fellow Angeleno John Wilson.

The Death of Martin Ganz

Manhattan Beach Officer Martin Ganz.

An armed robber and killer is apprehended and convicted after killing the first Manhattan Beach police officer to die in the line of duty in 1993.

Two days after Christmas of 1993, in the affluent but quiet Los Angeles suburb of Manhattan Beach, Officer Martin Ganz was on patrol, with his 12-year-old nephew in the passenger seat. He pulled over a motorist for a routine traffic stop near the Manhattan Village shopping center. Leaving his nephew in the car, Ganz walked up to the driver's side of the Daihatsu he'd stopped. As he approached the car's window, the driver turned and shot Ganz. The police officer ran back to his patrol car. The gunman got out of his car and chased Ganz, continuing to fire at him. Ganz lunged over the rear of his car. As he crouched on the ground, the gunman shot Ganz in the head. Then he went back to his own car, pointed the gun at the boy, but didn't shoot. He drove off.

Two witnesses at the scene helped police produce a composite drawing of the suspect. Detectives investigated more than a thousand tips, but the gunman could not be identified. Then Oregon law-enforcement officials sent to Southern California authorities the description of a suspect they were hunting for a robbery and murder near Portland in 1994. A witness in that incident had managed to follow the killer long enough to get a license-plate number and good description of the automobile, a Daihatsu similar to the one spotted at the scene of Ganz's murder.

The license plate led to Roger Hoan Brady, 27, son of a former television reporter, who was arrested six hours later at his parents' home in Vancouver, Washington. He was on parole after two years in prison on a federal bank robbery conviction, from a 1989 holdup in Agoura, California. He had also been ordered into a drug-treatment program at the time.

One of the two Manhattan Beach witnesses to the Ganz killing went to Oregon and identified Brady as the shooter. Ballistics tests also showed that a gun in Brady's home was used to kill the Manhattan Beach officer.

In February 1996, Brady was sentenced to life in prison for the murder of a hospital nurse in a Safeway parking lot in Beaverton, Oregon, after he had robbed the supermarket. He was extradited to Los Angeles for trial in the Ganz death.

Deputy District Attorney Barbara Turner prosecuted the case in 1998, in Torrance Superior Court. The jury deliberated two days, finding Brady guilty of murder with special circumstances—that the murder was of a police officer and that it was committed to avoid a lawful arrest. Early in 1999, Brady was sentenced to death.

The Death of William C. Getman

A new Los Angeles County Sheriff dies in a gun battle with a suicidal killer in 1858.

On January 8, 1858, District Attorney Ezra Drown told the Court of Sessions, the state criminal court at the time, "The painful duty devolves upon me to announce to this honorable Court, the mournful intelligence of the death of Wm. C. Getman, late Sheriff of Los Angeles County. Mr. Getman was yesterday, while in the discharge of his official duties, struck down by the hand of an assassin—hurried into eternity without a moment's warning. His death has cast a gloom over our city and county, which time alone can dissipate."

Billy Getman had only been sheriff for four months, having run a popular gambling house in a one-story adobe before that. But Drown praised the "brave and energetic" officer for much improving the security of citizens in the rough-and-ready town since he had been elected.

On January 7, a livery-stable owner on Aliso Street complained to Getman that an insane man wandering about should be picked up before he hurt someone. Getman had heard other reports of this maniac, known only as Reed, a man newly arrived from Texas. Getman took two deputies and found Reed barricaded in a pawnshop called Monte Pio. He had asked the pawnshop owner, among other bystanders, to kill him. "I want to speak to you," Getman told Reed.

"Keep away from me, don't come near me," Reed replied. Then he ran outside and pulled a pistol he'd taken from the pawnshop.

"You don't want to shoot me," Getman told him. "I merely want to speak a few words to you—don't shoot." But Reed fired, hitting Getman in the left breast.

"Boys, I am shot," were the Sheriff's last words, delivered as he fell.

The gunman ran back into the Monte Pio, where he held off the deputies for a time, armed with two derringers, two pistols and a bowie knife. He wounded one of the officers, but was finally shot and killed, as he had earlier requested.

Los Angeles Star headline on Sheriff Getman's death.

"Alphabet Bomber" Muharem Kurbegovic.

Notorious

Journalists, the saying goes, make the first cut of history. And when that history-in-the-making sets readers' interest on fire, the news usually appears on the front page. It should be no surprise that thirty percent of newspapers' front-page stories are about criminals and their prosecutors, the courts and the police, according to a study a few years ago by Roy Edward Lotz, a sociology professor at the John Jay College of Criminal Justice, City University of New York.

Certainly readers and those who follow the news on television and radio deserve to know developments that could literally mean life or death. There is a practical and civic-duty side to a report that an Alphabet Bomber is on the loose in Los Angeles, planting bombs at Los Angeles International Airport and at the Greyhound bus station; or that a preschool staff in a quiet beach town has been accused of more than a hundred counts of child molestation. The McMartin Pre-School case not only made Los Angeles parents reconsider their own children's safety but brought national attention to the crime itself, spurring both improvements in day care monitoring and, in some cases, overzealous responses.

The notoriety of many Los Angeles criminal cases, in fact, has made the Los Angeles County District Attorney's Office well known around the world and a highly sought-after place to work by well-trained young lawyers who want to make their mark in the justice system.

Los Angeles has always offered a stimulating array of true-crime stories that for reasons rooted in human nature are difficult to ignore. Former *New York Daily News* crime reporter David Krajicek once described what he considered his specialty's journalistic origins: "Going back to the Middle Ages, traveling balladeers made their daily bread by going from village to village singing songs and reciting poems about war and atrocity in the neighboring villages, and we sat in those villages and said, 'Yeah, give us more, give us more.' We're still sitting around saying, 'Give us more, give us more.'"

The *Los Angeles Times* managed to put out an edition on the bombing; publisher Harrison Gray Otis (top right); bodies were removed from rubble in caskets.

Clarence Darrow and the *Los Angeles Times* Bombing

After union-management relations explode in 1910, the celebrated attorney faces bribery charges.

At the turn of the last century, battles between business and organized labor were intense and often violent. In Los Angeles, labor-management antagonists were particularly belligerent and the then-conservative *Los Angeles Times* was an emblematic non-union shop. In 1890, Harrison Gray Otis, *Times* editor and publisher—"his face beet red, his neck veins bulging purple," as historian Kevin Starr described it in *Inventing the Dream*—had ordered all union typographers off the premises. He had cut his printers' salaries by twenty percent, then replaced them with non-union workers when they went on strike. Otis and other Los Angeles boosters were convinced that only an open-shop, cheap-labor town could grow and compete in the industrial world. A strike by metal workers was the focus of the Los Angeles labor struggle in 1910.

On Saturday, October 1, eight sticks of dynamite went off in the *Times* building at First and Spring Streets, killing twenty workers, most of whom were burned to death in the fire that raged after the explosion. Otis had no doubts about the culprits from the first instant. The next day's front page carried a headline that read: "Bomb Exploded by the Enemies of Industrial Freedom" and under a photo of the destruction, "The *Times* Building Yesterday, After the Unionist Bomb and Fire Had Destroyed the Great Newspaper Plant."

District Attorney J.D. Fredericks and his Chief Deputy W. Joseph Ford preferred an investigation, however. The City of Los Angeles hired private detective William J. Burns to do its share of the inquiry. An Otis-backed business group hired renowned criminal attorney Earl Rogers to act as a special prosecutor under Fredericks.

Burns named as the bombers two brothers, James B. and John J. McNamara of Indianapolis, who were members of the International Association of Bridge and Structural Iron Workers. Another key figure was veteran union dynamiter Ortie McManigal. The suspects apparently were spirited back to Los Angeles by Burns without benefit of extradition. But before coming West, McManigal had confessed and implicated the McNamara brothers, promising to testify against them. When the McNamaras reached Los Angeles, they were charged with murder.

Union supporters and the McNamaras maintained that they were innocent and being railroaded. Various theories were developed about the *Times*

catastrophe. Most McNamara supporters believed that it had been a simple, if catastrophic, accidental gas explosion—and Darrow was pondering the use of a scale model to prove this at the trial. The extremist view was that Otis had arranged the bombing himself, to discredit organized labor.

The national labor movement put up two hundred fifty thousand dollars as a war chest, hiring Clarence Darrow, the best-known criminal lawyer in the country, to head the defense team. Attorneys Joseph Scott and LeCompte Davis, a former deputy district attorney, assisted Darrow, as did in a lesser capacity, Cyrus McNutt and Job Harriman. Harriman was a strong labor supporter who was leading the field in the upcoming mayoral elections, running on the Socialist ticket.

By December 1, 1911, the trial had dragged on almost seven weeks and jury selection hadn't even been completed. The stakes were mounting. Otis wanted the brothers to hang. A victory for the McNamara brothers would greatly improve labor's tarnished image, which would enhance their organizing efforts and, in Los Angeles, would strengthen Harriman's chance to become mayor. The election was only four days away.

Unknown to the public, muckraking journalist Lincoln Steffens, who was reporting the trial for a newspaper syndicate, had been quietly engineering a compromise among Fredericks, Darrow, the McNamara brothers, city officials and Harrison Gray Otis and Harry Chandler of the *Times*.

By Thanksgiving, Steffens and Darrow had known that the prosecution had a strong case against the brothers—James McNamara for making and planting the bomb, and his brother, John, for orchestrating the dynamite campaign from Indianapolis. For one thing,

District Attorney Fredericks (top left), Defense Attorney Earl Rogers (right); charred interior of Times building.

Darrow had hired almost a hundred investigators to try to find holes in McManigal's damning confession, but without success.

There was strong physical evidence. President William Howard Taft had interceded by directing the U.S. Attorney General to have federal officers search the Iron Workers' Indianapolis headquarters. They had found incriminating books, letters, notes and clippings, as well as a store of dynamite in the basement.

But Darrow had another problem as well. In late November,

James and John McNamara.

a prospective juror, and then a seated juror, accused a detective for the defense of trying to bribe them to acquit. Bert Franklin, the detective, had previously worked for the U.S. Marshall's Office and the District Attorney's Office. He was arrested in the act of handing over one of the payoffs—with the implication that Darrow was involved. The detective was arrested and an indictment for Darrow seemed likely.

Steffens's attempt at an agreement wasn't easily accomplished, but he finally forged—or thought he forged—a city-wide labor-business settlement. The deal was to trade guilty pleas from the McNamaras in exchange for non-death penalty sentences—life for James McNamara, the bomber, and ten years for his brother. Any investigations of other union members involved in the bombing would be dropped. Finally, a labor-capital summit conference would be scheduled to help to heal the city's wounds. But this version of the deal, if there ever was one, was only honored by the defendants.

On December 1, the brothers pleaded guilty. On election day, December 5, they were sentenced. But contrary to the apparent peace agreement, Judge Walter Bordwell stridently attacked the defendants. James McNamara got his life sentence, but his brother was given fifteen—not ten—years.

The guilty pleas were an enormously deflating surprise to union supporters, though they were no surprise to the major figures involved. District Attorney Fredericks explained the turnaround simply: "Because they were guilty." Darrow told incredulous supporters: "They had it on us. The County had a complete case. There was no loophole." James McNamara said that he pleaded guilty to save his brother.

Outside the courtroom was pandemonium. Around the country, unions denounced the McNamaras and Darrow for betraying

the cause. Disgusted Job Harriman supporters threw their campaign buttons into the Los Angeles gutters and defeated him at the election. Historians agree that the the union movement in Los Angeles was set back for the next three decades.

The following January, Bert Franklin, the defense detective, pleaded guilty to the juror-bribing charge and testified before the grand jury. The grand jury indicted Darrow on two counts of bribery, which the District Attorney's Office chose to prosecute at separate trials.

Darrow hired his recent adversary, Earl Rogers, to defend him in the first trial. District Attorney Fredericks, Chief Deputy District Attorney Ford and Deputy District Attorney Arthur Keetch prosecuted Darrow.

The case of the first alleged bribe was angrily argued by both sides, but ended with a standing-room-only courtroom of spectators when Darrow gave a final, emotional plea for his good name. "I am on trial," said Darrow, his eyes overflowing with tears, "because I have been a lover of the poor, a friend of the oppressed, because I have stood by labor for all these years." More convincingly, perhaps, he also argued that no one who had spent thirty-five years in court would be so stupid as to attempt such a transparent bribe. In twenty-seven minutes, the jury came back with a not-guilty verdict.

At the second trial, in which Darrow represented himself, the jury hung. Fredericks declined to try Darrow again on the second charge and Darrow left town.

Five years after the bombing, in a final breach of the long-lost labor-management agreement, District Attorney Thomas Woolwine and future District Attorney Asa Keyes prosecuted two more figures in the *Times* bombing. Milton A. Schmidt and David Caplan were convicted and sentenced to life and ten years in prison, respectively.

Clarence Darrow.

David H. Clark

A former deputy district attorney, known as "Debonair Dave," is charged with two murders in 1931.

Political insider and crime boss Charles H. Crawford, also known as the Gray Wolf, and Herbert Spencer, publisher and editor of the political magazine *Critic of Critics*, were waiting in Crawford's fortified Sunset Boulevard office in Hollywood. It was May 30, 1931, in the late afternoon. Crawford controlled the bootlegging trade in Los Angeles, and his office—equipped with four phones, various bars, locks and other security devices—was a star chamber of power-brokering behind the scenes. Crawford himself, as one political reporter described him, was the "white-haired stormy petrel of local politics." Whatever ensued when their visitor finally arrived, he left both men dead or dying of gunshot wounds. Spencer died right away, with a bullet in his heart. Crawford, hit in the abdomen, was taken to the Georgia Street Receiving Hospital. There, police officers he knew asked who did it.
At first, Crawford said he didn't recognize the man. Then he admitted that he had, but would go to his grave before identifying him. Then the Gray Wolf died.

Witnesses who had seen a man leaving the scene had a detailed description, however. And the next evening, David H. Clark, "Debonair Dave," a highly regarded if flamboyant former deputy district attorney, surrendered to District Attorney Buron Fitts in the Hall of Justice parking lot. Clark was charged with both murders. The motive was money, prosecutors believed.

Fitts brought back former Chief Deputy District Attorney W. Joseph Ford as special prosecutor in the Clark cases, assisted by Deputy District Attorney A.H. Van Cott. And in an unusual prosecutorial move, Ford would try Clark separately for each crime, in a separate trial. Ford didn't deny that his strategy of filing the murder charges one at a time was to force the defense to reveal its arguments in the first trial, giving him a second chance to convict Clark if the first failed. Defense attorney Leonard Wilson complained that the ploy was "unworthy, unfair, and a needless burden to the taxpayers." Clark's co-defense attorney was W.I. Gilbert.

Ford first tried the Spencer murder, arguing that Clark had been in financial trouble and had bought the murder weapon only the day before the killing. In his defense, Clark blamed the Gray Wolf, contending that Crawford had tried to induce him to help frame the police chief on a morals charge. When Clark angrily refused, Crawford and Spencer pulled their guns and Clark shot them in self-defense. The jury deadlocked eleven to one for acquittal. Ford tried Clark a second time for the Spencer murder, and this time Clark was acquitted. Noting how juries had rejected prosecution arguments in the Spencer trials, the District Attorney's Office declined to go to trial on Crawford's death and dropped the charge. Clark continued his career in private practice and became known for representing various local mobsters.

More than two decades later, Clark, who was again in difficult financial straits, was living with a former law partner. When the law partner's wife accused Clark of taking advantage of the couple's generosity, he killed her with a shotgun blast. Clark pleaded guilty to second-degree murder. He died of a stroke a month after he began his term in Chino State Prison.

David Clark with wife, Nancy Malone Clark.

Chief Deputy District Attorney W. Joseph Ford examining weapons evidence.

W. JOSEPH FORD

SPENCER THORPE JR.

W. I. GILBERT

LEONARD WILSON

A. H. VAN COTT

DAVE CLARK

Newspaper photo of prosecution and defense in Clark case.

Sirhan Bishara Sirhan

In 1968, the killer of Robert F. Kennedy goes on trial to determine what form his inevitable punishment will take.

At 12:15 a.m. on June 5, 1968, having won the crucial California primary in his bid for the presidency, Senator Robert F. Kennedy was shot by Sirhan Sirhan, a 24-year-old Palestinian immigrant. Just over a day later, Kennedy died.

With more than two-dozen people in the room, and the murder weapon in Sirhan's hand when he was subdued, there was little serious doubt that he had pulled the trigger. Some witnesses claimed to have seen a woman in a polka-dot dress leaving the hotel with a male companion after the shots were fired, claiming, "We killed him." But ultimately, the Los Angeles Police Department dismissed the notion of a second killer or conspiracy, speculating that the woman, who was never found, had said, "*They* killed him." During the trial, both sides agreed that Sirhan had been the lone shooter.

Sirhan pleaded not guilty on August 2. He had asked for an attorney from the American Civil Liberties Union. The ACLU attorney had helped to put together a group of lawyers who had experience representing minority defendants. Attorney Grant Cooper would lead the team, which included Russell Parsons, a former deputy district attorney, and Emile Zola Berman. Chief Deputy District Attorney Lynn D. Compton was lead attorney among the prosecutors, who included Deputy District Attorneys John Howard and David Fitts. Superior Court Judge Herbert V. Walker would hear the case.

The trial opened on January 7, 1969. Early on, both sides proposed a plea-bargain—Sirhan would plead guilty in return for life in prison, instead of risking a death sentence before a jury. District Attorney

Clockwise from top: Campaign button; Sirhan escorted to court; prosecution team, **Chief Deputy District Attorney Compton (center), Deputy District Attorneys Howard (right) and David Fitts (left).**

Mortally wounded Kennedy supported by hotel employee (right).

Evelle Younger and the prosecutors liked the deal because their psychiatric examinations of Sirhan, who claimed not to have any memory of the shooting, strongly suggested that he was schizophrenic. In Judge Walker's chambers with Younger and the other prosecutors, and Cooper and his defense team, Younger urged Walker to approve the plea bargain, in the interests of avoiding a long, traumatic and expensive trial that would inevitably result in the same sentence. Younger agreed that the major evidence, reports and interviews that would have come out in a full trial, would be made public.

But Judge Walker, uncomfortable with the idea of another non-public resolution of a high-profile assassination—just as Lee Harvey Oswald's killing precluded a full public trial in the John F. Kennedy assassination—was reluctant to give his approval. Another plan

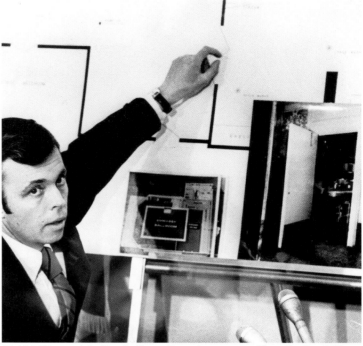

District Attorney John Van de Kamp discussing re-opened investigation,1975.

was developed: Sirhan would plead guilty, but there would be a trial in the penalty phase, where the basic arguments of both sides would be heard. This looked more reasonable to Walker.

Then a *Los Angeles Times* story about the secret plea-bargain meetings appeared. Sirhan and defense attorney Parsons now resisted. Sirhan, they said, had a right to tell his story and to support Palestinian rights, as he had intended. Attorney Abdeen Jabara had also joined the defense team by then. Jabara represented a group of wealthy Arab-Americans who saw the Sirhan trial as a political platform as well. Jabara opposed a plea bargain. The trial went ahead.

The prosecution argued that Sirhan had killed Kennedy after Kennedy publicly supported selling fifty U.S. Phantom jets to Israel. Notes found at his home had included the phrase "R.F.K. Must die!" The defense, as expected, pleaded diminished mental capacity. Sirhan did not like being called crazy. At one point, Sirhan yelled, "I request that my counsel disassociate themselves from this case completely. Just execute me!" Nevertheless, the defense put seven doctors on the stand to state that Sirhan's mental capacity was much reduced, making premeditated murder impossible.

Compton summed up the prosecution with a tough speech that one observer described as "an ice cold shower." Compton said, "If you buy those so-called experts, you have to turn him loose. But if you don't...there's nothing left but a plain old cold-blooded first-degree murder." The jury voted guilty of first-degree murder. On May 21, Sirhan was condemned to the gas chamber. That changed to a life term when the California Supreme Court abolished the death penalty in 1972.

Shortly after taking office in 1976, District Attorney John Van de Kamp reinvestigated the Kennedy death because of continuing speculation about a conspiracy and a possible second gun being fired. The Sirhan gun was test-fired and the Ambassador Hotel pantry was re-examined, under the direction of Deputy District Attorney Stephen Trott. Former prosecutor Vincent Bugliosi was present, representing critics of the original findings. Most of those who had been suspicious came to agree that Sirhan was solely responsible for Kennedy's death.

Ehrlichman in press interview.

John D. Ehrlichman, G. Gordon Liddy, David R. Young, Egil "Bud" Krogh Jr.

Watergate West brings the first subpoena issued by a state court judge for the testimony of a sitting President in 1974.

Setting the stage for the June 1972 Watergate burglary was the September 1971 burglary of the office of Daniel Ellsberg's Beverly Hills psychiatrist, Dr. Lewis Fielding. Three months before, *The New York Times* had begun publishing articles based on the Pentagon Papers, the top-secret history of U.S. involvement in Vietnam. Ellsberg, a senior researcher at the Massachusetts Institute of Technology's Center for International Studies, had leaked the documents to the newspaper. John D. Ehrlichman, President Richard Nixon's domestic affairs advisor, had formed an extralegal intelligence unit called the Plumbers—to plug information leaks and to do political intelligence work. Now angry and embarrassed by the Pentagon Papers leak, Nixon told Ehrlichman to find damaging information on Ellsberg before Ellsberg's upcoming espionage trial. Ehrlichman, Egil Krogh and David Young sent G. Gordon Liddy and E. Howard Hunt, two fellow Plumbers, to Beverly Hills.

Deputy District Attorney Stephen Trott.

Ehrlichman had heard that Ellsberg suffered from "emotional and moral problems." Psychiatric reports to prove this would help to discredit him. When Nixon later learned about the Fielding burglary, he and his top aides termed it a national-security matter, which became part of the Watergate coverup and impeachment charges.

On September 4, 1973, the Los Angeles County Grand Jury indicted Ehrlichman, Liddy, Krogh and Young on burglary, conspiracy to commit burglary and other charges stemming from the Fielding break-in. Deputy District Attorney Stephen Trott was in charge of the investigation of the case. Less than a month later, the "Saturday Night Massacre" took place, in which Watergate Special Prosecutor Archibald Cox, the U.S. Attorney General and deputy attorney general were either fired or resigned. With that, Watergate West was the sole active case in the Watergate scandal.

Attorneys for the defendants planned to argue at trial that the four had been lawfully working on a national-security mission for the White House. Defense attorneys petitioned Superior Court Judge Gordon Ringer for a subpoena to require President Nixon's testimony to support this argument. Ringer issued the subpoena, but Nixon rejected it. Then the subpoena was overtaken by a federal case that took priority.

On March 7, 1974, just five months before Nixon would resign, new Watergate special prosecutor Leon Jaworski indicted Ehrlichman, Liddy and four others on federal charges for the Fielding burglary. Jaworski asked District Attorney Joseph Busch to dismiss all but one of the Los Angeles charges, which he did. Busch and Jaworski issued a joint statement noting that the issues in the case "involve matters of national interest and therefore would be decided in the federal court system."

Deputy District Attorney Richard Hecht (right) and District Attorney Investigator Bill Burnett arriving in Washington, D.C.

Eulia Love

In 1979, when LAPD officers shoot a resident who owes $22.09 on her gas bill, the District Attorney's Office changes its response to such officer-involved incidents.

Eulia Mae Love, age 39, a South Central Los Angeles housewife, was a recent widow. Her husband, William Earl Love, had died from sickle-cell anemia in June 1978. Now her sole income was his Social Security benefit of six hundred eighty dollars a month. As Christmas of 1978 drew near, money was so tight that she asked her oldest daughter, age 17, to support herself and to find another place to live. Among the many bills that Love owed was a six-months overdue Southern California Gas Company bill that required payment of $22.09 by the first of the new year—or the gas would be shut off.

On the morning of January 3, 1979, a meter man came to either collect or turn off the gas. In an altercation, Love hit him in the arm with a shovel and he withdrew from the scene, reporting what had happened to his supervisor. Love then walked to a local supermarket and bought a money order for $22.09, and returned home. At 4:00 p.m. that afternoon, a Gas Company supervisor came, this time waiting in his car for LAPD officers to accompany him. According to Love's teenage daughter, Love tried to give the supervisor the money order, but he only rolled up his car window while he waited. An enraged Love went back into her house and returned to the front lawn with an eleven-inch boning knife. Edward Hopson, a veteran police officer, and Lloyd O'Callaghan, a four-year LAPD veteran, arrived in a squad car. They told her to drop the knife.

Love swore at the officers, then turned to walk back into her house. O'Callaghan knocked the knife out of her hand with his riot baton. She picked it up as Hopson said, "Don't do it, lady; don't do it." She was throwing it at O'Callaghan, according to a District Attorney's Office investigation, when the officers fired their weapons. Twelve rounds were discharged. Eight hit her, and she died on the spot. South Central residents were outraged.

District Attorney John Van De Kamp ordered a three-month investigation of the shooting. He concluded that, "There is no legal or evidentiary basis for a murder charge [against the officers] because the evidence shows the killing was in self-defense." Van de Kamp also ruled out involuntary manslaughter charges. As one offshoot of the incident, however, Van De Kamp created special roll-out teams of District Attorney's Office investigators and lawyers to quickly respond to and assess officer-involved shootings.

Muharem Kurbegovic

The "Alphabet Bomber" kills three people and injures thirty-six in a 1974 bombing at Los Angeles International Airport.

The implausible saga began in 1971, when Muharem Kurbegovic, 28, a Yugoslavian immigrant, was tried for masturbating in a dance hall restroom. Municipal Judge Alan Campbell presided. Though Kurbegovic was acquitted, two years later he set fires at the homes of Campbell and two Los Angeles police commissioners, Emmet C. McGaughey and Marguerite Justice. He also planted an arson device in the gas tank of McGaughey's car, but the gasoline failed to ignite. The police commission had denied Kurbegovic a license to open his own taxi-dance ballroom.

On August 6, 1974, he set off a bomb in a locker in the overseas lobby at Los Angeles International Airport. More than three hundred people were packed into the lobby, many of them in the check-in line for a 9:00 a.m. Pan American flight to Hawaii. Three people were

Airport lobby after bombing.

Kurbegovic in court.

killed instantly and thirty-six wounded, fourteen of them seriously. He left a tape-recorded message directing police to an even larger bomb hidden in the Greyhound bus station. Police recovered and safely detonated the device. Through this period, using the name Isak Rasim, ostensibly the chief military officer of a group called Aliens of America, Kurbegovic was also making phone calls and planting tape-recorded messages that claimed credit for other crimes and demanded changes in U.S. immigration and sex statutes. He became known as the "Alphabet Bomber" because he vowed to set off bombs at sites with names that would eventually spell out Aliens of America, "until our name has been written on the face of this nation with blood."

Two weeks after the airport bombing, LAPD officers arrested him after he placed another taped message in the restroom of a Western Avenue take-out restaurant. Kurbegovic, who entered the country legally, had been working as a design engineer with a research and development company. He was charged with felony

counts that included three counts of murder with special circumstances, multiple counts of violating the state dangerous weapons law by exploding a destructive device causing great bodily injury, charges stemming from the Greyhound terminal bomb and the arsons of the officials' homes.

Deputy Public Defender Gerald Chaleff was appointed to defend Kurbegovic, though Kubegovic would later act as his own attorney during the trial. At his arraignment, Deputy District Attorney Stephen Trott argued successfully that he be held without bail because one of the special charges could bring the death penalty. Deputy District Attorney Dinko Bozanich prosecuted the case at trial.

The trial, in 1980, took eight months—following six years of legal procedures surrounding the question of Kubegovic's competency to face prosecution. Thoughout the trial he ridiculed the judge, jurors, attorneys and the audience. He called himself "the Messiah." Occasionally, he wore a vest bearing the seven-headed cobra of the extinct Symbionese Liberation Army.

Bozanich obtained convictions on all twenty-five counts. The death-penalty statute under which Kurbegovic had been charged was abolished while he was in custody, eliminating the chance of a death sentence. When he received a life term, he held up a sign reading "I shall return!" Superior Court Judge Nancy B. Watson said at the sentencing, "I don't know if Mr. Kurbegovic is the most dangerous man in custody but I consider him the most dangerous person that I know of."

"Bite your tongue," snapped Kurbegovic.

Bozanich, pointing to the long delays Kurbegovic had forced in the case, said he "tried to sabotage the system and it didn't work." Twenty years after his conviction, Kurbegovic's bomb-making capability and past experimentation with nerve gas still set him apart, Bozanich said. "There is no doubt in my mind that he is still the most dangerous man in custody in California."

Raymond and Peggy McMartin Buckey

One of the longest criminal trials in history,
over alleged child molestation at the McMartin Pre-School,
ends in 1990 with no one satisfied.

The preliminary hearing by itself took eighteen months. The trial took almost three years. Half the jurors were replaced by alternates by the time deliberations began. And in the end, the two remaining defendants were set free. It was both one of the longest and likely most expensive criminal trials in history.

In the early 1980s, child molestation was just being recognized by the general public. So in 1983, when the mother of a two-and-a-half year-old boy told Manhattan Beach police that her son said he'd been sodomized at a local preschool, the matter was taken seriously. Examination showed that he had in fact been sexually abused. The mother said he had told her that "Mr. Ray" had done it. During the investigation, Manhattan Beach police sent parents a form letter with questions that prompted hundreds of families to be concerned that their children had been exposed to a ring of child molesters and pornographers.

In the end, eleven Manhattan Beach families would testify that their children had suffered from incidents that included rape, sodomy, oral copulation, being photographed in pornographic settings, playing "naked games," being forced to watch animal mutilations, sacrifices and satanic rituals. At the beginning of the preliminary hearing, seven people—Raymond Buckey, his mother Peggy McMartin Buckey, his sister, his grandmother and three teachers—were charged with more than three hundred counts of criminal conduct. Deputy District Attorneys Christine Johnston, Lael Rubin and Glenn Stevens were assigned the prosecution.

By the end of the preliminary hearing, however, the scope of the impending trial had been narrowed to sixty-five counts. Then District Attorney Ira Reiner, who in 1984 succeeded Robert H. Philibosian, dropped charges against all but Raymond Buckey and his mother. The trial of the two remaining defendants, on fifty-two counts, began in July 1988.

It was a bruising ordeal for the prosecutors and defense attorneys, as well as the families on both sides. Deputy District Attorneys Roger Gunson and Lael Rubin prosecuted the Buckeys. Attorney Daniel Davis represented Raymond Buckey. Dean Gits defended his mother. In a clamorous development, Stevens publicly expressed doubt that the Buckeys were guilty. He eventually testified for the defense and signed a deal to help make a movie of the trial—much to the disgust of the testifying families.

But the deepest controversy developed

Deputy District Attoneys Lael Rubin and Roger Gunson.

over the credibility of the interviews of the children. They had been conducted by Children's Institute International, which, with the deluge of terrified parents, had hired extra, untrained therapists to interview many of the suspected victims. When videotapes of these interviews were shown at trial, the therapists often seemed to be suggesting responses to the youngsters. As jurors later stated, this caused doubt

McMartin Pre-School, Manhattan Beach, California.

even when bolstered by testimony from physicians that the children had truly been molested. Also confusing to jurors were hard-to-believe testimony—such as one child who said that Raymond Buckey had killed a horse with a baseball bat—and references to child pornography that could never be found.

In January 1990, the jury acquitted Raymond Buckey and his mother on all but thirteen counts, on which it deadlocked. Superior Court Judge William Pounders dismissed the one remaining count of conspiracy against the mother. District Attorney Reiner decided to retry the remaining twelve counts against Raymond Buckey. Deputy District Attorneys Joseph Martinez and Pamela Bozanich were assigned to that case. But after an eight-week trial, the new jury deadlocked as well. Reiner decided against a third trial and dropped the remaining charges.

Afterward, most jurors in the first trial said that they believed that some of the children had been abused, but that they weren't confident that the Buckeys were responsible. The videotaped interviews were also unconvincing to most on the panel. In fact, most criticism from the jury was directed at Children's Institute International.

"We ultimately must respect the jury's decision," prosecutor Rubin said after the first verdicts came in, "even though I personally disagree with it." Reiner would later blame "incredibly weak" evidence for the problems that plagued the prosecution.

Left to right: Raymond Buckey, defense attorney Danny Davis, Peggy Buckey, defense attorney Dean Gits; interviewing therapists used dolls to role-play with suspected victims (inset).

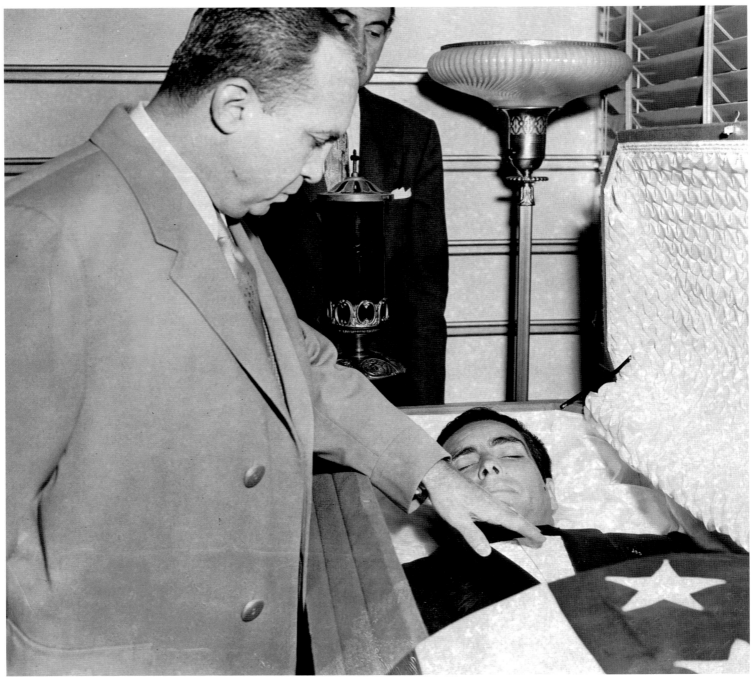

Mickey Cohen visits the coffin of his pal, Johnny Stompanato.

Criminal Cohorts

ven mobsters themselves call the California organized crime world the "Mickey Mouse Mafia." Los Angeles, San Diego, San Jose and San Francisco have always been considered places of lesser organized criminals, not cities dominated by a single powerful family syndicate as in many East Coast cities. Part of the reason is that California is considered, in mob geography, to be an "open territory," as are Las Vegas and Miami. The open territories are simply too big, with too much money to be made, for any one mob family to be able to control. The open territories are constantly subject to intruders from other organized gangsters.

In Los Angeles, this meant that even Jack Dragna—dubbed by reporters and public officials as the "Al Capone of Los Angeles"—had to give way in 1937 when East Coast syndicate bosses sent Benjamin "Bugsy" Siegel to Los Angeles. Charles "Lucky" Luciano had sent word to Dragna warning him to accommodate Siegel, who was "coming West for the good of his health and the health of all of us." Siegel was sent to develop gambling and other rackets, without regard for Dragna's modest efforts. Siegel soon had a nationwide bookmaking operation and began the creation of Las Vegas as a gambling oasis, without calling upon Dragna for assistance, or cutting him in. And even after Siegel's death, Dragna had to put up with Siegel's successor, Mickey Cohen.

Los Angeles has spawned other home-grown criminal groups as well—clannish criminals who haven't always taken the form of traditional organized crime. Members of the Symbionese Liberation Army considered themselves revolutionaries. And the Manson Family or the Nazi Low Riders are worlds apart from the expensive suits and big plans of a Bugsy Siegel. Yet to the victims of criminal cohorts, the distinction may not be too important.

Benjamin "Bugsy" Siegel

The East Coast syndicate sends a handsome killer to Los Angeles, in 1937, to build a gambling and rackets empire.

Charming, occasionally psychopathic Benjamin "Bugsy" Siegel got his nickname, which he hated, from his maniacal fits of anger—he went bughouse. Yet he became a popular figure, especially in Hollywood, after he came to Los Angeles in 1937 at the behest of East Coast organized crime bosses who wanted a piece of the lucrative Southern California vice market. Siegel prospered running a national book-making business, smuggling drugs, blackmailing and in other rackets.

But on the night of November 22, 1939, Harry "Big Greenie" Greenberg was Siegel's main concern. Greenberg was a New York mobster who had unwisely threatened to give information to federal prosecutor Thomas Dewey's New York racket-busting investigation unless mob bosses Meyer Lansky and Frank Costello sent him five thousand dollars right away. Instead, they had sent a hit man named Allie "Tick Tock" Tannenbaum. But in Canada, Tannenbaum learned that Greenberg was hiding in Los Angeles. The East Coast hoods decided to have their Los Angeles representative, Siegel, assist in the matter. "Big Greenie" was gunned down that night after buying a newspaper near Hollywood and Vine Streets.

Then in 1940, Tannenbaum himself started talking to New York investigators, and he gave up several names, including Siegel's, as Greenberg's killers. District Attorney Buron Fitts brought Tannenbaum before the Los Angeles County Grand Jury, which indicted Siegel for the murder. When LAPD detectives came to arrest Siegel at his mansion in the Holmby Hills, he hid in the attic until they found him. But the charges were dropped when the Brooklyn, New York, district attorney said he couldn't spare two key witnesses from a trial in New York.

One of those key witnesses was Abe "Kid Twist" Reles. In 1941, Reles became available. District Attorney John Dockweiler decided to try again, and Siegel and one Frankie Carbo went on trial in January, 1942. Deputy District Attorney Arthur Veitch prosecuted the case. Attorney Jerry Giesler defended Siegel. Tannenbaum testified against

Left to right: "Bugsy" Siegel; his trial jury; Deputy District Attorney Arthur Veitch with Detective Leroy Sanderson points to a map; headline (note spelling of "Bugsie"); Siegel smiling with attorney Geisler; coroner's toe tag on Siegel.

Siegel. But Tannenbaum said he had been in the killers' car too. Under California law, as Giesler argued, testimony of a single participant in the same crime isn't sufficient corroboration to convict a defendant. Then in a highly suspicious development, the witness who could add that second testimony, "Kid Twist," fell out of a hotel window to his death while under police protection in New York. Superior Court Judge A. A. Scott dismissed the charges against Siegel.

In 1944, District Attorney Fred N. Howser put Siegel on trial for bookmaking. Actor George Raft—the gritty bad-guy star of such gangster films as *Johnny Allegro* and *Rogue Cop*—appeared as a character witness. Siegel claimed he had only been placing a bet, not running the operation. But he pleaded guilty to misdemeanor bookmaking and was fined two hundred fifty dollars.

By 1945, Siegel had begun to build his dream gambling metropolis, Las Vegas. He wasn't to see much of it, however. On June 20, 1947, Siegel was shot to death in his girlfriend's living room.

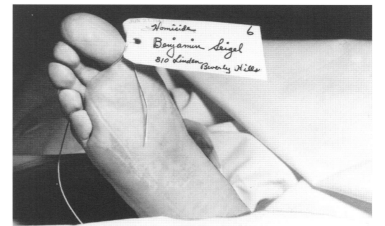

The gambling ship *Rex*; (inset) D.A. Investigator Aldo Corsini escorts
Tony Cornero (right) off ship.

Tony Cornero

**A persistent vendor of popular vices goes to sea
with his offshore gambling ships, which are shut down
in 1938 and 1946.**

From the beginning, Anthony Cornero Stralla—or Tony Cornero,
the name he preferred—worked near the ocean. In the 1920s, during
Prohibition, Cornero broke into the crime business by hijacking,
at shotgun-point, illegal liquor that bootleggers were landing at night
on Southern California beaches. Before he was 30 years old, he was
off-loading liquor, had accrued a million dollars and was known
as "King of the Rum-runners." He branched out to shipping liquor
on ships, once bringing four thousand cases of booze from Vancouver,
Canada, to a point offshore Los Angeles, aboard the *S.S. Lilly*. He used
small, fast boats to bring the bootleg liquor ashore. He branched out
again, with international operations in South America and Europe. In
one nefarious deal, he apparently bought the *S.S. Prezmysl* in Germany,
loaded it with a million dollars worth of fine spirits and sent it off
to the parched U. S. market.

He next turned up in Los Angeles in 1938, with a new attraction.
His gambling ship *Rex* was parked three and a half miles off the
California coast, in Santa Monica Bay. At the time, federal and state
territorial sovereignty extended three miles from the shore. The *Rex*
offered not just gambling—slot machines, dice tables, roulette wheels
and blackjack tables—but luxurious dining and dancing, with a live
orchestra. The *Rex* became an instant success with the Los Angeles
night-life crowd. It was a place where men got off the water taxi in
expensive suits and women wore smart dresses and high heels.

Santa Monica police and Los Angeles County sheriff's deputies first
raided the *Rex* in 1938. Cornero, who went home every night to his
home in Beverly Hills, protested, as always, that the *Rex* was outside
territorial waters. But prosecutors in the federal, state and county effort
invoked international maritime law, holding that territorial waters
extended three miles from a straight line drawn from headland to
headland. Bays, like Santa Monica Bay, didn't count.

Cornero moved the *Rex* to twelve miles offshore. For a year, the *Rex* remained in business, along with three barges that Cornero added to his entertainment operation, anchored off Long Beach as well as Santa Monica. But California Attorney General Earl Warren invoked state nuisance laws, issuing an abatement order to close the *Rex* down. In August 1939, Cornero was raided again. Taking personal command of the *Rex*, Cornero battened down the hatches with a steel door and for nine days—known as the "Battle of Santa Monica Bay"— his crew used fire hoses to keep law officers from boarding. Then he surrendered, glibly claiming that he needed a haircut. Officers dumped his gambling machinery into Santa Monica Bay. His ships were sold at auction to pay back taxes. Cornero, represented by attorney Jerry Giesler, paid a hefty fine.

Cornero, who had now become known in gambling circles as "The Admiral," made a brief comeback with an offshore gambling ship named the *S.S. Lux*, in 1946. He hoped to participate in the post-World War II economic boom. An added attraction this time was horse-race betting. Otherwise, the amenities remained: At the Charcoal Broiler on-board restaurant, the New York cut sirloin steak, with potatoes and vegetables, was only $2.50. District Attorney Fred N. Howser didn't think he had the authority to move against the ship. But Earl Warren, now governor of California, assured him that he did.

The U.S. Coast Guard seized the former Navy airplane tender after only three days of operation. District Attorney's Investigators Aldo Corsini and Chet Sharp escorted Cornero off the ship. The gambling equipment went overboard again. Cornero, as owner of the Panama Steamship Company, ostensibly went into the legitimate shipping business from then on.

Water taxi unloading gambling-ship passengers (top); crowd waiting at Long Beach dock to board *Lux*.

Mickey Cohen

Cohen and some of his "Seven Dwarfs" go on trial in 1961 for the murder of Jack "The Enforcer" Whalen.

Meyer Harris "Mickey" Cohen was a professional boxer before he became the most visible Los Angeles mobster, after Bugsy Siegel's assassination in 1947. Cohen ran his rackets out of a Sunset Boulevard men's goods store. In the mid-1940s, Cohen claimed to be taking in six hundred thousand dollars a day in bets from the Hollywood film crowd alone. When the East Coast syndicate tried to force him to pay protection money to keep his gambling and loan-sharking operations in business, the bloody "Sunset Wars" broke out. Several of Cohen's associates, including his lawyer, were gunned down in the battles. Cohen's house, near the Brentwood Country Club was bombed. He only escaped because of his newly installed radar security system. Despite his many friends in Hollywood, and his ready availability to reporters, he became widely known as "Nuisance No. 1."

In 1961, future District Attorney Joseph Busch prosecuted Cohen and four of a group of henchmen known as the "Seven Dwarfs," for conspiracy to murder Jack Whalen. Whalen had been gunned down in 1959 in Rondelli's restaurant in Sherman Oaks, then a popular meeting place for West Coast mobsters. Samuel Frank LoCigno, once a confederate of Cohen's, had confessed in 1959 to pulling the trigger and had been given a life sentence. But when his conviction was overturned and he was going to be retried, Cohen and the Dwarfs were charged as well.

Cohen's trial ended in a hung jury. LoCigno was tried a third time and convicted of voluntary manslaughter.

Cohen had less luck with federal prosecutors. He was imprisoned in the late 1950s for tax evasion. Then in 1962 he began what became a decade spent in prison for evading more than four hundred thousand dollars in taxes. He died in 1976 of stomach cancer.

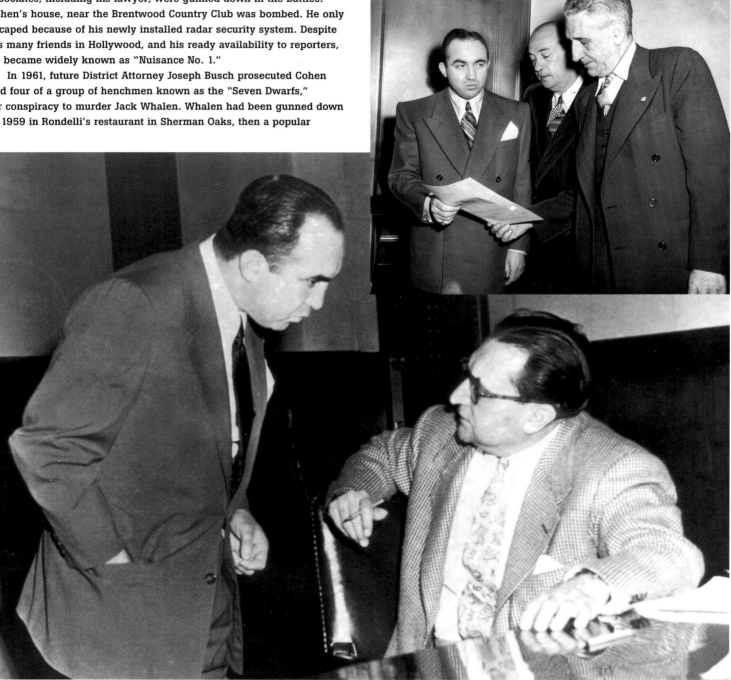

Mickey Cohen, standing, confers with defense attorney Maurice Blumenthal during trial recess; (inset) subpoenaed mobster Mickey Cohen (left), and Chief District Attorney Investigator H. Leo Stanley flank attorney Sam Rummel.

suits and had just filed lawsuits for two former Synanon members. The day of the snakebite, Morantz had sat down with two representatives of the California Attorney General's Office to discuss death threats he had been receiving as a Dederich-designated "enemy" of the group.

A neighbor had seen two suspicious men put something in the Morantz mailbox and had jotted down a license number. It was a Synanon-owned car. Founder Charles Dederich and two of his Imperial Marines, as they were known in Synanon—Joseph Musico and Lance Kenton, son of big-band leader Stan Kenton—were charged with attempted murder.

Deputy District Attorneys John Watson and Mike Carroll were assigned to the case until Carroll's promotion to director of Central Operations. He was replaced by John Hayes. Carroll handled the search warrant for Synanon's Northern California facility.

Dederich was ill at the time and appeared in court in a wheelchair. During the seven-week-long preliminary hearing, the prosecutors played a tape recording that Carroll had discovered, on which Dederich in a rage tells Synanon members, "I'm quite willing to break some lawyer's legs, and then tell him, 'Next time, I'm going to break your wife's legs, and then we are going to cut your kid's ear off.'"

Dederich and his two enforcers pleaded no contest to conspiracy to commit murder. Synanon attorneys pleaded for leniency and rehabilitation for Musico and Kenton. But Hayes argued for punishment—at least a year in jail. Superior Court Judge William P. Hogoboom agreed, saying that there was nothing to rehabilitate. The two were also forbidden to live at or have further contact with Synanon, though Kenton's wife was still a member.

Hogoboom sentenced Dederich to a five-thousand-dollar fine and five years' probation, with the condition that he no longer be an officer or director of Synanon. Without his strict control, Synanon faded from prominence.

Dederich escorted to court.

Synanon

Charles Dederich, promoter of "tough love," and two of his Imperial Marines are charged with attempted murder by rattlesnake in 1978.

On the afternoon of October 10, 1978, when attorney Paul Morantz reached into the mailbox at his Pacific Palisades home, a four-and-a-half-foot rattlesnake was waiting in its dark recesses. There was no warning because its rattles had been cut off. The snake bit him in the hand and he spent five days in the County-USC Medical Center, but lived. Morantz was a frequent critic of Charles Dederich and his cult-like rehabilitation organization Synanon. Dederich had begun Synanon as a substance-abuse rehabilitation group that used "tough love" personal confrontations—including the "game"—to bring addicts around. But as Synanon grew, Dederich had declared it a church and had used Synanon funds to build several thriving businesses—all under his hard-headed control.

Morantz was also a legal opponent, having just the month before won a three-hundred-thousand-dollar default judgment against Synanon for a couple who contended that the wife had been kidnapped and harmed by Synanon members. He had also won several child-custody

An ill Dederich at court arraignment.

The Manson Family

The fanatical followers of criminal con-man Charles Manson kill actress Sharon Tate and others in a demented Armageddon scheme in 1969.

On July 31, 1969, music teacher Gary Hinman was brutally murdered in his home. "Political Piggy" was scrawled on Hinman's living room wall in his own blood. Nine nights later, actress Sharon Tate, eight months pregnant, and four friends were slaughtered at her Benedict Canyon home. "Pig" was written on the front door in Sharon Tate's blood. The next night, in Los Feliz, Leno LaBianca, a supermarket-chain president, and his wife, Rosemary, were killed. "Death to Pigs" was written in blood on the wall of their home. And on the refrigerator door was the misspelled phrase, "Healter Skelter," also scrawled in blood.

When investigators over time reconstructed the events and motives

Manson escorted to his cell; Manson family members kneeling in front of the Hall of Justice (inset).

behind the deaths, they discovered a grotesque plan. Charles Milles Manson, a 34-year-old ex-convict who had been in prison so often that he considered it home, had gathered a tribe of mostly runaway teenage women and was trying to start a race war. Manson predicted that African-Americans would soon invade and dominate white America while the Family hid safely in the desert, acquiring more recruits. When the Family was more than a hundred thousand strong, it would return to the cities and take charge. Manson used "Helter Skelter," the title of a 1968 Beatles's song, as the name of this coming racial Armageddon. But he had forecast a black uprising for the summer of 1969. When the summer wore on with no sign of a black invasion of L.A.'s westside, Manson told one of his true believers, "I'm going to have to show [them] how to do it."

Manson and his deadly followers were rounded up. In an almost eight-month trial before Superior Court Judge Charles H. Older, Manson and three female Family members—Patricia Krenwinkel, Susan Denise Atkins and Leslie Sue Van Houten—were convicted of murder. Deputy District Attorney Vincent Bugliosi led the prosecution team,

Clockwise from top: Aerial view of the Tate house; the La Bianca house (inset); witness talking to Deputy District Attorney Vincent Bugliosi with Deputy District Attorney Stephen Kay in background.

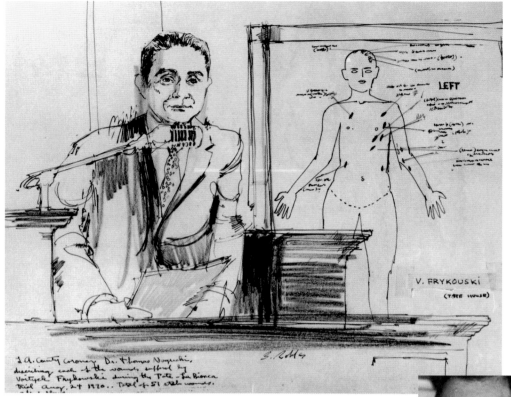

Clockwise from top: Coroner Thomas Noguchi testifying; Tex Watson; Manson; Manson-family members Leslie Van Houten, Patricia Krenwinkel and Susan Atkins.

which included Steven Kay and Donald Musich. Bugliosi summed up his argument for death sentences for all the defendants by contending that this was surely a death-penalty case, "If the death penalty is to mean anything in the State of California, other than two empty words...." The jury recommended death sentences for all.

In 1971, Bugliosi also won a death sentence for Charles Denton "Tex" Watson, another Family member. The same year, Kay and fellow Deputy District Attorneys Anthony Manzella and Burton Katz obtained more murder convictions of Manson as well as Family members Robert Kenneth Beausoleil, Steven Grogan and Bruce McGregor Davis in the deaths of a cowboy named Donald Jerome "Shorty" Shea and Gary Hinman, the music teacher.

In 1972, with the overturning of the California death-penalty law, the death sentences were converted to life in prison. Prosecutor Kay has since attended more than fifty parole hearings of Manson Family members to argue that they should remain in prison for the rest of their lives.

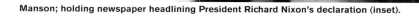

Manson; holding newspaper headlining President Richard Nixon's declaration (inset).

Patricia Hearst

In her brief life as a revolutionary in 1974, the newspaper heiress sprays gunfire to cover an SLA robbery at Mel's Sporting Goods Store. She faces prosecution in 1977.

![Patricia Hearst goes to trial; her attorney, F. Lee Bailey, in court.]

Patricia Hearst goes to trial; her attorney, F. Lee Bailey, in court.

The tiny but violently aggressive Symbionese Liberation Army kidnapped Patricia Hearst, the 21-year-old granddaughter of legendary publisher William Randolph Hearst, on February 4, 1974. After two months of terror, intimidation and physical and sexual abuse, Patricia Hearst announced that she had joined her captors and had adopted the name Tania. She took part in a San Francisco bank robbery. Then a month later she played a part in an armed robbery in Los Angeles.

On May 16, 1974, Hearst shot at the front of Mel's Sporting Goods Store in Inglewood, to cover the escape of SLA members William and Emily Harris, who were inside shoplifting. She fired thirty-three cartridges at the front of the building. The three got away by commandeering two occupied cars at gunpoint. The following day, six members of the SLA died in a flaming shootout with LAPD SWAT units.

More than a year later, in September 1975, Hearst and the Harrises were arrested in San Francisco. They were eventually brought to Los Angeles to be tried—separately—for the Mel's Sporting Goods robbery. The Harrises went first, with Deputy District Attorney Samuel Mayerson, assisted by Deputy District Attorney Richard Harbinger, prosecuting. William Harris represented himself, assisted by attorney Mark Rosenbaum, while Leonard Weinglass

and Mark Meltzer defended Emily Harris. Weinglass had been on the Daniel Ellsberg defense team in his Pentagon Papers case. On August 31, 1976, the Harrises were each sentenced to eleven years to life in prison on convictions for two counts of kidnapping, two counts of auto theft and one count of armed robbery. Mayerson had recommended concurrent sentences and Superior Court Judge Mark Brandler agreed, despite harsh personal attacks from the pair during their remarks before sentencing—remarks which Mayerson described as "stooping to a new low in offering such gratuitous insults to both the judge and the system."

Hearst was convicted of the San Francisco bank robbery and would serve fewer than two years of a seven-year prison sentence. In her Los Angeles trial, prosecuted again by Mayerson, Hearst pleaded no contest to assault with a deadly weapon and armed robbery. At her sentencing hearing, her lead defense attorney, F. Lee Bailey, argued for leniency, reminding the court that her crimes were "not the result of tendencies of the defendant prior to the kidnapping but primarily, in the opinion of the probation officer, from influence, both psychological and physical, that was brought to bear upon her while she was in the custody of her captors."

Hearst could have been sentenced to as much as fifteen and a half years to life on the charges. But Mayerson recommended five years probation. Superior Court Judge E. Talbot Callister agreed, adding as a condition of her probation that she pay restitution to the owner of Mel's Sporting Goods. When some commentators questioned the disparity between the sentences for Hearst and the Harrises, co-defense counsel Albert Johnson and Mayerson firmly declared that no deal had been made for Hearst. Mayerson wrote in an opinion article in the *Los Angeles Times* that he had followed the same penalty policies he would have done with any other defendant. "The only thing her family's wealth got her," he wrote, "was a kidnapping."

The Lancaster Skinheads

Three young Lancaster white supremacists beat a homeless man to death two days after Thanksgiving in 1995.

Sometimes he worked as a mechanic, but for the most part he lived on the kindness of strangers and slept in a vacant lot behind a McDonald's restaurant in Lancaster. Milton Walker Jr., 43, was African-American and a chronic alcoholic. And when three young white supremacists went out looking for someone to kill on a Saturday night, Walker became their victim. They found him and beat him to death with a board and a metal pipe.

In the mid-1990s, the Antelope Valley, in northern Los Angeles County, had seen an explosion of racial hate crimes. A special effort was launched by the District Attorney's Office, the United States Attorney's Office and community leaders, cooperating as part of the Antelope Valley Hate Crimes Task Force. There had been beatings, stabbings and shootings of minorities by white-power youths. A gang called the Nazi Low Riders was active. The gang was made up of white supremacists and Latinos who supported the white-power movement, sharing the goal of starting a race war in which all minorities would be killed. For the gang, a lightning-bolt tattoo indicated that they had killed someone.

Finding witnesses to these assaults was particularly difficult for prosecutors. "Many of the witnesses were not you or I... having some confidence in the judiciary and the police," noted Deputy District Attorney John Spillane, head of the Antelope Valley branch of the District Attorney's Office. But the Federal Bureau of Investigation found several witnesses to the Walker beating, and eventually one of the skinheads turned informant and led the FBI to the suspects.

Eighteen months after the killing, Randall Lee Rojas, 19 years old, Ritch Bryan, 17, and Jessica Anne Colwell, 16, were charged with murdering Walker because of his race. All were associated with the Nazi Low Riders.

Deputy District Attorney Jacquelyn Lacey prosecuted the case, which was tried simultaneously in front of three separate juries. She argued that the three were out to earn their lightning bolts by killing a minority person that night. Attorney Donald Calabria, who represented Rojas, described the act as a spur-of-the-moment incident, lacking the malice needed for first-degree murder.

Rojas and Bryan were convicted of first-degree murder. The jury also agreed that the murder was racially motived. Each was sentenced to life in prison without possibility of parole. Colwell was convicted of involuntary manslaughter because the jury decided, despite her later bragging, that she had not intended to kill.

After the verdicts, Rojas juror Fred Totten said that he thought Rojas, "was looking for an opportunity to kill a minority and here was a great opportunity. Here was a black man who was vulnerable."

Deputy District Attorney Jacquelyn Lacey presenting evidence to jury.

175

CRIMINAL COHORTS

"Freeway Killer" William G. Bonin.

Driven to Kill

What makes a criminal infamous is seldom difficult to discern. Something about the sheer scale of the crimes, or their grotesqueness, or how far they have gone beyond the pale of everyday life catches the public's fascination—or terror. When Richard Ramirez, the murderously intrusive Night Stalker, was on the loose, people bolted their windows and doors, no matter the summer heat. Yet in the end, with killers whose methods are often surrealistic in their rituals, as well as horrifying in their brutality, the biggest question often is: What made them do that? In some cases—thieves, or the sexually obsessed—the answer is not difficult to fathom. But in others, the reasons are more elusive.

In 1978, Patrick Wayne Kearney, known as the Trash Bag Killer—because he dumped the dismembered parts of his victims in trash bags—explained his motives to a psychiatrist. He said his first killings had been done out of curiosity, as well as the desire to have sex with the victims after they were dead. He apparently chose most of his victims because they reminded him of a "blonde…and arrogant" man who had tried to force him into homosexual sex as a teenager.

Simpler may be the obsession of James "Bluebeard" Watson, who from 1900 to 1920 found his many wives—and victims—by placing personal ads in newspapers. He ended up in Los Angeles in 1920, living with one of his most recently married wives. She became suspicious, however, had him tracked by a detective, and found that he had another wife living less than a mile away.

District Attorney Thomas Woolwine interrogated Watson personally, day after day, until he confessed to killing at least seven wives and having married twenty-two, in his quest for their money. He spent the rest of his life in San Quentin. But was there something else behind his elaborate search for a fortune?

"Something just told me to go and marry them," Watson told Woolwine as his compulsion began to reveal itself, "and yet something told me not to. Yet, I would go do it, and it seemed all at once an impulse came over me to go someplace and make away with [kill] them. It seemed like I had done something I was ordered to."

Louise Peete

After more than twenty years in prison, an infamous killer is released in 1939 and promptly kills again.

Louise Peete had a long history in crime. From her well-off upbringing in Louisiana at the turn of the last century, she married, moved on to other men and became an expensive and successful call girl. By 1915, she was in Denver, Colorado, where she married yet another man, Richard Peete, had a child, but five years later headed to Los Angeles.

There Peete learned that a wealthy businessman, Jacob Denton, was planning to travel and wanted to rent out his mansion. Peete used the opportunity to exert her well-educated, sweet, southern charm to get him into bed. She moved into his house. At the end of Peete's first month in Los Angeles, Denton disappeared. Peete maneuvered to get control of his assets but failed. Denton's suspicious family hired an attorney who hired a detective and Denton's body was found in a shallow grave in the basement. He had died from a single gunshot wound to the back of the neck. The trial was a Los Angeles sensation. Peete was witty, strangely seductive and of interest to the press. But the jury deliberated only four hours before convicting her of first-degree murder. She was sent to prison for life.

After eighteen years in state prisons at San Quentin and Tehachapi, Peete was paroled. Many had believed her dramatic claims of innocence in the Denton murder. These included her parole officer and an elderly couple, Margaret and Arthur Logan, who had a graceful home in

the Pacific Palisades. Peete was invited to move in. She did, using the name Anna B. Lee to avoid alarming the Logans' neighbors and friends. Margaret Logan paid Peete seventy-five dollars a month, plus room and board, to watch after Arthur Logan, age 74. Margaret Logan, as part of her effort during World War II, was working at an aircraft plant.

Soon Peete was involved in elaborate schemes to gain control of the Logans' money. Margaret Logan, finally suspicious, may have been making a phone call to probation officers when Peete shot her in the back of the head at close range. Peete buried Logan's body in the back yard. She got rid of Arthur Logan by bringing him in to the psychiatric ward of Los Angeles General Hospital and making artful declarations about his sanity, alleging recent violent acts against his wife. Arthur Logan was committed and died six months later, confused to the end, in Patton State Hospital in San Bernardino County. Peete appropriated the Logans' house, car and even Margaret Logan's clothing, which she had altered to fit herself. Peete kept telling the neighbors ever-changing stories to explain the Logans' absence. She was breaking open the home safe when Captain Thaddeus Brown, head of the LAPD homicide division, rang the front doorbell.

In April 1944, Peete was tried for the death of Margaret Logan. Deputy District Attorney John Barnes, who prosecuted the case, told jurors "Mrs. Peete, who was a Dr. Jekyll and a Mrs. Hyde, must have sat in her prison cell figuring what went wrong the first time and plotting this new crime." The jury took only three hours to convict Peete of first-degree murder. She was given a death sentence.

Ever upbeat and charming, Peete told reporters that she hoped for a pardon from Governor Earl Warren, because, "The governor is a gentleman, and no gentleman could send a lady to her death." But he did. Louise Peete died in the San Quentin gas chamber on April 11, 1947.

Clockwise from opposite top: District Attorney Fred Howser kneels while stenographer Mildred Evans poses as victim and Ray Rinker of the police crime lab details the Logan crime scene during court reenactment; Peete and her attorneys rise to hear her death sentence; public defenders Robert Antrom (right) and George Chatterton flank Louise Peete as her husband Lee Judson listens to court proceedings; Judge Frank R. Willis watches Peete who appears in court wearing a startling veiled hat, in this heavily doctored news photo taken during the 1921 trial.

Kenneth Bianchi and Angelo Buono

Two cousins become the Hillside Stranglers when they discover a mutual obsession with rape and murder, beginning in 1977.

They were rapists and killers of women. At first, because the Los Angeles Police Department didn't reveal that two murderers were involved, they were known by the singular, the Hillside Strangler, a name originally created by the press. Many of the women's corpses were found on hillsides. Their first alleged killing was in October 1977, the friend of a prostitute they knew. Later they killed anyone they could overwhelm—including two Catholic school girls, the youngest only 12 years old. The women usually had been tortured in some way—poison gas, electrocution, lethal hypodermic injections—and had ligature marks around ankles, wrists and throat, where they had been tied or handcuffed and strangled. Often with the prostitutes they killed, they impersonated vice cops until they could handcuff them.

Their deadly spree ended after twelve killings. In May 1978, Kenneth Bianchi moved to Bellingham, Washington, to follow his girlfriend and their new son. There, by himself, he killed two more women at the same time. The women were applying for a house-sitting arrangement. But the women had told friends Bianchi's name before they came to be interviewed. When police searched Bianchi's home, they found jewelry that had belonged to some of the Los Angeles victims. Bianchi implicated his cousin, Angelo Buono.

Bianchi began to fake a multiple-personality disorder, telling investigators and psychiatrists that another personality, "Steve Walker," had done the killings. Bianchi was an accomplished liar. Investigators worried that he could win with an insanity defense. The district attorney's offices in Los Angeles County and Washington's Whatcom County jointly offered Bianchi a plea bargain. Instead of seeking the death penalty, prosecutors would settle for life without parole if Bianchi pleaded guilty to the Washington murders as well as some of those in Los Angeles and testified against his cousin. Bianchi agreed.

Buono went to trial in 1981, defended by Katherine Mader—who would later become a deputy district attorney, the first Los Angeles Police Department Inspector General and a judge—and attorney Gerald Chaleff—

future Police Commission president—both appointed by the court. Deputy District Attorneys Roger Kelly and James Heins prosecuted. Superior Court Judge Ronald George, who later became chief justice of the California Supreme Court, presided.

At Buono's trial, Bianchi testified that he had no idea whether he was telling the truth when he told investigators his cousin had been involved. It was a clear attempt to persuade the court that his testimony would be useless. Kelly saw Bianchi's latest ruse as damaging to his case, and despite much collaborating physical evidence, he moved to dismiss the ten counts of murder that had been filed against Buono and to proceed initially only with such lesser charges as rape, sodomy and pimping. The prosecutor's plan was to continue investigating the killings to develop more corroborating evidence and then to take the murders to trial. In an unusual response, Judge George denied the motion to dismiss the murder charges, saying that he believed there was enough evidence to convict Buono of all charges.

Judge George, a former California deputy attorney general, referred the case to his former office for evaluation. The Attorney General's Office prosecuted Buono on all charges. Buono was convicted of nine of the ten murders. In 1984, he was sentenced to life without parole.

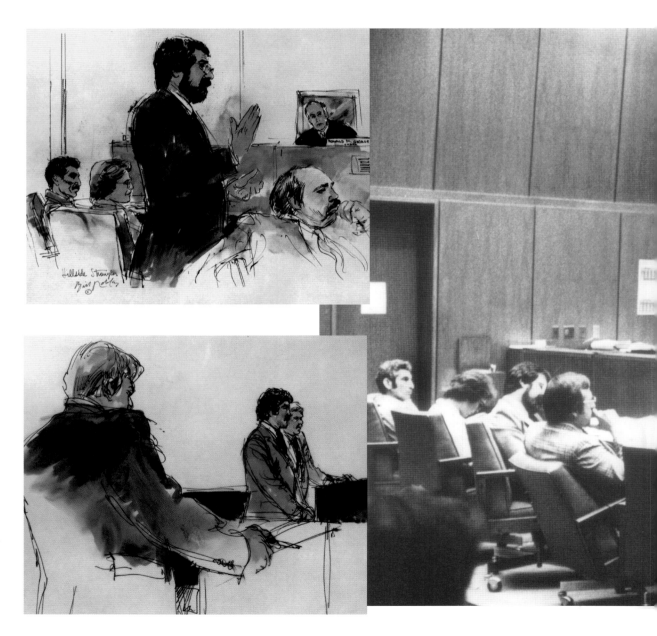

Clockwise from top left: Bianchi; Buono; courtroom scene during trial; Bianchi trial drawing; defense attorney Gerald Chaleff, Buono (far left).

Douglas Daniel Clark

The "Sunset Strip Killer" preys on prostitutes and young revelers in the celebrated entertainment district in 1980.

When police investigators began to collect evidence and testimony to connect vocational nurse Carol Bundy to the murder of John R. Murray, they also got interested in her apartment-mate and boyfriend, Douglas Clark. Bundy, it turned out, had killed Murray and decapitated him, because she was worried that he would go to the authorities with what she had told Murray about Clark—that he was responsible for a notorious string of murders on the Sunset Strip. Ironically, it was Bundy herself who finally turned Clark in. Clark, 32 years old, was arrested on August 12, 1980, and charged with aiding and abetting Bundy, 37, in the murder of Murray. For his own part, he was charged, ultimately, with the murder of six women, most of them prostitutes, as well as attempted murder of another woman and lewd conduct and oral copulation with an 11-year-old girl.

At the trial, Deputy District Attorney Robert N. Jorgensen told jurors how most of Clark's victims died—a gunshot to the head during oral copulation. Bundy, who said that she had been "overwhelmed by his sense of dominance and charm," testified against Clark. "If the girl were rude, crude or vulgar, or did not commit the sex act in the way that she had agreed to do it... then he would kill her," she told the jury.

Bundy also said that while they had cruised Sunset Strip together, scouting prostitutes for Clark, she had nothing to do with killing them. She did, however, make a suggestion to him once that she was surprised to see him carry out. "If you're going to go around killing people, killing hookers," she said she told him, "you might as well make it as gruesome as possible and do some weird thing like cut off their head [to] make it look like some psychotic did it." He brought home a victim's head and put it in their apartment freezer. It also turned out that Clark was a necrophiliac and had had sex with some of his victims after they were dead.

Jorgensen, the prosecutor, apologized to the jurors in his final arguments, for the "grotesque and disgusting evidence" that he had had to use in court. The jury convicted Clark on all counts of murder and attempted murder, as well as mayhem and mutilation of human remains. Clark's co-defense attorney, Maxwell Keith, argued in the penalty phase that Clark's life should be spared, saying "He is the sickest person I ever saw." Superior Court Judge Ricardo Torres sentenced Clark to death.

"Sunset Strip Killer" Douglas Clark as charges against him are read.

Lawrence Sigmond Bittaker

Two convicts form a grisly plan to record the murders of teenage girls. As soon as they get out of prison, in 1978, they begin to carry out their plot.

Planning what to do when they were released from prison, Lawrence Bittaker and Roy Norris concocted the appalling idea of using audio tape and film to record thrill killings of teenage girls. Free in 1978, they lured their first victim inside the van they called "Murder Mack," raped and killed her by twisting a wire coat hanger around her neck, tightening it with a pair of pliers. Though Bittaker would later describe the young women as "whores," they were ordinary girls ranging in age from 13 to 18. In late 1979, the pair were arrested for an assault that took place in Hermosa Beach. In jail, Norris broke down and began talking about the murders. Investigators searched the van and found, among other evidence, a tape recording of one of the victims, pleading for her life as she was tortured and killed.

To avoid the death penalty, Norris agreed to testify that Bittaker committed at least five murders. Investigators believed that the two could have killed as many as thirty to forty women before they were caught. Norris also pleaded guilty to five counts of murder, two counts of rape and one robbery.

Bittaker's trial, in 1981, was a gruesome portrait of the men whom Deputy District Attorney C. Ramsey Randolph termed "two mutates from hell." In his closing argument, Deputy District Attorney Stephen Kay, the co-prosecutor, pointed to Bittaker and asked jurors, "Can you imagine anything worse than dying at the hands of that abominable man?"

After three days of deliberation, the jury convicted Bittaker of all twenty-six felony counts. He was condemned to death.

William G. Bonin

A relentless sex offender dubbed the "Freeway Killer" goes on a murderous rampage, raping and killing a dozen young men and boys before he is caught in 1980.

Bonin; Deputy District Attorney Sterling E. Norris (inset).

William Bonin, a Vietnam veteran, had a long history of sex offenses, including conviction in 1969 for attacking a young boy in Redondo Beach. He was imprisoned in a Mentally Disordered Sex Offenders facility. Released, he was convicted again in 1975 of assaulting a boy in Garden Grove. Back in prison, he told a fellow inmate that the next time, he would leave no witnesses. In 1979, after his release, the nude, raped corpses of young men began to turn up on Los Angeles and Orange County freeways. On June 11, 1980, in Hollywood, Bonin was arrested in the act of sodomizing a 14-year-old runaway boy in the back of his van.

Bonin went to trial in 1981 on twelve counts of murder. Deputy District Attorney Sterling E. Norris prosecuted, while attorney William Charvet defended the case. Norris described the "callousness and malice" with which Bonin would pick up young boys, tie them up in the back of the van, sodomize them, often while beating them, then strangle or stab them to death—frequently using an ice pick. "He has an insatiable appetite for this type of killing," Norris told the jury. "He fully enjoys the whole episode." Norris argued that Bonin had been planning the series of killings for the past ten years. He also presented evidence including blood and semen stains, carpet fibers and hair that tied Bonin to the crimes.

Bonin was convicted on ten murder counts. His attorney argued for life imprisonment, citing his Vietnam experience. "He functioned in a semi-controlled system fairly well," Charvet noted. Norris strongly argued for the death penalty, which was returned. On February 23, 1996, after a pizza and coffee ice cream, Bonin became the first convict in California to be executed by lethal injection.

California's Mentally Disordered Sex Offenders program, which did not systematically track offenders after their release, was dismantled and replaced after the Bonin case.

Richard Ramirez

Los Angeles nights become fearful in 1985 when law-enforcement officials announce that the Night Stalker, a serial killer who breaks into people's homes, is on the loose.

In the spring and summer of 1985, Los Angelenos bought extra locks and guns when Sheriff Sherman Block confirmed that a particularly vicious serial killer was slipping into homes at night. Richard Ramirez was an accomplished burglar, sometimes robbing three homes a night. He liked cocaine, heavy-metal rock music, to dress in black and to have sex with prostitutes. Then he began to enjoy murder. Ramirez was also a Satanist. He began to leave satanic pentagrams behind after some of his attacks. One was scrawled on a bedroom wall, another on the thigh of a victim. He told Philip Carlo, author of *The Night Stalker*, that he believed that the more brutal his assault, the better Satan would like it, and that when he died he would go to hell as a hero.

The murders were among the most ghoulish in Los Angeles history. Typically, Ramirez would sneak into a house late at night, cut the phone wires and immediately shoot any man in the house.

Los Angeles Times

739 Sunday   Thursday, September 21, 1989   CC††/ 202 Pages   Copyright 1989/The Times Mirror Company   **Daily 25¢**   Designated Area Higher

Ramirez Guilty on All Night Stalker Murder Charges

By EDWIN CHEN, *Times Staff Writer*

Richard Ramirez, whose murderous crime rampage four years ago terrorized Southern California and baffled police for months, was found guilty Wednesday of all 43 Night Stalker crimes, including 13 murders.

The verdict raises the possibility of a death sentence.

Before the verdicts were read, the sullen, 29-year-old defendant asked for, and was granted, permission to leave the packed courtroom, which included several relatives of his murder victims. He heard the verdicts—a virtual clean sweep for the prosecution—through a speaker in a holding cell.

The Los Angeles Superior Court jury of seven women and five men, which deliberated for 22 days, next must decide whether to condemn the devil-worshiping drifter from El Paso to die in the gas chamber at San Quentin or order him imprisoned for life without parole.

As he was taken from the courthouse, Ramirez flashed a two-fin-

■ **OTHER VICTIMS**
The grandson of one of Ramirez's victims is one of many whose lives were tragically touched by murders. Page 26

■ **RELATED STORIES**

Then he would wake the woman of the house, tie her up or restrain her with thumb cuffs or handcuffs, then rape, sodomize and torture her until she revealed the location of jewelry or money. If she resisted or fought back, he killed her. He cut one savagely slain woman's eyes out after he tried, but failed, to cut out her heart.

Investigators had already identified Ramirez as their suspect on August 30, 1985, when he returned to Los Angeles by Greyhound bus after trying to visit his brother in Tucson, Arizona. At a liquor store, he saw why people were pointing at him: His picture was on the front page of every newspaper. He needed a car to get away. He started to run. He tried to steal a car from a woman who was sitting in it, but her boyfriend and others came

to her aid. They chased him as he started jumping fences, running through peoples' backyards, now in a predominantly Mexican-American neighborhood. Because Ramirez was Mexican-American too, these neighbors were particularly aware of his crimes and his picture. As soon as people saw him, they yelled "*El matador!*" "The killer!" Then they called the police. Men throughout the neighborhood joined the chase. When he slugged one woman in the stomach to get her car keys, her husband ran out with a heavy metal bar and beat Ramirez over the head. He and the rest kept after him as he staggered down the street. The enraged husband hit him over the head again and Ramirez collapsed. Sheriff's Deputy Andres Ramirez, no relation, who had grown up in the same neighborhood, was the first officer on the scene. Nineteen men who caught Ramirez later shared rewards totaling $36,777.

Ramirez was charged with thirteen murders and thirty other felonies from fifteen attacks—though investigators strongly suspected there were more. Other charges were filed in San Francisco and in Orange County. He was prosecuted in Los Angeles County by Deputy District Attorneys Phil Halpin and Alan S. Yochelson, who had a strong case based on statements from eight surviving witnesses, ballistics tests, fingerprints and other evidence. Ramirez had left distinctive shoe prints behind, including one on a victim's face. Three hundred seventy-five pieces of jewelry or other stolen valuables were also linked to him.

He was defended by Daniel V. Hernandez, Arturo Hernandez and Ray G. Clark. Superior Court Judge Michael A. Tynan faced a difficult ruling when a motion was made for a mistrial after one of the jurors was murdered in a family dispute. The concern was that this might prejudice the jury against another killer, Ramirez. But Tynan ultimately denied the motion and the trial went on.

He was convicted on all forty-three counts and was condemned to death in November 1989. His parting words at the sentencing hearing were, "I will be avenged."

Clockwise from top: courtroom drawing of Ramirez; Deputy District Attorneys Alan Yochelson and Phil Halpin; headline on Ramirez verdict.

Winnie Ruth Judd

A beautiful but mentally unbalanced young woman kills
her two best friends in a rage in 1931. She is caught with
the bodies in two steamer trunks at Union Station.

Winnie Ruth Judd had a deadly jealous streak. She was also a
former mental patient. In a bungalow in Phoenix, Arizona, on the night
of October 16, 1931, Judd shot and killed her two best friends—Helwig
Samuelson, age 23, and Agnes Ann LeRoi, 30. Judd had decided that
they preferred their own company to hers. Her girlfriends were also
going to parties with men that she considered her own.

Judd decided to take the corpses back with her to Los Angeles,
where she had once lived. She stuffed them into two steamer trunks—
having to dismember one of the bodies to make it fit—then called
a baggage service to lug the trunks to the railway station. When the
Golden State Limited arrived at Union Station in Los Angeles, Judd left
the trunks at the baggage check and went to get her older brother,
who was a law student at the University of Southern California. She told
him she needed his help to carry the heavy trunks to the ocean,
where the two of them would dispose of them.

Deer poachers had lately been transporting venison from Arizona
to Los Angeles in steamer trunks. So when the baggage clerk noticed

that one of Judd's trunks had the smell of meat, and was exuding
a dark red liquid, he told Judd to open it up. She said she would have
to get the keys and come back. As she and her brother drove away,
the clerk copied the license-plate number and called the police, who
pried open the trunks.

Judd disappeared but within days turned herself in. The District
Attorney's Office helped to arrange extradition to Tucson. She was
convicted of murder. But three days before she was to hang, a panel
of psychiatrists declared her insane. Her sentence was changed to life
in the Arizona State Mental Hospital. She escaped seven times over
the years, but was paroled in 1971. Judd died in her sleep in Phoenix,
at age 93, in 1998.

Baggage agent checks trunks; Winnie Judd's booking photo (inset).

Gang violence: the victims.

Gangs

Karen Toshima's death in 1988 was the point in time when many Americans realized how little they knew about modern street gangs and how vulnerable they were to the gangs' random violence. High-stakes drug deals and high-powered weapons had changed the nature of neighborhood gangs. Rivalries were no longer settled with fist fights. Semi-automatic pistols became the norm. Deaths and injuries for gang members and innocent bystanders alike increased dramatically.

The indiscriminate slaying of Toshima, in a supposedly safe, upscale neighborhood in Westwood, prompted a massive enforcement effort from the Los Angeles Police Department. Just months after Toshima was killed, the City of Los Angeles earmarked $6 million in emergency funds and six hundred fifty new police officers to beef up anti-gang work. LAPD Chief Daryl Gates initiated Operation Hammer as well, a controversial but forceful series of sweeps through gang territories in South Central Los Angeles, to interrogate and, where appropriate, arrest thousands of gang members.

The Toshima killing drew national attention, not least from other district attorneys' offices and police departments. Suddenly, law-enforcement personnel from around the country were reading the gang graffiti in their own towns, and taking the threat more seriously.

"After the Toshima case hit the papers, I got calls from places like Tulsa, Chicago, Detroit and Cleveland," Deputy District Attorney Michael Genelin, long-time head of the District Attorney's hard-core gang division, told a *Los Angeles Times* reporter a dozen years after the Toshima killing. "There were civic officials saying, 'Who the hell are these Crips, and why is their graffiti going up on the walls around town?' Within two or three years, we had fifty cities reporting some kind of dangerous gang activity."

More than thirteen hundred criminal gangs, with more than one hundred fifty thousand members, were still on Los Angeles County streets in 2000. In 1997, more than a third of all Los Angeles murders were committed by gang members. To cope with the problem, the District Attorney's Office assigned more than forty prosecutors to the Hardcore Gang unit, which boasted a ninety-four percent conviction rate.

Karen Toshima

A Crips gang member kills an innocent bystander in 1988 and Los Angeles takes a new look at gang violence.

Westwood Village is in many ways a small college town, a relaxed commercial neighborhood of narrow streets, trees and shops at the main gate to the sprawling UCLA campus. Late-evening window-shopping and strolling around town always seemed safe there.

Karen Toshima, a 27-year-old graphics artist, had just been promoted at the ad agency where she worked, and to celebrate, she and boyfriend Eddie Poon went to dinner in Westwood. The streets

were crowded. It was a Saturday night, January 30, 1988. At about 11:00 p.m. they were window-shopping, ambling down a sidewalk full of people on Broxton Avenue. She and Poon hadn't noticed that two rival gangs were forming ranks on either side of the street and were yelling at each other. On one side were members of the Westside Rolling 60s Crips, one of the most violent gangs in Los Angeles. On the other was a group from the Mansfield Hustlers.

Tyrone Swain, a Mansfield Hustler, had recently survived an attempted drive-by shooting that he blamed on the Rolling 60s Crips. When Durrell DeWitt "Baby Rock" Collins, his hair braided in blue beads—blue being the Rolling 60s Crips gang color—recognized Swain across the street, Collins asked another gang member for a loaded gun. Then Collins yelled at Swain, "C'mon, I've got something for you!"

Swain walked past Toshima into the street toward Collins, mocking his rival by holding a milk crate over his head. Collins pulled the .38-caliber pistol out of his leather bomber jacket and fired twice.

Eddie Poon had taken in the situation just before Collins fired

and he tried to pull Toshima down to safety. But a bullet hit her in the temple. She was rushed to the nearby UCLA Medical Center. Twelve hours later she was declared dead and taken off life support.

Deputy District Attorney Sandra Goen-Harris volunteered to take on the prosecution because she knew it would be an important and difficult case and she had had experience with gang members. She helped police with such routine business as filing search warrants, to speed the investigation as much as she could. "We felt it was critical to make an arrest as soon as possible," she recalled. "The whole community had become unglued."

Clockwise from left; Karen Toshima; Deputy District Attorneys Duarte and Harris.

A week after the killing, Collins was awakened in his bed and arrested. He was charged with one count of murder, with the added factor of having murdered with a handgun, and one count of attempted murder, also with a handgun, for trying to shoot Tyrone Swain. Deputy District Attorney Michael Duarte became Collins's prosecutor when Goen-Harris went on maternity leave near the end of the trial.

In September 1989, Collins was convicted of all counts. He was sentenced to twenty-seven years to life in state prison.

Stephanie Kuhen

When a family driving home from a birthday party takes
a wrong turn, members of the Avenues gang in Cypress Park
open fire, killing a three-year-old girl.

In the Los Angeles suburb of Cypress Park, at 1:30 in the morning
of September 17, 1995, Tim Stone made the fatal decision to take
a shortcut home from a birthday party. In the 1986 Thunderbird with
him were his girlfriend, Robynn Kuhen, her 3-year-old daughter
Stephanie and 2-year-old son Joseph, their uncle David Dalton,
and Stone's young brother Christopher. Soon after 26-year-old Tim
Stone turned down dimly lit Isabel Street, they began to pass Avenues
gang members drinking beer and having a party outside. Stone
drove slowly past, and he, Robynn Kuhen and Dalton avoided
eye contact, looking straight ahead. But it turned out
to be a dead-end street. Stone had to make a U-turn.
As they made their way back through the gauntlet,
gang members put a trash can in the middle of
the street in front of them. Stone gunned the
accelerator, speeding to get around the barrier
and to get away. The gang opened fire. More
than a dozen bullets crashed through the car
windows and into the tires. But Stone still
managed to drive to the Kuhens' home.

Tim Stone and young Joseph Kuhen
had been injured, though not severely. But
Stephanie Kuhen was motionless in the back
seat. She had a single gunshot to the head. Her
uncle discovered that she wasn't breathing.

The District Attorney's Office charged Anthony

Stephanie Kuhen; bullet-riddled Thunderbird.

Gabriel Rodriguez, 28 years old, Manuel Rosales Jr., 22, and Hugo
David Gomez, 17, each with one count of murder and five counts
of attempted murder. Later, 16-year-old Augustin Lizama and Marcos
Antonio Luna, 24, were charged with the same counts. Marvin Pech,
another Avenues gang member, had been charged but given immunity
when he agreed to testify for the prosecution.

Deputy District Attorneys Patrick Dixon and Eleanor Hunter tried

Rodriguez, Rosales, Gomez and Lizama together. Separately, Luna
would later plead guilty to one count of assault with a deadly weapon
for his role in putting the trash can into the street.

"This is a city street," Dixon reminded jurors. "Every one of us
has a right to drive a city street safely without being blown up
in the manner this car was."

Defense attorneys contended that the gang members thought
they were in danger from a rival gang, and that the suspicious
movements of the car looked like the beginning of a drive-by shooting. The defense also argued that the family knew the neighborhood
well enough to have avoided the area. And, outside the courtroom,
family members of the defendants asked, why would they go there?
Defense attorneys unsuccessfully tried to introduce to the jury
the possibility that Stone drove into the area so that someone in
the car could buy drugs. But Superior Court Judge
Edward Ferns cited a lack of evidence
of any kind to support that theory.

Rodriguez, Rosales and Gomez
were convicted of first-degree
murder and other charges
in 1997 and, finding a "high
degree of callousness and
viciousness" in their crime,
Judge Ferns sentenced
the three to fifty-four years
and eight months to life.
After sentencing, and
outside the court, Robynn
Kuhen told reporters,
"If we were there to buy
drugs, how come we never
stopped? How come they shot
up the car? They knew there
were children in the car."

The jury deadlocked with Lizama,
who had helped Luna drag the trash can
into the street but had apparently not fired a
weapon. Three weeks after the others were
sentenced, Lizama pleaded guilty to a reduced
charge of assault with a deadly weapon.

"We achieved what we wanted to achieve,
by getting guilty verdicts with the three shooters,"
said Hunter. "That was our main objective."

As one response to the Kuhen case,
District Attorney Gil Garcetti instituted a new
crime-prevention program aimed at gangs.
The Community Law Enforcement and Recovery
program, or CLEAR, is a partnership among
gang-impacted cities and law-enforcement
agencies that provides toll-free hotlines to report
gang crime, to have graffiti painted over and
to arrange for gang-prevention experts to speak
to community groups. It joined the existing
Strategy Against Gang Environments, or SAGE, set up in 1994, which
places experienced deputy district attorneys in troubled communities
to support local law-enforcement efforts to control the gangs.
A key SAGE tool is the civil injunction, a court order that can ban
gang members from drinking in the street, being out after midnight,
harassing residents, or carrying cellular phones, walkie talkies
or beepers.

The Halloween Murders

In a case of mistaken identity, gang killers murder Pasedena teenagers as they trick-or-treat.

On Halloween night in 1993, Stephen Coats and Reggie Crawford, both 14 years old, and Edgar Evans, 13, were leaving a birthday party when Deborah Bush, Coats's mother, offered them a ride. "No," said her son, kidding his mom, "your car is so slow I can probably beat you home." The three boys and five other teenagers began to walk back to their homes, trick-or-treating at houses along the way, through the Pasadena neighborhoods.

Earlier the same night, Herbert Charles McClain Jr., 26 years old, along with several friends, all members of the same Pasadena street gang, were in the emergency room of Huntington Memorial Hospital. A friend and fellow gang member, Fernando Hodges, had been shot that night and was dying of his wounds. Prosecutors believed that Hodges had been shot because three days before this, McClain had tried to kill Robert Lee Price, a member of the rival Crips. Now, with Hodges dying, McClain and the rest of the group left the hospital and began driving around Pasadena, McClain carrying a .44-caliber handgun. They were hunting Crips, to take their revenge for Hodges. The gang spotted the young teenagers, who were tall for their ages,

Death for Halloween killers

Judge imposes sentence on three defiant defendants

By Frank C. Girardot
STAFF WRITER

OS ANGELES — A Superior Court

25 cents plus tax

at a corner market. One had a blue bandanna hanging from his pocket, the identifying color of the rival Crips. McClain and his friends drove their cars around the block, where they parked. Then they waited in the path of the unsuspecting teenagers.

Lorenzo Alex Newborn, 25 years old, and Karl Holmes, 20, hid in bushes while McClain waited nearby with others in parked cars. According to prosecution testimony, Holmes later described the scene to a friend: "We were lying in the bushes and we jumped out and said, 'Trick or treat,'" and started blasting." Before he learned that they had killed three children, McClain bragged of his role to an acquaintance and said, "Boom boom, pow pow pow—I can still hear the noise."

Deborah Bush, Coats's mother, happened to be a crime-scene investigator for the Pasadena Police Department. She heard the gunfire just after she pulled into the driveway of her home. She ran to the nearby site to offer help. "I saw it was my son," she said later. "He had a bullet in his head and he was already gone." Another son

was among those teenagers who survived. The dead boys lay surrounded by spilled Halloween candy.

An outraged city offered a forty-thousand-dollar reward to find the killers. Five gang members were eventually charged in the crimes: McClain, Newborn, Holmes and two others—Solomon Bowen and Aurelius Bailey, who pleaded guilty in separate trials to lesser charges and were given suspended sentences.

Deputy District Attorneys Antony Myers and Jonlyn Callahan prosecuted the three key figures. One of the most difficult aspects of the case was the lack of physical evidence—no fingerprints, footprints, DNA, or recovered murder weapons. And none of the survivors could identify their assailants from that night. Defense attorneys stressed that the defendants were identified by informants and felons who received pay—the reward money.

Yet the jury of eight women and four men convicted all three men on all murder counts, as well as McClain on the separate charge of attempted murder for earlier trying to kill Robert Lee Price. Myers credited the successful convictions to the innocence of the three victims, eyewitnesses who had seen two of the defendants near the ambush

Clockwise from opposite top: Edgar Evans; Reggie Crawford; self-portrait of Stephen Coats Jr.; headline on sentence for defendants in Halloween murders.

site, and testimony that McClain gave, against his attorney's advice.

When McClain took the stand, he first denied killing any of the boys, but admitted that he had intended to kill a rival Crip in revenge for the death of his friend Hodges. Under Myers's cross-examination, he admitted, "I felt I was going to get some 'get back' for that; I was going to retaliate. I was going to kill a Crip."

The jury deadlocked, however, in the penalty phase, where the decision was between life without parole or the death penalty. Most jurors voted for death. The prosecutors decided to bring in a new jury and to retry the penalty phase. After a month-long retelling of the case, the new jury deliberated for eight days before returning death-penalty sentences for all three. "These defendants were the worst of the worst," said Myers.

Corie Williams

Gang members kill high-school senior Corie Williams and wound her friend aboard a municipal bus in 1997.

On January 15, 1997, a Watts gang called the 118th Street East Coast Crips discussed the news that members of a rival gang, the Bounty Hunter Bloods, some of whom attended Compton's Centennial High School, were riding home from school through Crips territory, on the Route 53 public bus. The Crips decided what to do about these Blood "slobs." They would ambush the bus.

The next afternoon, Corie Williams, 17 years old, a good student who hoped to go to law school, and her friend, Tammi Freeman, 18, were riding home from school on the standing-room-only bus. While the bus picked up passengers at a bus stop, Wilbert "L'il Evil" Eric Pugh, 20, a Crip, got on the bus and spotted a young man, Tyrone Lewis, 16, who was

Corie Williams.

wearing a red Tommy Hilfiger shirt. Lewis was seated behind Williams and Freeman. Pugh took him to be a Blood, since red is the Bloods' gang color. "Slob on the bus!" he yelled. Then Randall Amado, 16, who was associated with the gang, got on. One of them yelled at Lewis, "This is Eleven-8 East Coast Crips! You all got a problem with us, f——g slob! This is BK [blood killer] all day!" Outside, Robert "Baby Kiko" Johnson, 16, poked a .44 caliber semiautomatic pistol through a window and began firing into the bus, trying to hit Lewis. Pugh and Amado got off the bus and the driver drove off before they could get back on.

Tammi Freeman had been hit by gunshot in the shoulder. But a bullet had broken Corie Williams's neck. Among the first people to call Corie Williams's mother, to extend his sympathy for her death, was entertainer Bill Cosby, whose only son had been killed the same day, also by a young gang criminal.

Deputy District Attorney Robert Grace prosecuted Pugh, Amado and Johnson, though Johnson was tried before a separate jury. Pugh and Amado were convicted of the murder of Corie Williams, the attempted murder of Tyrone Lewis, assault on Tammi Freeman, and shooting at an occupied bus. As the verdicts were announced, Pugh tried to leave the courtroom and Amado lunged at Grace, the prosecutor. Four quick-acting deputies wrestled Amado to the floor while a fifth ushered Grace to safety. Later the same day, Johnson, who was judged the shooter, was convicted on a similar array of charges.

Pugh and Amado received sentences of twenty-seven years to life; Johnson, thirty-five years to life. Grace spoke directly to Amado, whose supporters had maintained that he wasn't technically a Crip, "If you had not been part of the group, if you had not shared the intent of the group, you wouldn't be sitting there today."

Asian Boyz

An Asian-American gang that preys on other Southeast Asian immigrants, becomes known for its drive-by shootings and violent home-invasion robberies in a 1995 killing spree.

The Asian Boyz gang, estimated at more than three hundred strong during the mid-1990s, had members not only in California but in Texas, Massachusetts and Florida. Members wore tattoos with a large dragon wrapped around the letter "A." In everyday life, they were typically good students and respected young businessmen, often modest and well-liked. But in their gang lives, the Asian Boyz were violent and ruthless criminals. The gang specialized in the extortion of Southeast Asian immigrants. Many were fluent in Vietnamese, or were the U.S.-born children of Cambodian, Filipino and other Southeast Asian immigrants who came to the United States in the 1970s. They took full advantage of Southeast Asian immigrants' reluctance to complain to the authorities, from years of experience with gangs and corrupt officials in their former countries.

The gang stole and sold cellular phone numbers, jewelry, computers and credit cards, and they became one of the first criminal groups to make money by breaking into cars and stealing air bags. The Asian Boyz also made a horrific name for themselves in drive-by shootings and home-invasion robberies. During one robbery in the San Fernando Valley, Asian Boyz members bound an 84-year-old Filipino woman with duct tape while they ransacked her home. In a Sacramento invasion, they used duct tape to quiet a baby. In one shooting, the Asian Boyz chased a victim in a vehicle and fired at it until it swerved and crashed into a streetlight pole. Then, as the victim sat trapped in his wrecked car, gang members walked up and executed him.

On May 21, 1997, Deputy District Attorney Laura Baird filed thirty-two counts—including seven counts of murder, eighteen counts of attempted murder and five counts of conspiracy to commit murder against seven ringleaders of the Asian Boyz. The incidents cited were six drive-by shootings in 1995, some of them attacks on members of the rival Valerio Street gang, but others were against non-gang people mistakenly identified as gang enemies. Two violent Asian Boyz members, Troung Dinh and Paulo Prado, had testified against their fellow gang members before the grand jury in return for leniency in their own sentencing.

In late 1998 and early 1999, Deputy District Attorneys Baird and Hoon Chun prosecuted the case against Bunthoeun Roeung, Sothi Menh, David Evangalista, Roatha Buth, Son Bui, Kimorn Nuth and Ky Tony Ngo.

Truong Dinh became the central prosecution witness. Despite some contradictions in his testimony, he was ultimately credible since he had been on the inside—the defendants were all former friends of his. One was a cousin. In more than two weeks on the stand, Dinh detailed the ambush of a rival gang in Van Nuys, the shooting of innocent people the gang mistook for rivals and other crimes.

Some defense attorneys argued that their clients had been damaged children—Roatha Buth, for instance, had seen thousands of people executed in the Cambodian killing fields. But the main

The brother of witness Truong Dinh stands on the porch of the San Jose home where his father was slain.

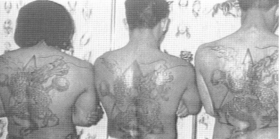

Clockwise from top: tattooed Asian Boyz gang members; gang crime scene; Deputy District Attorney Laura Baird; defendant Roatha Buth is led into courtroom.

defense argument was that Dinh and Prado, the other gang member who testified for the prosecution, were themselves responsible for the killings, not the defendants.

Prosecutors Baird and Chun agreed that Dinh, in particular, was central to the case but they pointed out that his testimony was supported by a mass of circumstantial evidence, including eyewitnesses and ballistics tests based on cartridge casings and murder weapons. "Attacking Dinh is not enough," Chun said of the defense efforts. The crimes were difficult to reconstruct, but prosecutors were able to do so in such detail that they could credibly connect individuals to their specific roles. For instance, in an attack in which two gang rivals were killed, defense attorneys claimed that Dinh was the true killer. Prosecutors argued persuasively that the defendants could only be innocent of the shootings had Dinh shot nine different guns while walking down a street.

At the time Dinh was testifying, jurors were not told that Dinh's father had just been murdered in front of his home in San Jose. Dinh knew, but continued his testimony for the next two days. Security

in the court and for the two prosecution witnesses had been tight, and it was beefed up even more after the killing. Prosecutors and the judge had round-the-clock security. But authorities had heard of no threats to the families of the hundreds of witnesses in the trial. They also believed it was taboo for the gang to kill a relative. Two jurors inadvertently learned of the murder of Dinh's father and asked to be excused.

All seven defendants were convicted of one to six murders each. Baird and Chun gained convictions on ten murders and twenty-one counts of attempted murder. The jury deadlocked over the sentencing of the four defendants who could have been given the death penalty. In the end, all seven were sentenced to multiple terms of life without parole. Baird and Chun still believed the gang leaders should have gotten death. "They're responsible for so many victims," said Baird. "There was no reason for it, and they took great pride in it. They enjoyed killing."

Two gang members were later arrested and jailed in San Jose for gunning down Dong Dinh, Truong Dinh's 64-year-old father. Investigators said that the pair had also intended to kill Truong Dinh and two other witnesses for the prosecution. On June 14, 2000, Santa Clara County prosecutors announced that they would seek the death penalty for the two alleged killers.

Los Angeles County District Attorneys, 1850-2000

1850-1851	WILLIAM C. FERRELL
1851-1852	ISAAC OGIER
1852-1853	KIMBALL H. DIMMICK
1853-1854	BENJAMIN EATON
1854-1857	CAMERON E. THOM
1857-1859	EZRA DROWN
1859-1861	EDWARD J.C. KEWEN
1861-1863	EZRA DROWN
1863-1867	VOLNEY E. HOWARD
1867-1869	ALFRED B. CHAPMAN
1869-1873	CAMERON E. THOM
1873-1876	VOLNEY E. HOWARD
1876-1877	RODNEY HUDSON
1877-1879	CAMERON E. THOM
1879-1882	THOMAS BROWN BRUEN
1882-1884	STEPHEN M. WHITE
1884-1886	GEORGE M. HOLTON
1886-1887	GEORGE S. PATTON
1887-1888	J.R. DUPUY
1888-1890	FRANK P. KELLY
1890-1892	JAMES MCLACHLAN
1892-1894	HENRY C. DILLON
1894-1898	JOHN C. DONNELL
1898-1902	JAMES C. RIVES
1902-1914	JOHN D. FREDERICKS
1914-1923	THOMAS LEE WOOLWINE
1923-1928	ASA KEYES
1928-1940	BURON FITTS
1940-1943	JOHN F. DOCKWEILER
1943-1946	FRED N. HOWSER
1946-1951	WILLIAM E. SIMPSON
1951-1956	S. ERNEST ROLL
1956-1964	WILLIAM B. MCKESSON
1964-1971	EVELLE J. YOUNGER
1971-1975	JOSEPH P. BUSCH
1975-1983	JOHN K. VAN DE KAMP
1983-1984	ROBERT H. PHILIBOSIAN
1984-1992	IRA REINER
1992-2000	GIL GARCETTI

1850

1850-1851 William C. Ferrell

1851-1852 Isaac Ogier

Isaac Ogier
1851-1852

The County's second District Attorney was also a founder of the Rangers, a vigilante group.

Ogier, an attorney from Charleston, South Carolina, came to California as a Forty-Niner, then turned up in Los Angeles in 1851. He formed a law partnership with a Peruvian named Don Manuel Clemente Rojo, who also worked as a journalist for the *Los Angeles Star*. Ogier served a year as District Attorney. In 1853, in the El Dorado Saloon, Ogier, Judge Agustin Olvera and other leading citizens organized the Rangers, a vigilante group that would grow to a hundred members and would lynch at least twenty-two people between 1854 and 1855. Ogier's reputation seemed to survive, however. From 1854 to 1861, Ogier served as federal District Judge for the Southern District.

Kimball H. Dimmick
1852-1853

The third District Attorney comes to California as an army commander during the Mexican-American War.

New Yorker Kimball Dimmick came west as a U.S. Army officer. He then became an *alcalde* and Judge of the First Instance in San Jose under the military transition to statehood in 1849. After moving to Los Angeles he held various posts, including District Attorney, justice of the peace, county judge and finally U.S. Attorney for the Southern District. In private practice, Dimmick most often represented horse thieves, gamblers and their ilk. According to historian W.W. Robinson, Dimmick had a standard, simple plea to the jury: "The District Attorney prosecuting my client is paid by the County to convict this prisoner, whether he is guilty or innocent; and I plead with you, gentlemen, in the name of Impartial Justice, to bring in a verdict of 'Not Guilty!'"

1859-1861 Edward J.C. Kewen

1852-1853 Kimball H. Dimmick

1857-1859; 1861-1863 Ezra Drown

1867-1869 Alfred B. Chapman

Cameron E. Thom
1856-1857; 1870-1873; 1877-1879

An immigrant from the South, Thom serves as L.A.'s District Attorney, returns to the South to fight for the Confederacy, then comes back for two terms as chief prosecutor.

Cameron Thom came to California from Virginia as a Forty-Niner. He moved to Los Angeles in 1854. One of his first cases as a defense attorney was a controversial murder charge against Dave Brown, a well-known gambler. Brown had killed a man in a livery stable on Main Street. In the heyday of the vigilantes, a crowd gathered and decided to string up Brown and be done with him. Los Angeles Mayor Stephen Foster—not the songwriter of "Camptown Races," though they were alive at the same time—convinced the would-be lynchers to give the courts a chance to

1853-1854 Benjamin Eaton

1856-1857; 1870-1873; 1877-1879
Cameron E. Thom

1867-1869 Volney E. Howard

1876-1877 Rodney Hudson

Ezra Drown

**An Iowa attorney has a rough passage to Los Angeles.
But he goes on to become District Attorney twice.**

General Ezra Drown, a brigadier-general of the militia in Iowa, came to Los Angeles in 1853. He, his wife and two small boys were aboard the steamship *Independence* as it traveled up the Mexican coast from the Isthmus of Panama. When the ship caught fire, burning to the waterline, Drown put his wife on a floating hencoop and swam to shore with the boys clinging to his back. When he returned to rescue his wife, she had been pushed into the sea by another passenger. In Los Angeles, as Harris Newmark recalled, Drown, though "broken in spirit... put his best foot forward." He worked as an attorney, then won election to the City Council. He was elected District Attorney in 1857. After another term as City Council president, Drown returned to the District Attorney's Office again in 1861.

1879-1882 Thomas Brown Bruen

1882-1884 Stephen M. White

1884-1886 George M. Holton

1886-1887 George S. Patton

act. Foster vowed that if justice wasn't expediently done, he would resign his office and lead a lynch mob himself. Brown was sentenced to death. But Thom and two colleagues, the high-priced defense lawyers of their day, were able to get a stay from the state Supreme Court. Foster, true to his word, resigned, led another lynch mob and Thom's client was hanged. Foster was re-elected as mayor two weeks later.

Thom was a California senator from 1859 to 1860. He returned to the South during the Civil War, fighting as a major in the Confederate army. Then he came back to Los Angeles and served two more terms as District Attorney. He was mayor of Los Angeles from 1882 to 1884 and also helped to found the city of Glendale.

1887-1888 J.R. Dupuy

1888-1890 Frank P. Kelly

1890-1892 James McLachlan

1892-1894 Henry C. Dillon

dollar bond, pledged allegiance to the United States and was taken off the island. Later, in a fight with another notorious hothead, Fred Lemberg, known as the "Flying Dutchman," Kewen shot and nearly killed him. Kewen was acquitted of assault in 1866.

In Los Angeles, Kewen and attorney James G. Howard formed such a successful criminal defense practice that a vigilante group once decided to lynch them. When Howard spoke to the group's leader, according to Robinson, he said, "We are old friends; be generous; let's compromise. Hang Kewen, he's the head of the firm."

Kewen survived to enjoy life at El Molino, his gracious home in present-day San Marino that was converted from the old gristmill of Mission San Gabriel.

Edward J.C. Kewen
1859-1861

A hot-tempered southern attorney makes his mark on both sides of the law.

Originally from Mississippi, Edward J.C. Kewen was California's first Attorney General. Later, he moved to Los Angeles and entered politics, becoming superintendent of the Los Angeles City schools in 1858 and District Attorney a year later. He was a man who "shot first and argued later," as historian W.W. Robinson described him in *Lawyers of Los Angeles*, "… a fire-eating, name-calling orator, violent in speech and in temper." In 1862, while a state assemblyman, and in the second year of the Civil War, Kewen was arrested and jailed for two weeks at the military prison on Alcatraz Island, for advocating secession. He paid a five-thousand-

George S. Patton
1886-1887

The father of the legendary World War II tank commander was District Attorney before running for higher office.

George S. Patton was the first city attorney of Pasadena, in 1877. He also opened a Los Angeles law practice before being elected District Attorney in 1886. Patton would also be the first mayor of San Marino. He was less successful, however, standing for other public offices—losing a bid for the U.S. Congress in 1894 and for the Senate in 1916. Patton swam against the tide as a stubborn opponent of women having the vote.

John D. Fredericks
1902-1914

Fredericks comes to national attention for his prosecution of the *Los Angeles Times* bombing in 1910.

John D. Fredericks came to California in 1891, taught at Whittier State School, and was admitted to the California Bar Association in 1895. He became a deputy district attorney in 1899 and was elected to three terms as District Attorney—in 1902, 1906 and 1910. At the *Times* bombing trial, in 1911, during the complicated negotiations that ended the trial, Fredericks insisted that both John and James McNamara, the accused bombers, must plead guilty.

Fredericks, who reminded some observers of Abraham Lincoln, lost the governor's race in 1914 but was elected to the U.S. Congress in 1923.

1894-1898 John C. Donnell

1898-1902 James C. Rives

1902-1914 John D. Fredericks

1914-1923 Thomas Lee Woolwine

Thomas Lee Woolwine
1914-1923

Public corruption and vice are high on the list of targets of this reform-minded prosecutor.

He even raided the prestigious California Club once in his zeal to control illegal liquor, gambling, prostitution and, most importantly, public corruption. Thomas Lee Woolwine, who began as a deputy district attorney in 1908, would go on as District Attorney to contribute to the downfall of two mayors, Charles Sebastian and Frederick Woodman, as well as leading an investigation of a particularly violent nest of Ku Klux Klansmen in Los Angeles. Woolwine obtained thirty-five grand jury indictments of Klansmen for assault with deadly weapons with the intent to commit murder after a Klan home-invasion slaying in Inglewood in 1922. None of the defendants were convicted, but Klan members heckled him from the audiences of his political campaign meetings from then on. Woolwine ran twice unsuccessfully for governor during his years as District Attorney.

Asa Keyes
1923-1928

An influential District Attorney is a major Los Angeles figure through much of the Roaring Twenties, until his term ends in scandal.

Asa "Ace" Keyes had been a deputy district attorney for two decades before taking over as District Attorney with the retirement of Thomas Woolwine in 1923. The descendant of a pioneer California family, Keyes's father had been a county clerk. In the five years before his conviction for bribery, in connection with the Julian Petroleum Corporation scandal, Keyes created new departments in the office, including Homicide, Special Cases, Juvenile Complaints, the Trials division and a unit specializing in the prosecution of bootleggers.

Buron Fitts
1928-1940

A feisty prosecutor becomes District Attorney during the Depression.

Buron Fitts was a proud veteran of World War I, returning with a knee injured in a gunshot wound that would require a score of operations over his life to avoid amputation. He became a leader in the American Legion, which always gave him a strong base of political support.

Fitts became a deputy district attorney in the Woolwine years and chief deputy under District Attorney Asa Keyes. In 1926, Fitts was elected California lieutenant governor. Two years later, when Keyes was indicted for bribery, Fitts was appointed special prosecutor to take charge of the case. Fitts ran for the District Attorney's

1943-1946 Fred N. Howser – lighting seized pornography on fire.

1923-1928 Asa Keyes

1928-1940 Buron Fitts

1946-1951 William E. Simpson

1940-1943 John F. Dockweiler – meeting with office staff.

Office as well and won.

In office, Fitts reorganized and cut the staff, while raising the salaries of the prosecutors and investigators who remained. He concentrated enforcement efforts on gambling and other crimes of vice. Then while making an unsuccessful attempt to run for governor in 1930 he ran into trouble himself.

A well-known District Attorney's Office investigator, Leslie T. White, had come upon a prostitution ring specializing in underage girls. The ring's madam said that she had supplied young girls to several wealthy businessmen, including John P. Mills, a real-estate developer and friend of Fitts. The madam claimed that she had delivered a young virgin every week to Mills. A sixteen-year-old girl was willing to testify against Mills and he was charged with statutory rape. Eventually, the other businessmen charged in the case were acquitted. Fitts dropped the remaining charge against Mills, saying that there wasn't sufficient evidence to take him to court and that the complaining witness had disappeared.

Political rival and future reform mayor Fletcher Bowron, then a superior court judge, urged the grand jury to take a close look at several politicians. The grand jury responded with an indictment of Fitts—and his sister, who worked as his secretary—for bribery and perjury. The grand jury charged that Fitts and his sister had sold Mills a useless orange grove that the family had owned, receiving much more than it was worth in the trade—essentially a bribe to Fitts to drop the rape charge. Two years later, Fitts was acquitted. His sister's charges were dismissed.

During World War II, Fitts went back into the military, joining the Army Air Force. He commanded combat operations in Europe and North Africa.

1951-1956 S. Ernest Roll – in his courtroom days prior to becoming District Attorney.

1956-1964 William B. McKesson   1964-1971 Evelle J. Younger

John F. Dockweiler
1940-1943

**The first big case for the new District Attorney
is the Bugsy Siegel murder trial.**

John Dockweiler served three terms in the U.S. Congress, from 1933 to 1939, before winning in the 1940 District Attorney's race against incumbent Buron Fitts. One of his first responsibilities was to prepare for the prosecution of Bugsy Siegel for a gangland murder in Hollywood. The case, which finally went to trial in January 1942, was dismissed by the judge after the prosecution's star witness conveniently fell to his death from a New York hotel room window.

Dockweiler instituted reforms in the District Attorney's Office, including a ban on office investigators working as security guards at the Santa Anita racetrack. He created the Bureau of Crime Research and Prevention and reorganized the Bureau of Investigation, bringing it under civil-service regulation. This ended the disruptive practice of treating investigators' jobs as a matter of political patronage. Dockweiler was investigating allegations of police brutality in Los Angeles when he died suddenly of pneumonia in 1943.

Evelle J. Younger
1964-1971

**A former war-time intelligence agent becomes
District Attorney for two terms.**

Evelle Younger served with U.S. Army intelligence during World War II and later worked as a special agent for the Federal Bureau of Investigation. In the 1940s, he acted as a prosecutor for the City of Los Angeles and the City of Pasadena. In the 1950s he became a judge, first of the municipal court in 1950, then superior court in 1958.

During his terms as District Attorney, he opened branches of the office in Norwalk and Van Nuys and reorganized the office bureaus. In 1967, Younger created the Special Investigations Division. Complex, headline-grabbing cases that were prosecuted on his watch included the assassination of Senator Robert Kennedy, the Manson Family murders and the Watts Riots.

In 1970 he was elected state Attorney General. In 1976 he ran an unsuccessful campaign to become governor of California.

Joseph P. Busch
1971-1975

**An experienced prosecutor from inside the office is picked
by the Board of Supervisors to replace Evelle Younger.**

Joseph Busch had been with the District Attorney's Office for almost two decades when he was chosen for the top job. He had risen through the ranks since joining as a deputy district attorney in 1952—serving as director of special operations, assistant district attorney and chief deputy district attorney.

Busch opened six new branch offices and instituted the Organized Crime and Pornography Division, Consumer and Environmental Protection Division and Bureau of Community Affairs, among other restructurings.

Busch died of a sudden heart attack, at age 49, in the summer of 1975.

1971-1975 Joseph P. Busch – demonstrating a non-lethal weapon.

John K. Van de Kamp
1976-1982

An experienced prosecutor from a famous local family is named District Attorney.

1975-1983 John K. Van de Kamp

It took the Board of Supervisors six months to pick a replacement after District Attorney Joseph Busch's sudden death. But John Van de Kamp, of the family that owned the bakery of the same name, was an understandable choice. He had served as U.S. Attorney and was the first federal public defender in Los Angeles.

Van de Kamp dramatically increased the number of women deputy district attorneys in the office, beginning with the appointment of Andrea Ordin as assistant district

1983-1984 Robert H. Philibosian

1984-1992 Ira Reiner

attorney. He also created special units focused on gangs, sexual assault, domestic violence, child-abuse, career criminals and a unit to monitor crime in the entertainment industry. He also set in place programs to help victims and witnesses of crime, as well as special teams to quickly respond to cases of police officer-involved shootings.

Van de Kamp was elected state attorney general in 1982.

Robert H. Philibosian
1983-1984

A former courtroom prosecutor has a brief term as District Attorney after appointment by the Board of Supervisors.

Robert Philibosian was picked to replace John Van de Kamp after his election as state attorney general in 1982. He had been a deputy district attorney, an active courtroom prosecutor from 1968 to 1979. Later he served as chief deputy attorney general.

During his administration, Philibosian installed advocates to aid crime victims in all branches of the District Attorney's Office as well as at ten police stations. Philibosian also created the Narcotics Section, to focus on large-scale drug dealers, and emphasized enforcement of sex crimes and child-abuse laws. He went into private practice after defeat in his first election.

Ira Reiner
1984-1992

The Los Angeles City Attorney wins the District Attorney's job in 1984.

When Ira Reiner was elected district attorney he was already a well-known public figure in Los Angeles. He had been a member of the Community Colleges Board of Trustees, a fire commissioner and City Controller. He began his career as a litigator in the City Attorney's Office and was Los Angeles City Attorney when he ran for district attorney in 1984.

In office he pursued criminal injuries of workers by organizing the Occupational Safety and Health Section. He also gave priority to prosecutions of illegal hazardous waste disposal and other environmental crimes, hate crimes, consumer protection, drunk-driving cases and abuse of patients in nursing homes. To discourage crime among young people, Reiner gave support to the Street Gang Enforcement Program and truancy mediation, to encourage students to remain in school.

He withdrew his bid for a third term in 1992

Gil Garcetti
1992-2000

A veteran of the District Attorney's Office takes charge in 1992.

Gil Garcetti was head deputy of the Torrance office when he was elected in 1992. Garcetti, District Attorney Ira Reiner's former chief deputy district attorney, had spent well over two decades working at various posts within the office, from trial prosecutor to a variety of management positions. Garcetti was elected to a second term in 1996.

During his tenure, Garcetti emphasized prosecution of family violence, stalking, hate crimes, workers compensation fraud, welfare fraud, gang violence, truancy and child-support violations. He created a number of new programs to stiffen enforcement in these areas, including the Family Violence Division, the Stalking and Threat Assessment Team, the Bureau of Crime Prevention and Youth

1992-2000 Gil Garcetti

Services, the Hate Crimes Unit, the High-Tech Crimes Unit, the Welfare Fraud Division and the Real Estate Fraud Section.

In 1994, Garcetti created the Strategy Against Gang Environments program, or SAGE, which places experienced deputy district attorneys in the field, able to use such enforcement techniques as civil injunctions, or court orders, to ban the paraphernalia of gang activity. In 1996, after the brutal gang slaying of a small girl, Garcetti instituted Community Law Enforcement and Recovery, CLEAR, an anti-gang partnership with the Los Angeles Police Department, Los Angeles Sheriff's Department and municipalities, to get the most violent gang members off the street. SAFE WAY OUT, a hotline, is another Garcetti program. It refers family violence victims, in six languages, to the nearest safe shelter.

2000

Bibliography

Gregory Alan-Williams, *A Gathering of Heroes: Reflections on Rage and Responsibility: A Memoir of the Los Angeles Riots*, Academy Chicago Publishers, Chicago, 1994

J.C. Bates, editor, *History of the Bench and Bar of California*, Bench and Bar Publishing, San Francisco, 1912

Daniel Beecher, *Office of District Attorney of County of Los Angeles*, Los Angeles County Bar Bulletin, 1942

Daniel Beecher, *A Study of the Office and Problems of the District Attorney of the County of Los Angeles*, Law Library of Los Angeles County Pamphlets, Vol. 33, 1931

Tony Blanche and Brad Schreiber, *Death in Paradise: An Illustrated History of the Los Angeles County Department of Coroner*, General Publishing Group, Los Angeles, 1998

Robert Blew, "Vigilantism in Los Angeles, 1835-1874," from *A Southern California Historical Anthology*, Centennial Publications, Los Angeles, 1984

Edith L. Blumhofer, *Aimee Semple McPherson: Everybody's Sister*, William B. Eerdmans Publishing Company, Grand Rapids, Michigan, 1993

Joseph L. Brent, *The Lugo Case: A Personal Experience*, Searcy & Pfaff, Ltd, New Orleans, 1926

Kitty Bruce, *The Almost Unpublished Lenny Bruce*, Running Press, Philadelphia, 1984

Vincent Bugliosi with Curt Gentry, *Helter Skelter: the True Story of the Manson Murders*, W.W. Norton & Co., New York, 1974

California Legislature, *New Initiatives for a New Los Angeles*, 1992

Robert Campbell, *Los Angeles County Sheriff's Department Commemorative Book 1850-1981*, Sheriff's Relief Association of Los Angeles County, Los Angeles, 1981

Lou Cannon, *Official Negligence: How Rodney King and the Riots Changed Los Angeles and the LAPD*, Times Books, a division of Random House Inc., New York, 1997

Philip Carlo, *The Night Stalker: The Life and Crimes of Richard Ramirez*, Pinnacle Books, published by Kensington Publishing Corp., New York, 1997

John Caughey and LaRee Caughey, editors, *Los Angeles: Biography of a City*, University of California Press, Berkeley, 1976

Lindsay Chaney and Michael Cieply, *The Hearsts: Family and Empire—The Later Years*, Simon and Schuster, New York, 1981

Caryl Chessman, *Cell 2455, Death Row*, Prentice-Hall, Inc., Englewood Cliffs, New Jersey, 1954

Caryl Chessman, *Trial by Ordeal*, Prentice-Hall, Inc., Englewood Cliffs, New Jersey, 1955

Arthur Christensen, *Politics and Crowd-Morality; A Study in the Philosophy of Politics*, translated from the Danish by A. Cecil Curtis, E.P. Dutton, New York, 1915

Marcia Clark, *Without a Doubt*, Penguin Books, New York, 1998

Robert Glass Cleland, *The Cattle on a Thousand Hills, Southern California 1850-1880*, The Huntington library, San Marino, California, 1941

Alfred Cohn and Joe Chisholm, *Take the Witness*, Frederick A. Stokes Company, New York, 1934

The Commission, *The Report of the Independent Commission on the Los Angeles Police Department*, Los Angeles, 1991

Antonio Coronel, edited by Doyce B. Nunis, Jr., *Tales of Mexican California*, Bellerophon Books, Santa Barbara, 1994

Geoffrey Cowan, *The People v. Clarence Darrow, The Bribery Trial of America's Greatest Lawyer*, Times Books, New York, 1993

Robert G. Cowan, *On the Rails of Los Angeles: A Pictorial History of Its Street-Cars*, Historical Society of Southern California, Los Angeles, 1971

Fred G. Crawford, *Organizational and Administrative Development of the Government of the City of Los Angeles: During the Thirty-year Period July 1, 1925 to September 30, 1955*, University of Southern California, School of Public Administration, Los Angeles, 1955

Michael J. Dear, H. Eric Schockman and Gred Hise, editors, *Rethinking Los Angeles*, Sage Publications, Thousand Oaks, California, 1996

Paul DeFalla, *Lantern in the Western Sky, Pts 1 & 2*, Historical Society of Southern California Quarterly, Vol. 42, 1960

James D. Delk, *Fires & Furies: The L.A. Riots*, ETC Publications, Palm Springs, California, 1995

John Douglas and Mark Olshaker, *Obsession: The FBI's Legendary Profiler Probes the Psyches of Killers, Rapists, and Stalkers and Their Victims and Tells How to Fight Back*, A Lisa Drew Book/Scribner, New York, 1998

Mike Eberts, *Griffith Park: A Centennial History*, Historical Society of Southern California, Los Angeles, 1996

Guy W. Finney, *Angel City in Turmoil: A Story of the Minute Men of Los Angeles in Their War on Civic Corruption, Graft and Privilege*, Amer Press, Los Angeles, 1945

Otto Friedrich, *City of Nets: A Portrait of Hollywood in the 1940s*, Harper & Row, New York, 1986, University of California Press, Berkeley, 1997

Robert M. Fogelson, *The Fragmented Metropolis: Los Angeles, 1850-1930*, University of California Press, Berkeley and Los Angeles, 1967

Robert M. Fogelson, compiled by, *Mass Violence in America: The Los Angeles Riots*, Ayer Company, Salem, New Hampshire, 1988

Neal Gabler, *Winchell: Gossip, Power and the Culture of Celebrity*, Alfred A. Knopf, Inc., New York, 1994

Jerry Giesler as told to Pete Martin, *The Jerry Giesler Story*, Simon and Schuster, New York, 1960

Robert Giroux, *A Deed of Death*, Alfred A. Knopf, Inc., New York, 1990

Albert Goldman, from the journalism of Lawrence Schiller, *Ladies and Gentlemen—Lenny Bruce!*, Random House, New York, 1971

Judson A. Grenier, editor, *A Guide to Historic Places in Los Angeles County: Prepared under the auspices of the History Team of the City of Los Angeles American Revolution Bicentennial Committee*, Kendall/Hunt Publishing Company, Dubuque, Iowa, 1978

Richard Griswold del Castillo, *The Los Angeles Barrio, 1850-1890*, University of California Press, Berkeley, 1979

Benjamin Hayes, *Pioneer Notes, Diaries of Judge Benjamin Hayes 1849-1875*, Private Printing, 1929

Abraham Hoffman, *Vision or Villainy: Origins of the Owens Valley-Los Angeles Water Controversy*, Texas A&M University Press, College Station, Texas, 1981

Burton L. Hunter, *The Evolution of Municipal Organization and Administrative Practice in the City of Los Angeles*, Parker, Stone & Baird Co., Los Angeles, 1933

Joan M. Jensen and Gloria Ricci Lothrop, *California Women in History*, Materials for Today's Learning, Inc., Parks, Nevada, 1988

Robert Blair Kaiser, *R.F.K. Must Die!: A History of the Robert Kennedy Assassination and Its Aftermath*, E. P. Dutton & Co., Inc., New York, 1970

Thomas Kiernan, *The Roman Polanski Story*, Grove Press, New York, 1980

William Klaber and Philip H. Melanson, *Shadow Play: The Murder of Robert F. Kennedy, the Trial of Sirhan Sirhan and the Failure of American Justice*, St. Martin's Press, New York, 1997

Ronald Markman and Ron LaBrecque, *Obsessed: The Stalking of Theresa Saldana*, William Morrow and Co., New York, 1994

Lary May, *Screening Out the Past: The Birth of Mass Culture and the Motion Picture Industry*, Oxford University Press, New York, 1980

Robert R. Mayer, editor, *Los Angeles, A Chronological and Documentary History, 1542-1976*, Oceana Publications, Inc., Dobbs Ferry, New York, 1978

Carey McWilliams, *Southern California: An Island on the Land*, first published 1946, Peregrine Smith, Santa Barbara, 1973

Carey McWilliams, *California: The Great Exception*, Current Books, New York, 1949

Douglas Monroy, *Thrown Among Strangers: the Making of Mexican Culture in Frontier California*, University of California Press, Berkeley, 1990

Michael Munn, *The Hollywood Murder Casebook*, St. Martin's Press, New York, 1987

Remi Nadeau, *City Makers: The Story of Southern California's First Boom, 1868-76*, Trans-Anglo Books, Corona del Mar, California, 1977

Harris Newmark, *My Sixty Years in Southern California 1853-1913*, The Knickerbocker Press, New York, 1926.

Doyce B. Nunis, Jr., editor, *Los Angeles and Its Environs in the Twentieth Century*, Ward Ritchie Press, Los Angeles, 1973

Doyce B. Nunis, Jr., editor, *Women in the Life of Southern California: An Anthology Compiled from Southern California Quarterly*, Historical Society of Southern California, Los Angeles, 1996

Doyce B. Nunis, Jr., editor, *Southern California's Spanish Heritage: An Anthology*, Historical Society of Southern California, Los Angeles, 1992

Darcy O'Brien, *Two of a Kind: The Hillside Stranglers*, New American Library, New York, 1985

Scott O'Dell, *Country of the Sun: Southern California An Informal History and Guide*, Crowell, New York, 1957

Terrys T. Olender, *For the Prosecution: Miss Deputy D.A.*, Chilton Co., Book Division, Philadelphia, 1961

Ethel Spector Person, *Dreams of Love and Fateful Encounters: The Power of Romantic Passion*, W. W. Norton & Co., New York and London, 1988

Leonard Pitt and Dale Pitt, editors, *Los Angeles A to Z: An Encyclopedia of the City and County*, University of California Press, Berkeley, 1997

Leonard Pitt, *The Decline of the Californios: A Social History of the Spanish-Speaking Californians, 1846-1890*, University of California Press, Berkeley and Los Angeles, 1970

James J. Rawls and Walton Bean, *California: An Interpretive History*, McGraw-Hill, New York, 1988

Craig Rice, editor, *Los Angeles Murders*, Duell, Sloan and Pearce, New York, 1947

W.W. Robinson, *Lawyers of Los Angeles*, Los Angeles Bar Association, 1959

W.W. Robinson, *People Versus Lugo: The Story of a Famous Los Angeles Murder Case and Its Amazing Aftermath*, Dawson's Book Shop, Los Angeles, 1962

Willoughby Rodman, *A History of the Bench and Bar of Southern California*, William J. Porter, Los Angeles, 1909

William B. Secrest, *Lawmen and Desperadoes: A Compendium of Noted, Early California Peace Officers, Badmen and Outlaws 1850-1900*, A. H. Clark Company, Spokane, Washington, 1994

Lynn Sherr and Jurate Kazickas, *Susan B. Anthony Slept Here: A Guide to American Women's Landmarks*, Times Books, New York, 1994

Lee Shippey, *The Los Angeles Book*, Houghton Mifflin, Boston, 1950

Carl Sifakis, *The Mafia Encyclopedia*, Facts on File, New York, 1999

Carl Sifakis, *The Encyclopedia of American Crime*, Facts on File, New York, 1982

Oscar T. Shuck, *History of the Bench and Bar of California*, The Commercial Printing House, Los Angeles, 1901

Joel Simon, *Endangered Mexico: An Environment on the Edge*, Sierra Club Books, San Francisco, 1997

Leland Ghent Stanford, *San Diego's LL.B. (Legal Lore, & the Bar): A History of Law and Justice in San Diego County*, San Diego County Bar Association, Law Library Justice Foundation, San Diego, 1968

Kevin Starr, *Material Dreams: Southern California Through the 1920s*, Oxford University Press, New York, 1990

Kevin Starr, *Inventing the Dream: California Through the Progressive Era*, Oxford University Press, New York, 1985

Kevin Starr, *The Dream Endures: California Enters the 1940s*, Oxford University Press, New York, 1997

Kevin Starr, *Americans and the California Dream: 1850-1915*, Oxford University Press, New York, 1973

Katherine Ames Taylor, *The Los Angeles Tripbook*, Putnam, New York, 1928

Lately Thomas [pseudonym], *The Vanishing Evangelist, The Aimee Semple McPherson Kidnapping Affair*, Viking Press, New York, 1959

Kevin Tierney, *Darrow – A Biography*, Crowell, New York, 1979

Jules Tygiel, *The Great Los Angeles Swindle: Oil, Stocks, and Scandal During the Roaring Twenties*, Oxford University Press, New York, 1994

Joseph Wambaugh, *The Onion Field*, Delacorte Press, New York, 1973

J.J. Warner, Benjamin Hayes and J.P. Widney, *An Historical Sketch of Los Angeles County California: From the Spanish Occupancy, by the Founding of the Mission San Gabriel Archangel, September 8, 1771, to July 4, 1876*, Louis Lewin & Co., Los Angeles, 1876

J.J. Warner, *An Illustrated History of Los Angeles County*, Lewis Publishing Company, Chicago, 1889

Matt Weinstock, *My L.A.*, Current Books, New York, 1947

Steve Wick, *Bad Company: Drugs, Hollywood, and the Cotton Club Murder*, Harcourt Brace Jovanovich, San Diego, New York and London, 1990

J. Albert Wilson, *History of Los Angeles County, California*, Thompson & West, Oakland, 1880

Paul A. Winters, book editor, *Crime: Current Controversies*, Greenhaven Press, Inc., San Diego, 1998

Marvin J. Wolf and Katherine Mader, *Fallen Angels: Chronicles of L.A. Crime and Mystery*, Facts on File Publications, New York and Oxford, England, 1986

Walton J. Wood, *Office of the Public Defender of Los Angeles County*, Los Angeles County Law Library Pamphlets, Vol. 13, 1914.

UNPUBLISHED DISSERTATIONS

Carrie M Broaded, "The Social Development of Los Angeles County During the Sixties," (Master's dissertation, University of Southern California, History, 1929)

Ed Escobar, "The Loss of Commitment: Crime and Punishment in Los Angeles 1836 to 1856," (Term paper, University of California, Riverside, History, 1973)

Robert Gerhart Lane, "The Administration of Fletcher Bowron as Mayor of the City of Los Angeles," (Master's dissertation, Political Science, 1954)

Leonard Ross Sanders, "Los Angeles and Its Mayors, 1850-1925," (Thesis, University of Southern California, History, 1968)

Thomas Joseph Sitton, "Urban Politics and Reform in New Deal Los Angeles: The Recall of Mayor Frank L. Shaw," (University of California, Riverside, History, 1983)

NEWSPAPERS

Los Angeles Star
Los Angeles Times
Los Angeles Herald
Los Angeles Herald-Examiner
Los Angeles Daily News
Los Angeles Record
Los Angeles Express
Los Angeles Evening Express
San Diego Union
Glendale News-Press

OTHER DOCUMENTS

"Our Fascinating Link to the Past: The Story of *El Molino Viejo—The Old Mill*." (pamphlet) Old Mill Foundation, San Marino, California

Ed C. King, "I Know Who Killed Desmond Taylor," originally published in *True Detective Mysteries*, October, November, 1930

"This Is Los Angeles," Los Angeles Chamber of Commerce

"Historical Record and Souvenir," Los Angeles County Pioneer Society, Times Mirror Press, Los Angeles, 1923

"Mayors of Los Angeles," Municipal Art Department of the City of Los Angeles, 1965

"Time Was: Los Angeles Senior Citizens Reminisce," Noelle Sickels, editor, City of Los Angeles Department of Cultural Affairs, 1992

Index

Acknowledgments

Thanks to the District Attorney Crime Prevention Foundation for its financial support, as well as to the staff of The Huntington Library, the Los Angeles Public Library, the University of Southern California's Regional History Museum, *El Pueblo de Los Angeles* Historical Monument, the Seaver Center for Western History Research at the Natural History Museum of Los Angeles County and Angel City Press. Special thanks to Carol Baker, Mark McKinniss, Jerri Patchett, Tom McDonald, Suzanne Childs, Sharon Matsumoto, Robert Heflin, Ken Price, Barbara Bolante-Martinez, Paddy Calistro, Scott McAuley, Sheila Perkins, Carolyn Cole, Linda Moussa, historian Doyce B. Nunis Jr., graphic designers Alex Luna and Maritta Tapanainen, and the constant Judie Lewellen.

Finally, my personal thanks to everyone who has faithfully served over the decades in the Los Angeles County District Attorney's Office. In good times and bad, in the headlines or not, your commitment to justice has been the final bulwark protecting all Los Angelenos.

— Michael Parrish
Los Angeles
July 2000

Photo Credits

Academy of Motion Picture Arts and Sciences Center for Motion Picture Study Margaret Herrick Library: 91 (right), 97 (top).

AP/Wide World Photos: 71 (2).

California Historical Society TICOR Collection at University of Southern California: 22 (bottom), 26 (bottom), 68, 110 (left), 132, 149 (top).

California State Archives: 23 (2).

Corbis: 55.

District Attorney's Bureau of Investigation: 31 (bottom), 166 (bottom).

District Attorney's Office: 2, 14, 23 (bottom right), 29 (middle and bottom), 30 (top), 31 (top), 35 (3), 51 (2), 74, 86 (top), 87, 112 (top), 127, 150 (top left), 188 (top right), 194, 195 (all except DA Thom), 196 (6), 198 (4), 199 (top left 2), 199 (bottom right), 200 (middle left), 201 (4).

Dunne, Dominick: 69.

Evidence: 50, 65, 186 (top left), 189 (2), 66, 73, 86 (bottom), 102, 103, 107 (bottom and background), 118 (4 images from video by George Holliday), 119 (2 images from video by George Holliday), 120.

Fox News: 193 (right 3).

Hayes, Benjamin: from *Pioneer Notes:* 25 (top right).

Heimann, Jim: 166 (top).

Huntington Library: 21, 22 (top), 24, 25 (top left), 27 (large), 28 (right and bottom), 29 (top), 111 (bottom), 144 (bottom), 145 (bottom), 195 (bottom right).

Los Angeles County: 133.

Los Angeles County Sheriff's Department: 106.

Los Angeles News Service: 120 (Bob Tur Video), 121 (Bob Thompson, Santa Monica Outlook, Santa Monica Historical Society).

Los Angeles Police Department: 51 (top), 143 (2), 186 (middle right).

Los Angeles Public Library: 6, 20, 22 (middle), 36, 38 (right), 40, 41 (middle right and bottom 2), 42, 44 (2), 46 (inset), 47 (2), 49 (2), 54, 57 (2), 58 (2), 59, 62, 63 (2), 76 (2), 78, 79, 80, 81 (2), 82 (top), 83 (top), 88, 90 (left), 92 (2), 93 (top and bottom), 95 (3), 96, 97 (bottom), 98 (2), 101, 103, 105, 112 (bottom), 114 (top and bottom), 115 (left), 116 (bottom), 124, 126 (3), 128 (3), 129 (2), 130 (top), 131 (top), 134 (2), 136, 138, 140, 141 (2), 142, 146, 148 (bottom), 149 (bottom), 150 (bottom left), 151 (2), 152, 153 (2), 154 (bottom), 155, 158 (right), 160 (2), 161 (bottom), 164 (2), 165 (4), 168 (bottom), 169 (top), 172 (top right, bottom right), 173 (bottom), 178 (2), 179 (2), 180 (right), 181 (2), 182, 184 (right), 185 (2), 202 (background).

Los Angeles Public Library *Herald-Examiner* Collection: 38 (left), 41 (middle left), 60, 61, 90 (left), 99 (2), 150 (bottom right), 170 (bottom), 172 (bottom left).

Los Angeles Public Library Security Pacific National Bank Collection: 27 (inset), 28 (left), 30 (bottom), 32 (top 2), 76 (right).

Los Angeles *Star*: 110 (right).

Los Angeles *Times:* 34, 41 (top), 43 (by Larry Bessel), 64 (by Larry Davis), 70 (top by Al Schaben, bottom by Rick Meyer), 71 (top), 90 (bottom), 93 (middle), 94 (2), 100 (by Bill Beebe), 108 (by John Malmin),

114 (background), 115 (right by George R. 117, 118 (top by Rick Meyer), 119 (right), 131 (middle and bottom), 135 (by Rick Meyer), 148 (top), 154 (middle and right), 156 (bottom), 162, 174 (background), 183 (top), 184 (left), 192, 193 (left).

Manhattan Beach Police Department: (top).

Natural History Museum of Los Angeles County: 25 (bottom), 111 (top).

Pasadena Historical Museum: 188 (bottom right).

Pasadena *Star-News*: 190 (bottom).

private collections: 139, 154 (left), 167 (2), 186 (all except top left and middle right), 188 (left), 190 (top), 191 (3).

Resar, Mike: 107 (top).

Robles, Bill: 51 (bottom), 77 (2), 85, 104 (2), 122, 158 (left), 161 (top), 169 (bottom), 172 (top left), 173 (top), 174 (right), 175, 180 (top left and bottom left), 183 (bottom), 184 (background).

Stephens, John: 72.

University of California, Los Angeles: 52, 56 (3), 84, 116 (top), 144 (top and middle), 156 (top), 157, 170 (top), 171 (3), 174 (left), 176, 200 (bottom).

University of Southern California: 10, 23 (top right), 26 (top), 33 (2), 39, 45, 46 (large), 48, 82 (inset), 83 (bottom), 168 (top), 199 (bottom left and top right), 200 (top and middle left).

Wesselmann Collection: 8, 130 (bottom).